# TOEFL® TEST スピーキング英単語

五十峰 聖・宇佐美 修
河合塾グローバル教育研究推進チーム

河合出版

## 著者紹介

**五十峰 聖**（いそみね・せい）
ETS Authorized Propell® Facilitator
立命館アジア太平洋大学（APU）教育開発・学修支援センター准教授
Eastern Washington University より社会学学士号，West Virginia University より高等教育経営学修士号を取得。
大学職員，International Student House（ワシントンDC）プログラムディレクターを経て帰国。大手留学支援機関，明治学院大学，神奈川大学等を経て2012年9月より立命館アジア太平洋大学勤務。2016年4月より現職。
専門：アカデミックイングリッシュ，アメリカ研究，学生育成

**宇佐美 修**（うさみ・おさむ）
ETS Authorized Propell® Facilitator
栄光学園中学校・高等学校 英語科教諭
国際基督教大学卒業。テネシー大学ノックスビル校より外国語および第二言語としての英語教育学修士号を取得。
ニューインターナショナルスクールでの日本語教諭を経て，2003年9月より現職。高校生パーラメンタリーディベート連盟（HPDU）理事，神奈川県高等学校英語ディベート推進委員会事務局担当。
専門：アカデミックイングリッシュ，批判的思考

**河合塾グローバル教育研究推進チーム**
学校法人河合塾の講師グループ。英語試験の分析を日々行い，従来の大学受験の枠組みにとらわれず，対策教材の作成や指導法の研究を，大学や外部の試験機関，各方面の専門家と積極的に連携し推進している。

# はじめに

　この本を手に取られた方は，本の構成や勉強の進め方が，従来の参考書とまったく違っていることに気づかれたことと思います。もしこの本を見た瞬間に，「新しい！」とか「おもしろそう！」と感じたのであれば，是非この『TOEFL® TESTスピーキング英単語』で勉強を始めてみてほしいと思います。

　ページを開いてみると，単語と絵が目に飛び込んできます。どのようなテーマが取り上げられているか，一目でわかりますね。そして絵の周りにちりばめてある単語は，既に知っている単語もあれば，はじめて見る単語もあるでしょう。書いてある単語と，そこに載っていなくても自分の知っている単語を組み合わせて，まず絵の説明を考え，次に絵のテーマを発展させていってください。参考となる文章や音声も用意してあります。話の展開は自由です。そして自分の考えた文章を声に出してみてください。何分で話せましたか？　最初は何秒かもしれません。でも考えて内容が膨らんでいくと自然と何分，という長さで話ができるようになります。

　あなたは小さいとき，好きな絵本がありませんでしたか？　声を出して読みませんでしたか？　そして自分でお話を作ったりしませんでしたか？　絵本で覚えた表現は今でも覚えているのではありませんか？

　音と文字と意味は一緒にして学ぶと，自然に身につき，しかも簡単に忘れたりしなくなります。本書を使って学ぶことで，TOEFL®テストが求める表現の適切さや話の組み立てが，小さいころに言葉を身につけたような自然な形で表現できるようになっていきます。TOEFL®テストにおける「話す」「書く」のセクションで問われる問題は，テンプレートにはめこんだような形だけの答えでは高い評価は得られません。教室の中で交わされる討議や会話は，型にはまったやりとりであるはずはありません。わかりやすく話の趣旨が展開されていく発言や意見であるからこそ，その場の人たちが耳を傾けるのです。

　TOEFL®テストが求める力は，皆さんの将来に必ず有益なものになるでしょう。英語を使って学ばなければならないことは，現在では過去に例を見ないほど多くなっています。英語を使って学ぶ経験や内容は，皆さんの将来に大きく影響します。教科の垣根にとらわれない多様な分野に興味をもち，それらを「英語で」学べるようになっていってください。皆さんが新しい挑戦を始めるとき，「英語で学ぶ力」はその挑戦を支える土台になります。そして本書がその挑戦への一歩を踏み出す大きな助けとなることを期待しています。

国際教育交換協議会（CIEE）日本代表部　TOEFL事業部

# Contents

本書の使い方 …………………………………………… 005
TOEFL iBT® テスト受験ガイド ……………………… 009

Unit 1  Moving Pyramid Stones …………… 011
Unit 2  Praying Hands ………………………… 033
Unit 3  Mpemba Effect ………………………… 055
Unit 4  Planetary Habitability ……………… 077
Unit 5  Da Vinci's Bird Sketches …………… 097
Unit 6  Dinosaur Metabolism ……………… 119
Unit 7  Biggest Bird Nests …………………… 141
Unit 8  Keystone Species …………………… 163
Unit 9  Decision Fatigue …………………… 185
Unit 10 Deceiving Eyes …………………… 207

---

協力　　　　　　国際教育交換協議会（CIEE）日本代表部
本文イラスト　　宇佐美 修
装丁デザイン　　阿部太一［GOKIGEN］
録音　　　　　　株式会社ブレーンズ ギア

# 本書の使い方

## ねらい

　本書では，様々な学術的な話題について「内容を理解し，それを説明する」ことを英語で繰り返すことで高い英語運用能力を身につけることを目指しています。使える英語の修得を目指す方，特に次のような英語学習者の皆様に本書を使っていただきたいと考えています。

- 語彙力を増強したいが，単語の羅列だけの単語集ではなかなか覚えられない。
- 語彙力だけでなく，同時にスピーキングやライティングの力も向上させたい。
- アカデミックイングリッシュを身につけたい。TOEFL® テストのスコアを上げたい。

　扱う話題は，心理学，生物学，考古学などTOEFL® テスト頻出分野から選びました。短い講義を聴き，理解した内容を絵や図をヒントに英語で説明することを繰り返すことで，語彙力そしてスピーキング力をつけていきます。本書で扱う10の学術的な話題を英語で詳しく話すことができるようになれば，大きな自信となることでしょう。

## 学習手順

各Unitは以下の5つのパートに分かれています。
1. Lecture 1 Original　　　1つ目の講義
2. Lecture 1 Paraphrase　講義の言い換え
3. Conversation　　　　　講義についての会話
4. Lecture 2 Original　　　2つ目の講義
5. Lecture 2 Summary　　2つ目の講義の要約

各パートでは，以下の手順で学習を進めます。
1. Listen:　　　　講義や会話を聴く
2. Understand:　内容を確認する
3. Read Aloud:　様々な形で音読する
4. Speak:　　　 理解した内容を英語で話す

　なお，音読には，ただ英文を読み上げるだけでなく，英文を見ながらCD音声を追うように読み上げる「オーバーラッピング」や，英文を見ずに音声を追うように読み上げる「シャドーイング」などの方法があります。

　以下に詳細な学習手順をページごとに示します。必要に応じてアレンジして学習を進めて下さい。

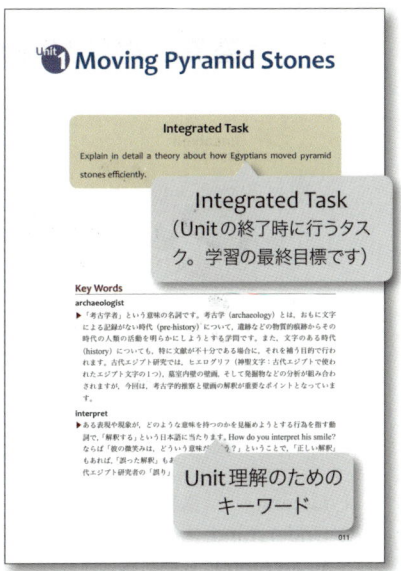

005

# Lecture 1

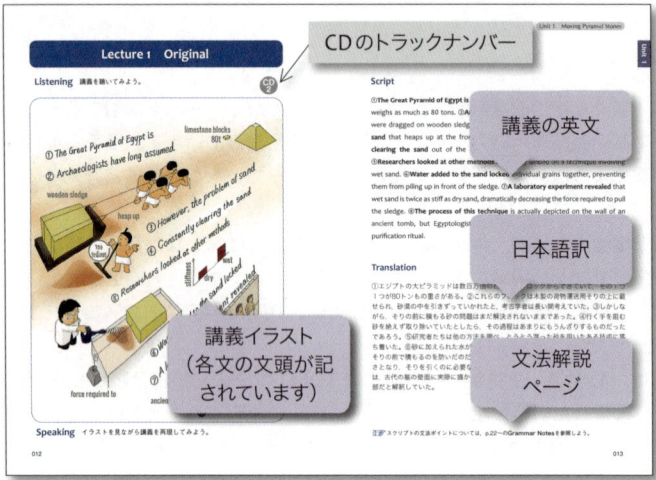

1. **Listen:** 講義を聴く（①何も見ずに→②イラストを見ながら）
2. **Understand:** 内容を確認する（Script，日本語訳，文法解説）
3. **Read Aloud:** 音読する（オーバーラッピング，シャドーイング）
4. **Speak:** イラストをヒントに講義を再現する

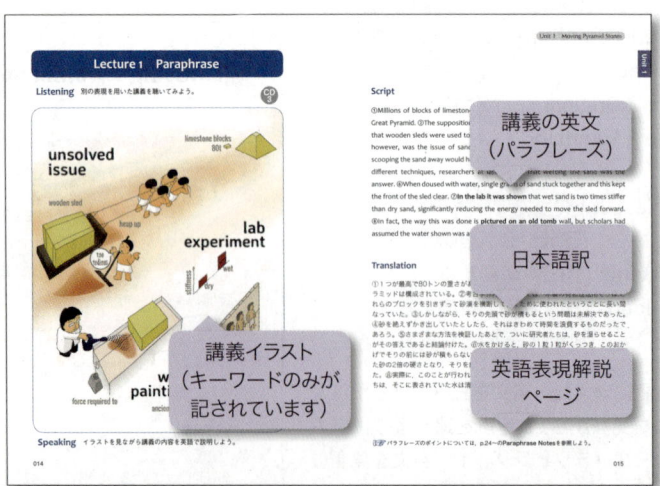

1. **Listen:** 講義（パラフレーズ）を聴く（①何も見ずに→②イラストを見ながら）
2. **Understand:** 内容を確認する（Script，日本語訳，パラフレーズ解説）
3. **Read Aloud:** 音読する（オーバーラッピング，シャドーイング）
4. **Speak:** 講義内容を説明する（①イラストを見て→②自分の言葉で説明）

## Conversation

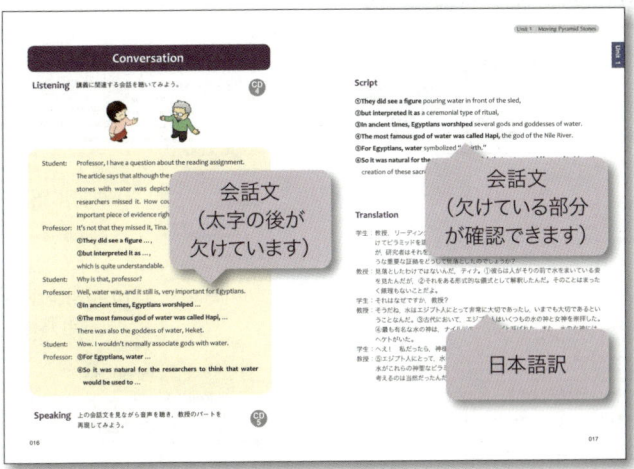

1. **Listen:** 会話を聴く（①何も見ずに→②吹き出しを見ながら）
2. **Understand:** 内容を確認する（Script，日本語訳）
3. **Read Aloud:** 音読する（オーバーラッピング，シャドーイング）
4. **Speak:** セリフを再現する（①吹き出しを見ながら→②何も見ずにロールプレイ）

## Lecture 2

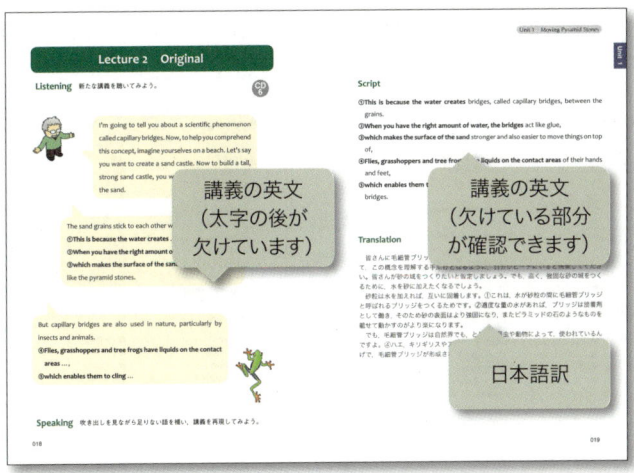

1. **Listen:** 講義を聴く（①何も見ずに→②吹き出しを見ながら）
2. **Understand:** 内容を確認する（Script，日本語訳）
3. **Read Aloud:** 音読する（オーバーラッピング，シャドーイング）
4. **Speak:** 講義を再現する（①吹き出しを見て再現→②講義内容を要約する）

007

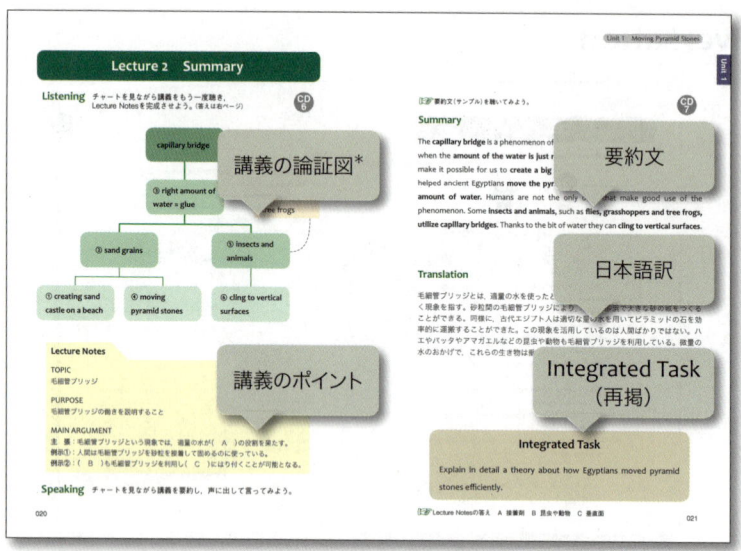

\*論証図の丸数字は講義で提示される順序です。緑色は支持文，赤色は反論です。
上のほうに講義の主要なポイントが示され，下に行くほど詳細な説明となります。

1. **Listen:** 講義をもう一度聴く（①何も見ずに→②チャートを見ながら）
2. **Understand:** 内容を確認する（前ページの Script，Lecture Notes）
3. **Read Aloud:** 音読する（オーバーラッピング，シャドーイング）
4. **Speak:** 論証図をヒントに要約する（①要約文の再現→②自分の言葉で要約）

最後に Integrated Task の質問に英語で答えてみましょう。

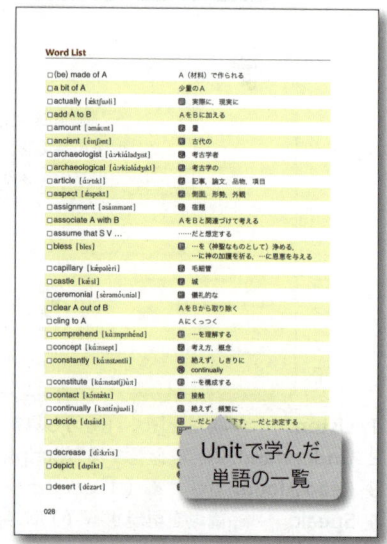

# TOEFL iBT® テスト受験ガイド

受験の申込から受験当日までを，簡単に記します。
これらは，国際教育交換協議会（CIEE）日本代表部のウェブサイト
（http://www.cieej.or.jp/toefl）から引用し，まとめたものです。
より詳しい内容は，当ウェブサイトを確認してください。

> TOEFL iBT® テスト申込までの流れ

### 1．Bulletin（受験要綱）の入手・熟読

"TOEFL Information and Registration Bulletin" の略で，TOEFL iBT® テストの受験要綱です。受験希望者は，申込前に必ずBulletinを読まなければなりません。

### 2．身分証明書（ID）の準備・確認

受験には，米国ETSの定める身分証明書（ID）が必要です。当日に提示できなければ，受験できず，返金も一切ありません。

### 3．My Home Pageの作成

米国ETSのTOEFL®テスト公式サイト上に無料で作成できる，個人のアカウントページのことです。
My Home Pageを作成すると，
- TOEFL iBT® テスト会場・実施スケジュールの最新情報の確認
- テスト申込
- 申込済みテスト日の変更・キャンセル
- スコアの確認
- 志望団体へのOfficial Score Reports（米国ETSから団体に直接送付される公式スコアレポート）の送付手続き

…などの機能がいつでも利用できます。

### 4．受験料の支払い方法の準備・確認

支払い方法には，クレジットカード・Pay Pal Account・国際郵便為替・送金小切手があります。
テスト日の7日前（通常の申し込み締切日）までに申込をすれば，受験料は，US$230＊です。
通常の申込締切日以降の申込も可能ですが，手数料US$40が加えられて，受験料はUS$270となります。

　＊2016年6月時点の料金です。

### 5．申込

オンライン・郵送・電話から選ぶことができますが，支払い方法により，利用できる申込方法は異なりますので，ご注意ください。

## TOEFL iBT® テスト受験の前に

### 1．申込済みテスト内容確認
テストに関する重要な変更がある場合がありますので，必ずテスト前日に My Home Page で確認してください。

### 2．Official Score Reports の送付手続き
公式スコアの提出を求められている場合，ETS に送付依頼をする必要があります。
テスト日前日の22時までに My Home Page で手続きすれば，4校まで無料で送付を依頼することができます。

### 3．受験キャンセル
テスト日の4日前（中3日）までに手続きすれば，受験料の半額の返金が行われます。

### 4．申込済みテスト日・会場変更
テスト日の4日前（中3日）までに手続きすれば，US$60の手数料を支払うことで，テスト日・会場変更が可能です（ただし，空席がある場合のみ）。

## TOEFL iBT® テスト当日

### 1．必ず持参するもの
- テスト当日に有効な身分証明書（ID）
- Registration Number（受験番号）
- テスト前日に My Home Page で確認した内容を印刷したもの

### 2．集合時刻
テスト開始30分前までに集合します。遅刻した場合は受験できず，受験料の返金もありません。

### 3．規約
テスト会場では，定められた規定・手順に従ってください。

＊受験料や手数料は，予告なく変更される可能性があります。最新の情報は，TOEFL® テスト公式ウェブサイト（http://www.ets.org/toefl）で必ずご確認ください。

# Unit 1 Moving Pyramid Stones

## Integrated Task

Explain in detail a theory about how Egyptians moved pyramid stones efficiently.

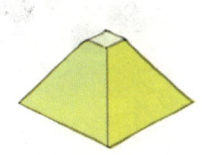

## Key Words

**archaeologist**

▶「考古学者」という意味の名詞です。考古学（archaeology）とは，おもに文字による記録がない時代（pre-history）について，遺跡などの物質的痕跡からその時代の人類の活動を明らかにしようとする学問です。また，文字のある時代（history）についても，特に文献が不十分である場合に，それを補う目的で行われます。古代エジプト研究では，ヒエログリフ（神聖文字：古代エジプトで使われたエジプト文字の1つ），墓室内壁の壁画，そして発掘物などの分析が組み合わされますが，今回は，考古学的推察と壁画の解釈が重要なポイントとなっています。

**interpret**

▶ある表現や現象が，どのような意味を持つのかを見極めようとする行為を指す動詞で，「解釈する」という日本語に当たります。How do you interpret his smile? ならば「彼の微笑みは，どういう意味だと思う？」ということで，「正しい解釈」もあれば，「誤った解釈」もありえるわけです。講義の最後で明らかにされる，古代エジプト研究者の「誤り」とは，どのようなものだったのでしょう。

011

# Lecture 1　Original

Listening　講義を聴いてみよう。

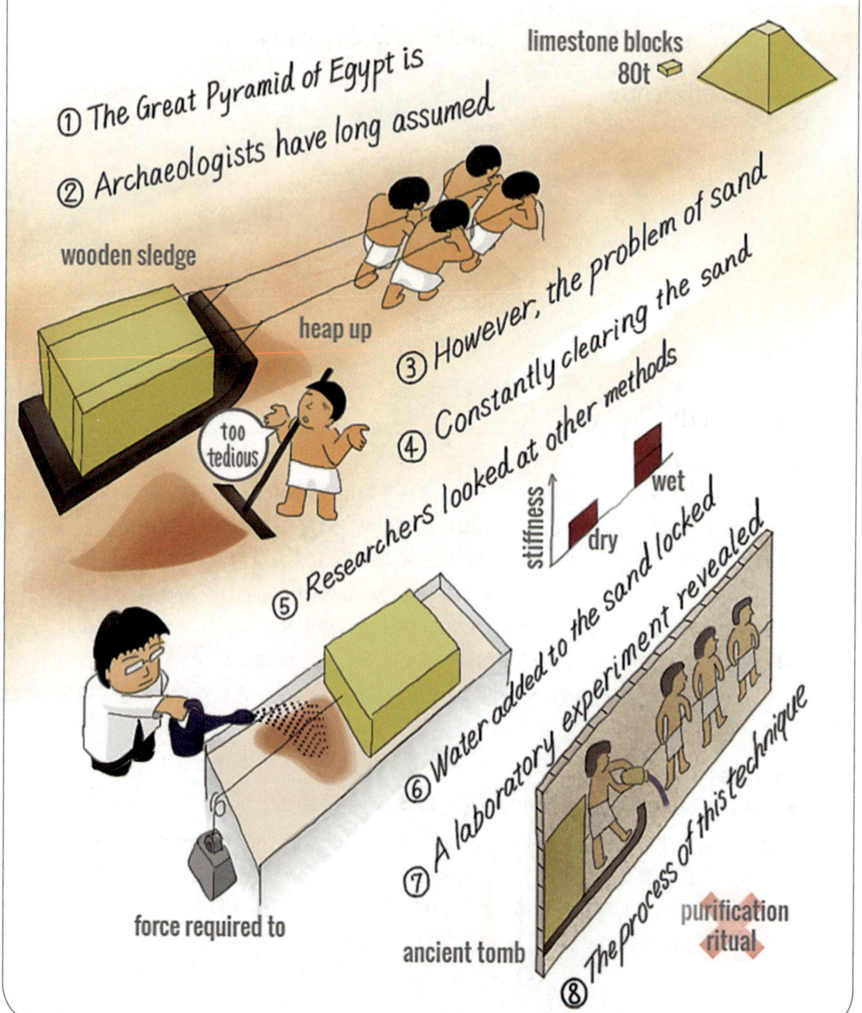

## Script

①**The Great Pyramid of Egypt is** made of millions of limestone blocks, each of which weighs as much as 80 tons. ②**Archaeologists have long assumed** that these blocks were dragged on wooden sledges through the desert. ③**However, the problem of sand** that heaps up at the front of the sledge remained unsolved. ④**Constantly clearing the sand** out of the way would have made the process too tedious. ⑤**Researchers looked at other methods** and finally landed on a technique involving wet sand. ⑥**Water added to the sand locked** individual grains together, preventing them from piling up in front of the sledge. ⑦**A laboratory experiment revealed** that wet sand is twice as stiff as dry sand, dramatically decreasing the force required to pull the sledge. ⑧**The process of this technique** is actually depicted on the wall of an ancient tomb, but Egyptologists had been interpreting the water as part of a purification ritual.

## Translation

①エジプトの大ピラミッドは数百万個の石灰石のブロックからできていて，その1つ1つが80トンもの重さがある。②これらのブロックは木製の荷物運送用そりの上に載せられ，砂漠の中を引きずっていかれたと，考古学者は長い間考えていた。③しかしながら，そりの前に積もる砂の問題はまだ解決されないままであった。④行く手を阻む砂を絶えず取り除いていたとしたら，その過程はあまりにもうんざりするものだったであろう。⑤研究者たちは他の方法を調べ，とうとう湿った砂を用いたある技術に落ち着いた。⑥砂に加えられた水が，砂の1粒1粒をしっかりかみ合わせて動かなくし，そりの前で積もるのを防いだのだ。⑦室内実験では，湿った砂は，乾いた砂の2倍の硬さとなり，そりを引くのに必要な力が劇的に減ることがわかった。⑧この技術の過程は，古代の墓の壁面に実際に描かれているが，エジプト学者はその水を清めの儀式の一部だと解釈していた。

☞ スクリプトの文法ポイントについては，p.022～の**Grammar Notes**を参照しよう。

## Lecture 1 Paraphrase

**Listening** 別の表現を用いた講義を聴いてみよう。 CD 3

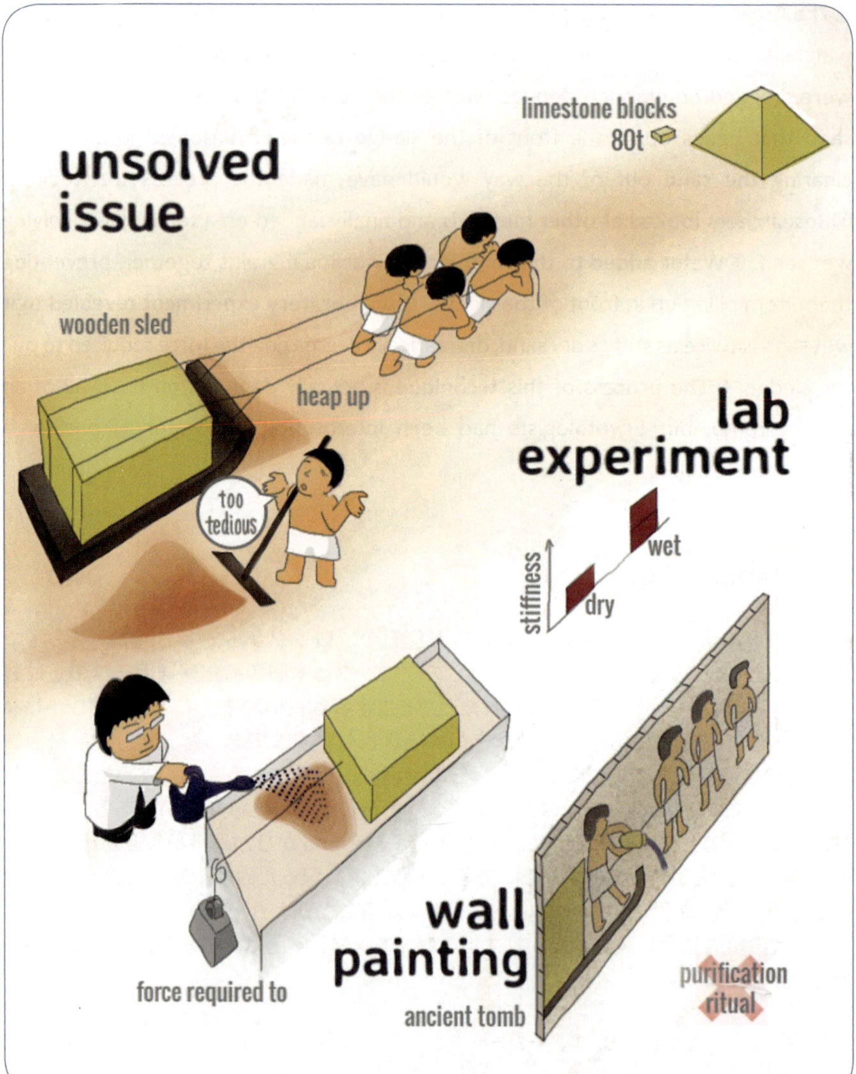


**Speaking** イラストを見ながら講義の内容を英語で説明しよう。

Unit 1　Moving Pyramid Stones

## Script

①Millions of blocks of limestone, weighing up to 80 tons each, constitute Egypt's Great Pyramid. ②The supposition within the archeological community has long been that wooden sleds were used to haul these blocks across the desert. ③**Unresolved**, however, was the issue of sand piling up at the head of the sleds. ④Continually scooping the sand away would have been extremely time-consuming. ⑤After testing different techniques, researchers at last decided that wetting the sand was the answer. ⑥When doused with water, single grains of sand stuck together and this kept the front of the sled clear. ⑦**In the lab it was shown** that wet sand is two times stiffer than dry sand, significantly reducing the energy needed to move the sled forward. ⑧In fact, the way this was done is **pictured on an old tomb** wall, but scholars had assumed the water shown was an aspect of a rite of purification.

## Translation

①１つが最高で80トンの重さがある数百万個の石灰石のブロックで，エジプトの大ピラミッドは構成されている。②考古学界内での仮説では，木製の荷物運送用そりは，これらのブロックを引きずって砂漠を横断して行くために使われたということに長い間なっていた。③しかしながら，そりの先頭で砂が積もるという問題は未解決であった。④砂を絶えずかき出していたとしたら，それはきわめて時間を浪費するものだったであろう。⑤さまざまな方法を検証したあとで，ついに研究者たちは，砂を湿らせることがその答えであると結論付けた。⑥水をかけると，砂の１粒１粒がくっつき，このおかげでそりの前には砂が積もらないようになったのだ。⑦実験室では，湿った砂は乾いた砂の2倍の硬さとなり，そりを前進させるのに必要な力を大幅に減らすことが示された。⑧実際に，このことが行われた様子が，古代の墓の壁面に描かれているが，学者たちは，そこに表されていた水は清めの儀式の一面であると仮定してきた。

☞ パラフレーズのポイントについては，p.024〜の**Paraphrase Notes**を参照しよう。

015

# Conversation

**Listening**  講義に関連する会話を聴いてみよう。

Student: Professor, I have a question about the reading assignment. The article says that although the process of moving the pyramid stones with water was depicted on an old tomb wall, the researchers missed it. How could they have missed such an important piece of evidence right in front of them?

Professor: It's not that they missed it, Tina.
①**They did see a figure …,**
②**but interpreted it as …,**
which is quite understandable.

Student: Why is that, professor?

Professor: Well, water was, and it still is, very important for Egyptians.
③**In ancient times, Egyptians worshiped …**
④**The most famous god of water was called Hapi, …**
There was also the goddess of water, Heket.

Student: Wow. I wouldn't normally associate gods with water.

Professor: ⑤**For Egyptians, water …**
⑥**So it was natural for the researchers to think that water would be used to …**

**Speaking**  上の会話文を見ながら音声を聴き，教授のパートを再現してみよう。

016

## Script

①**They did see a figure** pouring water in front of the sled,
②**but interpreted it as** a ceremonial type of ritual,
③**In ancient times, Egyptians worshiped** several gods and goddesses of water.
④**The most famous god of water was called Hapi,** the god of the Nile River.
⑤**For Egyptians, water** symbolized "rebirth."
⑥**So it was natural for the researchers to think that water would be used to** bless the creation of these sacred pyramids.

## Translation

学生：教授，リーディングの宿題について質問があるんです。その論文によれば，水をかけてピラミッドを建設するための石を動かす過程は古代の墓の壁に描かれていますが，研究者はそれを見落としていました。彼らは自分たちのすぐ目の前にあるそのような重要な証拠をどうして見落としたのでしょうか？

教授：見落としたわけではないんだ，ティナ。①彼らは人がそりの前で水をまいている姿を見たんだが，②それをある形式的な儀式として解釈したんだ。そのことはまったく無理もないことだよ。

学生：それはなぜですか，教授？

教授：そうだね，水はエジプト人にとって非常に大切であったし，いまでも大切であるということなんだ。③古代において，エジプト人はいくつもの水の神と女神を崇拝した。④最も有名な水の神は，ナイル川の神で，ハピと呼ばれた。また，水の女神には，ヘケトがいた。

学生：へえ！　私だったら，神様と水を結び付けて考えるなんて，普通はしませんね。

教授：⑤エジプト人にとって，水は「再生」のシンボルだった。⑥だから，研究者にとって水がこれらの神聖なピラミッドの建設に神の加護があるよう祈るために使われたと考えるのは当然だったんだ。

# Lecture 2　Original

**Listening**　新たな講義を聴いてみよう。

I'm going to tell you about a scientific phenomenon called capillary bridges. Now, to help you comprehend this concept, imagine yourselves on a beach. Let's say you want to create a sand castle. Now to build a tall, strong sand castle, you would want to add water to the sand.

The sand grains stick to each other when you add water.
①**This is because the water creates** …
②**When you have the right amount of water, the bridges** …,
③**which makes the surface of the sand** …
like the pyramid stones.

But capillary bridges are also used in nature, particularly by insects and animals.
④**Flies, grasshoppers and tree frogs have liquids on the contact areas** …,
⑤**which enables them to cling** …

**Speaking**　吹き出しを見ながら足りない語を補い，講義を再現してみよう。

Unit 1　Moving Pyramid Stones

## Script

①**This is because the water creates** bridges, called capillary bridges, between the grains.
②**When you have the right amount of water, the bridges** act like glue,
③**which makes the surface of the sand** stronger and also easier to move things on top of,
④**Flies, grasshoppers and tree frogs have liquids on the contact areas** of their hands and feet,
⑤**which enables them to cling** to vertical surfaces due to the formation of capillary bridges.

## Translation

　皆さんに毛細管ブリッジと呼ばれる科学現象についてお話ししようと思います。さて，この概念を理解する手助けとなるように，自分がビーチにいると想像してください。皆さんが砂の城をつくりたいと仮定しましょう。でも，高く，強固な砂の城をつくるために，水を砂に加えたくなるでしょう。
　砂粒は水を加えれば，互いに固着します。①これは，水が砂粒の間に毛細管ブリッジと呼ばれるブリッジをつくるためです。②適度な量の水があれば，ブリッジは接着剤として働き，③そのため砂の表面はより強固になり，またピラミッドの石のようなものを載せて動かすのがより楽になります。
　でも，毛細管ブリッジは自然界でも，とりわけ昆虫や動物によって，使われているんですよ。④ハエ，キリギリスやアマガエルは，手足の接触面に液体があり，⑤そのおかげで，毛細管ブリッジが形成されて，垂直面にぴったりとくっつくことができます。

# Lecture 2　Summary

**Listening**　チャートを見ながら講義をもう一度聴き，Lecture Notesを完成させよう。(答えは右ページ)

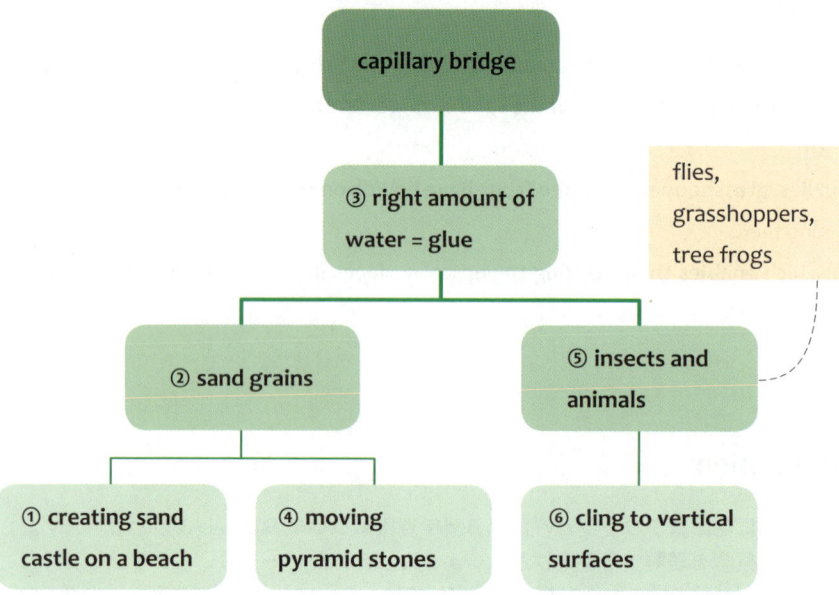

### Lecture Notes

TOPIC
毛細管ブリッジ

PURPOSE
毛細管ブリッジの働きを説明すること

MAIN ARGUMENT
主　張：毛細管ブリッジという現象では，適量の水が（　A　）の役割を果たす。
例示①：人間は毛細管ブリッジを砂粒を接着して固めるのに使っている。
例示②：（　B　）も毛細管ブリッジを利用し（　C　）にはり付くことが可能となる。

**Speaking**　チャートを見ながら講義を要約し，声に出して言ってみよう。

Unit 1　Moving Pyramid Stones

☞ 要約文（サンプル）を聴いてみよう。

## Summary

The **capillary bridge** is a phenomenon of water working as **glue** between tiny objects when the **amount of the water is just right**. Capillary bridges between **sand grains** make it possible for us to **create a big sand castle on a beach**. Similarly, they also helped ancient Egyptians **move the pyramid stones** efficiently, using just **the right amount of water.** Humans are not the only ones that make good use of the phenomenon. Some **insects and animals**, such as **flies, grasshoppers and tree frogs, utilize capillary bridges**. Thanks to the bit of water they can **cling to vertical surfaces**.

## Translation

毛細管ブリッジとは，適量の水を使ったとき，その水が微細な物体間の接着材として働く現象を指す。砂粒間の毛細管ブリッジにより，我々は砂浜で大きな砂の城をつくることができる。同様に，古代エジプト人は適切な量の水を用いてピラミッドの石を効率的に運搬することができた。この現象を活用しているのは人間ばかりではない。ハエやバッタやアマガエルなどの昆虫や動物も毛細管ブリッジを利用している。微量の水のおかげで，これらの生き物は垂直面にはり付くことができるのだ。

### Integrated Task

Explain in detail a theory about how Egyptians moved pyramid stones efficiently.

☞ Lecture Notesの答え　A　接着剤　B　昆虫や動物　C　垂直面

# Grammar Notes

①The Great Pyramid of Egypt **is made of** millions of limestone blocks**, each of which** weighs **as much as** 80 tons.

- be made of A は「Aでできている」という意味で，consist of A とほぼ同義です。ピラミッドが何でできているのかを説明しています。
- each of which weighs ... は，and each of them weighs ... と書き換えることができます。which は limestone blocks を先行詞とする関係代名詞で，「その石灰岩のブロックの1つ1つは…だけの重さがある」と limestone blocks に関する説明を添えています。
- as much as ...「…もの」は「80トン」という重量の大きさを強調する働きをしています。

②Archaeologists **have long assumed** that these blocks were dragged on wooden sledges through the desert.

- have long *done* は「長い間…してきた」という意味です。have *done* for a long time とほぼ同じ意味です。
- assume that ... は「…だと考える」という意味ですが，think などとは異なり，「根拠がないままに…だと決めてかかる」「当然…だと思い込む」という意味合いを含みます。講義の終盤で，この考古学者たちの考えが誤りであったことが示されますが，それに対応した表現です。

③However, the problem of sand **that** heaps up at the front of the sledge **remained unsolved**.

- that は関係代名詞で，先行詞（＝修飾される名詞）は sand です。sand that heaps up at the front of the sledge 全体で，「そりの前に積み重なる砂」という意味です。
- remained unsolved は「まだ解決されていなかった」という意味で，had not been solved yet と書き換えることができます。

④**Constantly clearing the sand out of the way would have made** the process too tedious.

- clear A out of B は「BからA（不要なもの）を取り除く」という意味です。ここでのBは the way ですが，これはそりの進む道筋を示しています。
- would have made ... は「仮定法過去完了」を用いています。したがって，主語である Constantly clearing the sand out of the way は，実際にはそうしなかったことを前提として，「もし絶えず前方の砂を取り除いていたら…」という仮定を示しています。
- make the process too tedious は「その過程をあまりにうんざりするものにする」という意味です。主語，および仮定法過去完了と結びついて「もし絶えず砂を取り除いていたら，その仕事はあまりにうんざりするものになっただろう」という意味が完成します。

⑤Researchers **looked** at other methods **and** finally **landed** on a technique **involving** wet sand.

- 1つの主語 Researchers に対して，述語動詞が looked at ... and landed on ... と2つ並んだ構造です。and などで2つ以上の要素が結び付けられている場合，「何を共有しているのか」

に注意が必要です。ここでは，主語が共有されています。

Researchers {　**looked** at other methods
　　　　　　　**and**
　　　　　　　**landed** on a technique involving wet sand.

▶ involvingは現在分詞で，involving wet sand全体が直前のa techniqueを修飾しています。

⑥Water **added** to the sand locked individual grains together, **preventing them from piling up** in front of the sledge.

▶ addedは過去分詞で，added to the sand全体が直前のWaterを修飾しています。Water (S) ... locked (V) individual grains (O) ...という文の骨格を見抜くことが大切です。
▶ preventing ...は分詞構文で，砂に加えられた水が砂粒を固く結びつけた結果，何が起きたかを追加的に説明しています。and it prevented them ...と書き換えても，それほど意味は変わりません。
▶ prevent A from *doing*は「Aが〜するのを妨げる」「Aが〜できない［しない］ようにする」という意味です。ここでは，結果的に砂粒がそりの前方に積もらなくなったことが述べられています。

⑦A laboratory experiment revealed **that** wet sand is **twice as stiff as** dry sand, **dramatically decreasing the force required** to pull the sledge.

▶ thatは接続詞で，動詞revealの目的語となる内容を導いています。「室内実験によって明らかになったこと」がthat節で述べられています。
▶ twice as 〜 as ...は「...の2倍〜」という意味です。twiceは「2倍」を表し，以降three times「3倍」，four times「4倍」…と続きます。分数の場合は，half as 〜 as ...「...の半分〜」，a third as 〜 as ...「...の3分の1〜」…となります。
▶ dramatically decreasing ...は分詞構文で，「湿った砂が乾いた砂の2倍の硬さである」ことが，どのような結果をもたらすかを追加的に説明しています。and (that) it dramatically decreases ...と書き換えても，ほぼ同じ意味です。
▶ requiredは過去分詞で，required to pull the sledge全体が，直前のthe forceを修飾しています。

⑧The process of this technique is actually depicted on the wall of an ancient tomb, but Egyptologists **had been interpreting** the water as part of a purification ritual.

▶ had been interpretingは過去完了形を用いた表現です。過去完了は，過去のある時点を基準にして，「その時点までの完了」に言及するため，過去の「ある時点」の前後で「変化」が生じていることを効果的に示すことができます。ここでは，「実験などによって，砂に水をかけることでそりを滑りやすくしたという事実が明らかになった時点」を基準として，それ以前において，「壁画は清めの儀式だと解釈されていた」（＝過去完了形で表現）が，それ以降は「水をかける動作だと解釈されるようになった」という「解釈の仕方の変化」が効果的に表現されています。

## Paraphrase Notes

①Millions of blocks of limestone, weighing **up to** 80 tons each, **constitute** Egypt's Great Pyramid.

▶オリジナル①では，A is made of B「AはBでできている」という表現を用いていましたが，こちらでは，B constitute A「BがAを構成する」という表現に変わっています。Aが「全体」，Bが「構成要素」である点に注意しましょう。

▶オリジナル①では，as much as を用いて表した「80トンもの重さ」という意味合いを，up to 80 tons「(最大で)80トンにも達する」と表現しています。

②**The supposition within the archeological community has long been** that wooden sleds were used to haul these blocks across the desert.

▶オリジナル②での「考古学者は…だと長い間考えてきた」という表現を，「考古学会での想定は，長い間…ということだった」とパラフレーズしています。

▶「そり」に当たる名詞は，sledge に代わって sled が用いられています。また，「引きずって運ぶ」という動作は，drag に代わって haul という動詞で表しています。

③**Unresolved, however, was the issue** of sand piling up at the head of the sleds.

▶下線部を平易な語順に直すと，However, the issue was unresolved となります。

▶the issue was unresolved の unresolved が文頭に置かれたことによって，the issue (S) was (V) が was (V) the issue (S) という語順になっています。このような語順の変化は，主語が修飾語を伴って長くなった場合などに生じます。

▶however「しかしながら」など，内容的なつながりを示す副詞句は，文頭に置かれるだけでなく，文の途中や文末に置かれる場合があります。主語の直後や，文頭の副詞句・節の直後に挿入されることが特に多いので，注意しましょう。

④Continually scooping the sand away would have been extremely time-consuming.

▶オリジナル④と同様に，仮定法過去完了を用いています。

▶Constantly → Continually，clear ... out of the way → scoop ... away，tedious → time-consuming といった語句レベルでの言い換えが行われています。

⑤**After** testing different techniques, researchers at last decided that wetting the sand was the answer.

▶順序の表し方に注目しましょう。オリジナル⑤では，Researchers looked at ... and finally landed ... と，and で動詞をつなぐことで順序を表していましたが，ここでは After testing ..., researchers at last decided ... と，前置詞 after によって，前後関係を表現しています。

▶decide that ... は「…だと結論付ける」という意味です。

Unit 1　Moving Pyramid Stones

⑥When doused with water, single grains of sand stuck together **and this kept the front of the sled clear**.

▶this は，「砂粒が結びついた」という内容を受けています。下線部全体は「そして，このことがそりの前方を砂のない状態に保った」，つまり「砂粒が結びついたので，そりの前には砂が積もらなかった」という意味になります。keep O C「OをCの状態に保つ」という表現がポイントです。

▶オリジナル⑥のように分詞構文を用いて書けば，下線部は (...,) keeping the front of the sled clear となります。

⑦**In the lab it was shown that** wet sand is **two times stiffer than** dry sand, significantly reducing the energy needed to move the sled forward.

▶オリジナル⑦の「室内実験は…ということを明らかにした」という表現が，「実験室では…ということが示された」と言い換えられています。

▶twice as stiff as という，as ～ as を用いた倍数表現は，two times stiffer than という比較級を用いた表現に変わっています。

⑧In fact, the way this was done is pictured on an old tomb wall, but scholars **had assumed** the water **shown** was an aspect of a rite of purification.

▶had assumed の過去完了時制は，「その思い込みは後に修正された」という「変化」を効果的に表しています。オリジナル⑧の解説で確認しましょう。

▶shown は過去分詞で，直前の the water を修飾しています。the water shown <u>in the picture on an old tomb</u> の下線部が省略されたものと考えられます。

025

# Expressions and Phrases

ヒントを手がかりにして，日本語に対応する英語表現を言ってみよう。

| 日本語 | ヒント | 英語 |
|---|---|---|
| ☐ 読書課題 | re___ as___ | reading assignment |
| ☐ 発表された記事 | pu___ ar___ | published article |
| ☐ 退屈な講義 | te___ le___ | tedious lecture |
| ☐ 古代 | an___ ti___ | ancient times |
| ☐ 考古学的側面 | ar___ as___ | archaeological aspect |
| ☐ 中心人物 | ce___ fi___ | central figure |
| ☐ 式服 | ce___ co___ | ceremonial costume |
| ☐ 石灰石のお墓 | li___ to___ | limestone tomb |
| ☐ 広大な砂漠 | va___ de___ | vast desert |
| ☐ 砂粒 | sa___ gr___ | sand grain |
| ☐ 個々の粒 | in___ pa___ | individual particle |
| ☐ 室内実験 | la___ ex___ | laboratory experiment |
| ☐ 時間のかかる過程 | ti___-co___ pr___ | time-consuming process |
| ☐ 研究技術 | re___ te___ | research technique |
| ☐ ある特定の方法 | pa___ me___ | particular method |
| ☐ 実際の量 | ac___ am___ | actual amount |
| ☐ 長距離 | lo___ di___ | long distance |
| ☐ 垂直方向 | ve___ di___ | vertical direction |
| ☐ 接触面 | co___ ar___ | contact area |
| ☐ 表面の固さ | su___ st___ | surface stiffness |
| ☐ 水分吸収 | li___ ab___ | liquid absorption |
| ☐ 毛細管現象 | ca___ ac___ | capillary action |
| ☐ 架橋 | br___ fo___ | bridge formation |
| ☐ 異常な現象 | ex___ ph___ | extraordinary phenomenon |
| ☐ 極端な例 | ex___ ca___ | extreme case |
| ☐ 劇的な減少 | dr___ de___ | dramatic decrease |
| ☐ 決定的証拠 | cr___ ev___ | crucial evidence |
| ☐ 似た発想 | si___ co___ | similar concept |
| ☐ 小さな虫 | ti___ in___ | tiny insect |
| ☐ 怠け者のキリギリス | id___ gr___ | idle grasshopper |

Unit 1　Moving Pyramid Stones

□木製のそりを引く

| dr___ the wo___ sl___ | drag the wooden sledge |
| ha___ the sl___ made of wo___ | haul the sled made of wood |

□重さが2トンもある

| we___ u_ to two tons | weigh up to two tons |
| be a_ he___ as two tons | be as heavy as two tons |

□摩擦力を低下させる

| de___ the fr___ force | decrease the frictional force |
| re___ the force due to fr___ | reduce the force due to friction |

□地面に岩を積み上げる

| he___ up rocks on the gr___ | heap up rocks on the ground |
| pi___ up rocks on the land su___ | pile up rocks on the land surface |

□清めの儀式を描写する

| de___ the pu___ ri___ | depict the purification rite |
| il___ how they pu___ things | illustrate how they purify things |

□それを神聖な儀式と解釈する

| in___ it as a sa___ ri___ | interpret it as a sacred ritual |
| un___ that it is a re___ ri___ | understand that it is a religious ritual |

□絶え間ない努力を必要とする

| in___ co___ ef___ | involve continuous effort |
| re___ co___ hard wo___ | require constant hard work |

□未だに解決されない

| still re___ un___ | still remain unsolved |
| be y_ to be so___ | be yet to be solved |

□重要な点を理解し損ねる

| mi___ the si___ point | miss the significant point |
| fail to co___ the ma___ point | fail to comprehend the major point |

□もともとの予測に固執する

| st___ to the or___ su___ | stick to the original supposition |
| cl___ to the in___ pr___ | cling to the initial prediction |

027

# Word List

| | |
|---|---|
| ☐ (be) made of A | A（材料）で作られる |
| ☐ a bit of A | 少量のA |
| ☐ actually [ǽktʃuəli] | 副 実際に，現実に |
| ☐ add A to B | AをBに加える |
| ☐ amount [əmáunt] | 名 量 |
| ☐ ancient [éinʃənt] | 形 古代の |
| ☐ archaeologist [àːrkiálədʒist] | 名 考古学者 |
| ☐ archaeological [àːrkiəládʒikl] | 形 考古学の |
| ☐ article [áːrtikl] | 名 記事，論文，品物，項目 |
| ☐ aspect [ǽspekt] | 名 側面，形勢，外観 |
| ☐ assignment [əsáinmənt] | 名 宿題 |
| ☐ associate A with B | AをBと関連づけて考える |
| ☐ assume that S V … | ……だと想定する |
| ☐ bless [bles] | 動 …を（神聖なものとして）浄める，…に神の加護を祈る，…に恩恵を与える |
| ☐ capillary [kǽpəlèri] | 名 毛細管 |
| ☐ castle [kǽsl] | 名 城 |
| ☐ ceremonial [sèrəmóuniəl] | 形 儀礼的な |
| ☐ clear A out of B | AをBから取り除く |
| ☐ cling to A | Aにくっつく |
| ☐ comprehend [kàːmprihénd] | 動 …を理解する |
| ☐ concept [káːnsept] | 名 考え方，概念 |
| ☐ constantly [káːnstəntli] | 副 絶えず，しきりに 類 continually |
| ☐ constitute [káːnstət(j)ùːt] | 動 …を構成する |
| ☐ contact [káːntækt] | 名 接触 |
| ☐ continually [kəntínjuəli] | 副 絶えず，頻繁に |
| ☐ decide [disáid] | 動 …だと結論を下す，…だと決定する 比較 decide to do「…しようと決心する」，decide that S V...「…だと結論を下す」 |
| ☐ decrease [diːkríːs] | 動 …を減らす，…が減る |
| ☐ depict [dipíkt] | 動 …を描く，…を描写する 類 describe |
| ☐ desert [dézərt] | 名 砂漠 形 砂漠のような，人のいない |

Unit 1　Moving Pyramid Stones

|  |  |
|---|---|
| □ douse [daʊs] | 動 …に（水などを）浴びせる，…をずぶ濡れにする<br>類 drench |
| □ drag [dræg] | 動 …を引きずる |
| □ dramatically [drəmǽtɪkəli] | 副 劇的に |
| □ due to A | Aのせいで，Aのおかげで<br>類 on account of A / owing to A / because of A |
| □ efficiently [ɪfíʃəntli] | 副 効率よく |
| □ enable A to do | Aが…するのを可能にする |
| □ evidence [évədəns] | 名 証拠 |
| □ experiment [ɪkspérəmənt] | 名 実験　動 実験する |
| □ extremely [ɪkstríːmli] | 副 極端に，極度に<br>類 exceptionally / extraordinarily |
| □ figure [fígjər] | 名 姿，図 |
| □ fly [flaɪ] | 名 ハエ |
| □ force [fɔːrs] | 名 力，影響力，軍事力<br>動 （強いて）…させる（force O to do） |
| □ formation [fɔːrméɪʃən] | 名 形成 |
| □ glue [gluː] | 名 接着剤，のり |
| □ goddess [gáːdəs] | 名 女神 |
| □ grain [greɪn] | 名 粒，粒子，穀物 |
| □ grasshopper [grǽshɔ̀pər] | 名 バッタ，キリギリス |
| □ haul [hɔːl] | 動 …をぐいっと引っ張る |
| □ heap up | …を積み上げる |
| □ in fact | 実際には |
| □ individual [ìndəvídʒuəl] | 形 個々の，個人の，独特の　名 個人，構成員 |
| □ insect [ínsekt] | 名 昆虫 |
| □ interpret A as B | AをBだと解釈する |
| □ involve [ɪnváːlv] | 動 …を含む，…を伴う，…を巻き込む<br>類 include<br>語法 involve oneself in A「Aに参加する，Aに熱中する」 |
| □ issue [íʃuː] | 名 問題，発行，出版物<br>動 …を発行する，…を支給する |
| □ lab [læb] | 名 実験室（=laboratory） |

029

| | | |
|---|---|---|
| □ laboratory [lǽbərətɔ̀:ri] | 名 | 実験室 |
| □ land on A | | Aに到達する，Aに着陸する |
| □ limestone [láɪmstòun] | 名 | 石灰岩 |
| □ liquid [líkwɪd] | 名 | 液体 |
| □ method [méθəd] | 名 | 方法 |
| □ miss [mɪs] | 動 | …を見逃す，…を免れる，…に乗り遅れる，…がいないのを寂しく思う |
| □ natural [nǽtʃərəl] | 形 | 当然の，自然の |
| □ object [á:bdʒɪkt] | 名 | 物体，目的 |
| □ particularly [pərtíkjəlɚli] | 副 | 特に |
| □ phenomenon [fɪnɑ́mɪnən] | 名 | 現象 |
| □ pile up | | 積み上がる，…を積み上げる |
| □ pour [pɔ:r] | 動 | …を浴びせる，…を注ぐ |
| □ prevent A from *doing* | | Aが…するのを妨げる |
| □ process [prá:ses] | 名 | 過程，プロセス |
| □ pull [pʊl] | 動 | …を引っぱる |
| □ purification [pjùərəfɪkéɪʃən] | 名 | 清めること，浄化 |
| □ rebirth [rì:bə́:rθ] | 名 | 再生 |
| □ reduce [rɪd(j)ú:s] | 動 | …を下げる，…を減少させる |
| □ remain [rɪméɪn] | 動 | …のままである |
| □ require [rɪkwáɪər] | 動 語法 | …を必要とする，…を要求する<br>require that S (should) *do*「…するよう要求する」 |
| □ researcher [rì:sə́:rtʃər] | 名 | 研究者 |
| □ reveal [rɪvíːl] | 動 | …を明らかにする，…であることを示す |
| □ rite [raɪt] | 名 | 儀式 |
| □ ritual [rítʃuəl] | 名 類 | 儀式<br>rite / ceremony |
| □ sacred [séɪkrəd] | 形 | 神聖な |
| □ scoop [sku:p] | 動 | …をすくい上げる |
| □ significantly [sɪgnífɪkəntli] | 副 類 | かなり，著しく，はっきりと，重要なことに<br>notably / remarkably |
| □ similarly [símələrli] | 副 | 同様に |
| □ sledge [sledʒ] | 名 | （荷物運搬用の）そり（=sled） |

## Unit 1　Moving Pyramid Stones

| | | |
|---|---|---|
| □ stick [stɪk] | 動 | くっつく，張りつける，…を突き刺す |
| | 類 | adhere |
| □ stiff [stɪf] | 形 | 堅い，まがりにくい |
| □ supposition [sʌ̀pəzíʃən] | 名 | 仮説　類 assumption / hypothesis |
| □ surface [sə́ːrfəs] | 名 | 表面　形 表面の |
| □ symbolize [símbəlàɪz] | 動 | …を象徴化する |
| □ technique [tekníːk] | 名 | 技術 |
| □ tedious [tíːdiəs] | 形 | うんざりするような，退屈な |
| | 類 | boring |
| □ thanks to A | | Aのおかげで |
| □ time-consuming [táɪmkəns(j)ùːmɪŋ] | 形 | 時間のかかる |
| □ tiny [táɪni] | 形 | ごく小さい，ごくわずかな |
| | 類 | minute / microscopic |
| □ tomb [tuːm] | 名 | 墓 |
| | 類 | grave |
| □ understandable [ʌ̀ndərstǽndəbl] | 形 | 理解できる |
| □ unsolved [ənsάːlvd] | 形 | 未解決の，解決されていない |
| □ up to A | | 最大Aまで |
| □ utilize [júːtəlàɪz] | 動 | …を利用する |
| □ vertical [və́ːrtɪkl] | 形 | 垂直の |
| □ weigh [weɪ] | 動 | …の重さがある，…の重さを量る，…を比較考察する |
| □ wet [wet] | 形 | 湿った　動 …を濡らす |
| □ wooden [wúdn] | 形 | 木製の |
| □ worship [wə́ːrʃəp] | 動 | …を崇拝する　名 崇拝，礼拝 |

## 参考文献

Gad A. Water culture in Egypt. In : El Moujabber M. (ed.), Shatanawi M. (ed.), Trisorio-Liuzzi G. (ed.), Ouessar M. (ed.), Laureano P. (ed.), Rodríguez R. (ed.). *Water culture and water conflict in the Mediterranean area*. Bari : CIHEAM, 2008. p. 85-96. (Options Méditerranéennes : Série A. Séminaires Méditerranéens; n. 83). 1. MELIA Workshop Water Culture and Water Conflict, 2007/11/22-25, Nabeul-Médenine (Tunisia). http://om.ciheam.org/om/pdf/a83/00800927.pdf

Persson, B. N. (2007, August 22). Wet adhesion with application to tree frog adhesive toe pads and tires. *Journal of Physics: Condensed Matter, 19* (37), doi:10.1088/0953-8984/19/37/376110

Feng, J. (2014, May 5). *Mystery Of How The Egyptians Moved Pyramid Stones Solved*. Retrieved September 9, 2015, from IFLScience.com website: http://www.iflscience.com/physics/mystery-how-egyptians-moved-pyramid-stones-solved

# Unit 2 Praying Hands

## Integrated Task

Do you agree or disagree with the following statement?

*Great art inspires great stories.*

Use specific reasons and examples to support your answer.

## Key Words

**works of art**

▶「芸術作品」という意味です。名詞workは,「作業そのもの」だけでなく,「作業の結果生じた（特に芸術の）作品」も意味します。ここで注意が必要なのは,前者は「数えられない名詞」として扱われるためa workやworksという形にはなりませんが,後者は「数えられる名詞」として扱われ,a work, two worksなどと数えることができる,という点です。また,artは芸術全般を指す語ですが,とりわけ「絵画」を指すことが多く,artistは芸術家全般というよりも,「画家」という訳語が当たることが多いことも知っておきましょう。今回の講義で扱われるのは『祈りの手』というタイトルの,素描による「絵画作品」です。

**inspire**

▶「息を吹き込む」という原義を持つ動詞で,「人を元気づける」,「人に着想を与える」などの意味で用いられます。今回の講義は,「偉大な芸術作品は偉大な物語をinspireする」という1文から始まります。これは,「優れた1点の芸術作品が人々の想像力を刺激し,イメージを膨らませ,優れた1つの物語が生まれるに至る」という過程を簡潔に述べたものです。生まれた物語は,必ずしも「実話」であるとは限りません。そのことが,続く1文のone legend（伝説,逸話）という表現に現れています。デューラーの『祈りの手』が喚起した物語とは,どのようなものなのでしょうか。

033

# Lecture 1　Original

**Listening**　講義を聴いてみよう。　CD 9

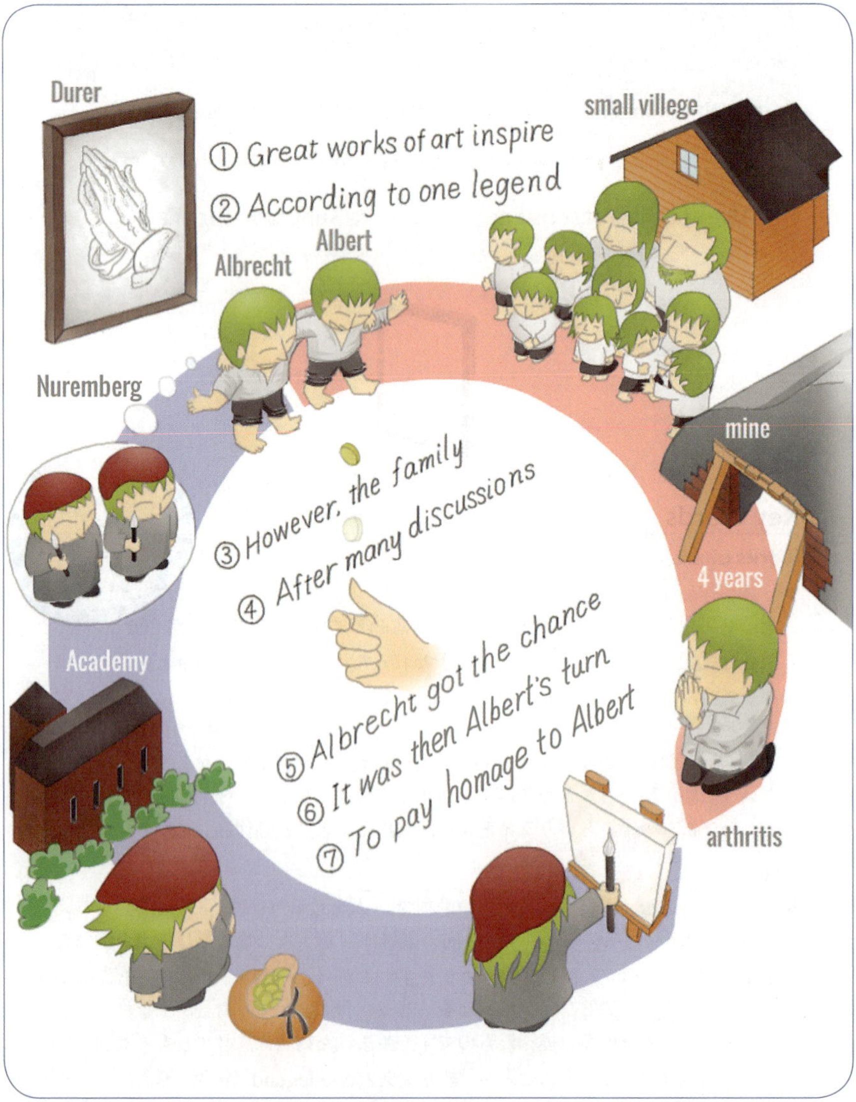


**Speaking**　イラストを見ながら講義を再現してみよう。

## Script

①**Great works of art inspire** great stories, and Albrecht Durer's "Praying Hands" is no exception. ②**According to one legend**, two brothers, Albrecht and Albert Durer, lived in a tiny village near Nuremberg, each dreaming about becoming an artist. ③**However, the family** did not have the money to send either of them to Nuremberg to study art. ④**After many discussions** the boys decided to toss a coin to choose the one who would first work at the nearby mine to help the other study art at the Academy. ⑤**Albrecht got the chance** to study first and became a successful painter by the time he finished his studies at the Academy. ⑥**It was then Albert's turn** to study art, but it was too late because his hands were damaged by the four years of hard work, and his right hand was suffering from arthritis. ⑦**To pay homage to Albert** for all that he had sacrificed, Albrecht carefully drew his brother's abused hands with palms together and thin fingers stretched skyward.

## Translation

①偉大な芸術作品はすばらしい物語を喚起する。そして，アルブレヒト・デューラーの「祈りの手」も例外ではない。②ある逸話によれば，アルブレヒト・デューラーとアルベルト・デューラーはニュルンベルク近郊のとある小さな村に住んでいて，2人とも芸術家になる夢を抱いていた。③しかしながら，家族には芸術を学ばすために彼らのどちらもニュルンベルクにやるお金がなかった。④何度も話し合った末，2人の少年はコインを投げて，どちらかが先に近くの炭鉱で働いて，もう1人が美術学校で美術を勉強するのを手助けするのかを決めることにした。⑤アルブレヒトが最初に学ぶ機会を得た。そして美術学校で勉強を終えるころまでには，画家として成功を収めるまでになった。⑥今度はアルベルトが美術を勉強する番だったが，あまりにも遅すぎた。なぜなら，4年間の厳しい労働の末に，彼は両手を痛めていて，さらに右手は関節炎を患っていたからだ。⑦アルベルトが犠牲にしたすべてのことに対し敬意を払うために，アルブレヒトは，弟の酷使された両手を，手のひらを合わせて，細い指が天に向かって伸びている格好で，入念に描いた。

☞ スクリプトの文法ポイントについては，p.044〜の**Grammar Notes**を参照しよう。

# Lecture 1　Paraphrase

**Listening**　別の表現を用いた講義を聴いてみよう。 CD 10

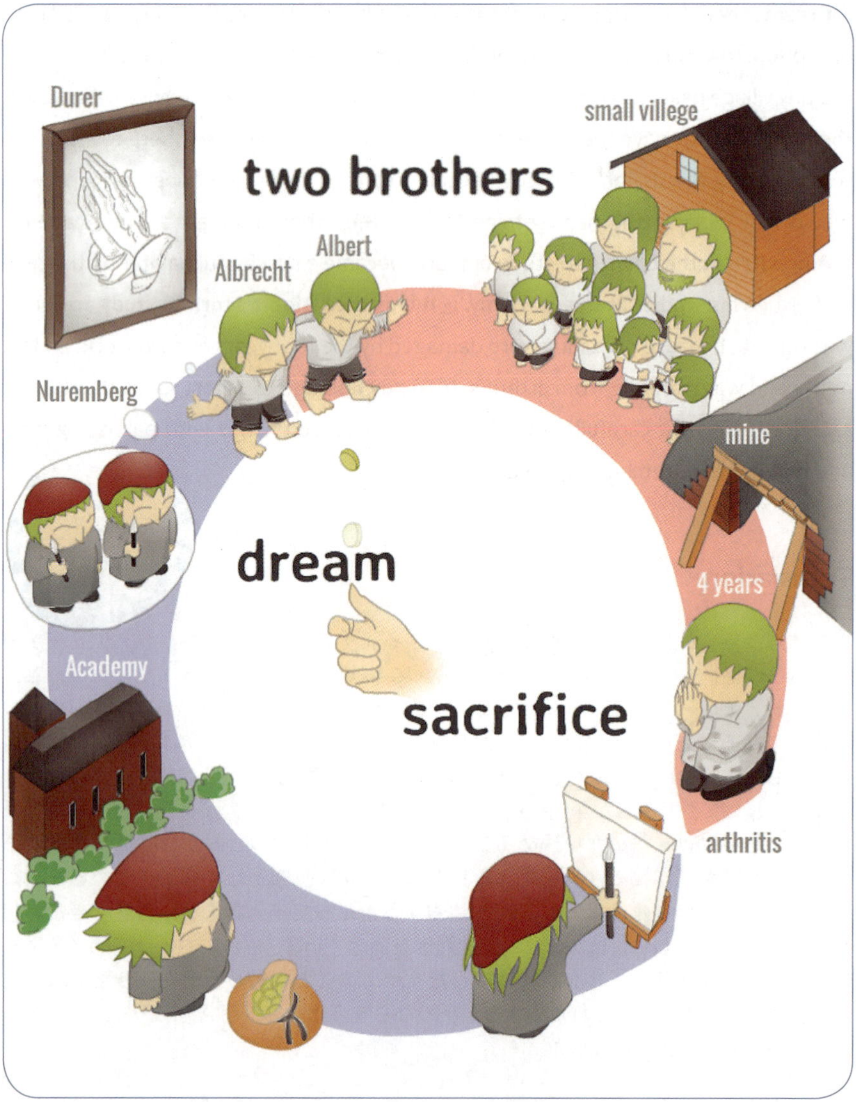


**Speaking**　イラストを見ながら講義の内容を英語で説明しよう。

Unit 2　Praying Hands

## Script

①Terrific pieces of art engender terrific tales, and "Praying Hands", by Albrecht Durer, does, too. ②One such story describes **Albrecht and his brother Albert** residing in a hamlet near Nuremberg and **aspiring** to be artists. ③Alas, the Durer family was too poor to send either boy off to Nuremberg to train. ④Following much discussion, the brothers chose to flip a coin to determine which one would start off working in a local mine and support the other going to study at art school. ⑤Albrecht had the initial opportunity to train, and he was a successful artist even before leaving the Academy. ⑥Albert's time to study had now arrived, but it was not soon enough: four years of difficult labor had injured his hands, plus his right hand was arthritic. ⑦To acknowledge Albert's huge **sacrifice** on his behalf, Albrecht painstakingly sketched the mangled hands of his brother, showing his palms pressed together and his thin fingers pointing to heaven.

## Translation

①すばらしい芸術作品はすばらしい物語を生み出し，アルブレヒト・デューラーによる「祈りの手」もまた同様である。②そのような話の１つによると，アルブレヒトと彼の弟であるアルベルトはニュルンベルク近郊のとある小さな村に住み，芸術家になることを熱望していたとある。③悲しいかな，デューラー家はあまりにも貧しかったので，彼らのどちらも教育をうけるためにニュルンベルクにやることができなかった。④何度も話し合った末に，兄弟はどちらが先に地元の炭鉱で働き始め，もう１人が美術学校に勉強をしに行くのを援助するかを決めるために，コインを投げることにした。⑤アルブレヒトが最初に絵を学ぶ機会を得て，彼が美術学校を卒業しないうちに，すでに画家として成功を収めるまでになっていた。⑥今度は，アルベルトが勉強する番がやってきた。しかし，手遅れであった。４年に及ぶ辛い労働で彼は両手を痛めてしまっていて，おまけに右手は関節炎を患っていた。⑦自分の代わりに大きな犠牲を払ってくれたアルベルトに感謝の意を示すために，アルブレヒトは弟の傷ついた両手を丹精込めて描き，手のひらを固く合わせて，細い指が天に向かっている姿を表現した。

☞ パラフレーズのポイントについては，p.046～の**Paraphrase Notes**を参照しよう。

## Conversation

**Listening** 講義に関連する会話を聴いてみよう。

Student A: I was really touched by the story behind "Praying Hands." What beautiful brotherly love!

Student B: ①Uh… I hate to break it to you, but …

Student A: You mean, it never happened?

Student B: ②Nope. Albrecht's father recognized his son's talent and sent him to apprentice with …

③He never needed his brother to …

Student A: The family was rich, then?

Student B: ④No, the part about …

⑤They had eighteen children, and the father had to …

Student A: Was Albrecht really close with his siblings like in the story?

Student B: Yes, but most of them died in childhood. Only three, including Albrecht, of the eighteen survived.

⑥Interestingly, though, Albrecht's younger brother, Hans, too, …

Student A: Wow. The story is very different than reality, but still a good story!

**Speaking** 上の会話文を見ながら音声を聴き、学生Bのパートを再現してみよう。

## Script

①**Uh... I hate to break it to you, but** that story is fictional.
②**Nope. Albrecht's father recognized his son's talent and sent him to apprentice with** a painter in Nuremberg at the age of fifteen.
③**He never needed his brother to** financially support him.
④**No, the part about** the family being poor is true.
⑤**They had eighteen children, and the father had to** work hard as a goldsmith to support the family.
⑥**Interestingly, though, Albrecht's younger brother, Hans, too,** became a successful artist.

## Translation

学生Ａ：「祈りの手」の背後に隠された物語にほんとうに感動したわ。なんとも美しい兄弟愛ね！
学生Ｂ：①実は，言いたくはないけど，その話は作り話なんだ。
学生Ａ：そんなことはなかったということなの？
学生Ｂ：②そうなんだ。アルブレヒトの父親は息子の才能に気づいて，15歳のときニュルンベルクのある画家のもとに見習いに出したんだ。③彼は経済的に自分を援助してくれる兄弟は決して必要ではなかったんだ。
学生Ａ：その頃，家族は裕福だったの？
学生Ｂ：④そうじゃないよ，家族が貧しかったというところは，本当なんだ。⑤家族には18人の子どもがいて，父親は家族を養うために金細工師として一生懸命に働かなければならなかったんだ。
学生Ａ：アルブレヒトはこの話にあるように，兄弟と本当に固い絆で結ばれていたの？
学生Ｂ：そうだよ。でも彼らのほとんどは子どもの頃に亡くなったんだ。18人中アルブレヒトを含めて3人しか生き残らなかったんだよ。⑥でも，興味深いことに，アルブレヒトの弟，ハンスも画家として成功したんだ。
学生Ａ：まあ，この話は現実とはだいぶ違うけど，それでもいい話よね！

# Lecture 2　Original

## Listening　新たな講義を聴いてみよう。

Some of you may be disappointed that the touching story behind Durer's "Praying Hands" was fictional.
①But you know, creating a good story inspired by a painting …
②There are some fictional stories that have been created …

Let me give you an example. Are you all familiar with the Dutch painter Johannes Vermeer? One of his most famous paintings is called "Girl with a Pearl Earring." It is a portrayal of a European girl wearing a large, blue hairband, or a turban, and a large pearl earring.

Now, this painting inspired two writers to create fictional novels about it.
③One describes the girl with the earring as a servant in Vermeer's house and the story of …
④The other novel is a collection of short stories about …
⑤They are so highly acclaimed that you may believe that …

## Speaking　吹き出しを見ながら足りない語を補い、講義を再現してみよう。

## Script

①**But you know, creating a good story inspired by a painting** isn't all that uncommon.
②**There are some fictional stories that have been created** based on good paintings.
③**One describes the girl with the earring as a servant in Vermeer's house and the story of** how she becomes the portrait's subject.
④**The other novel is a collection of short stories about** the lives of the owners of Vermeer's paintings.
⑤**They are so highly acclaimed that you may believe that** the stories are true!

## Translation

　皆さんの中には，デューラーの「祈りの手」の背後に隠された感動的な物語が作り話だということで，がっかりした人もいるかもしれません。①しかし，ご存じのように，1枚の絵によって感化されて良い話が生まれることは，それほどまれなことではありません。②良い絵をもとにして創り出された作り話が，いくつかあります。
　1つ例を挙げましょう。皆さんは，オランダの画家，ヨハネス・フェルメールを知っていますか。彼の有名な絵画の1つは，「真珠の耳飾りの少女」と呼ばれているものです。それは，大きな，青いヘアバンド，つまりターバンを巻き，大きな真珠の耳飾りをしているヨーロッパの少女の肖像画です。
　さて，この絵画が2人の小説家に影響を与え，彼らはその絵についてフィクションの小説を書いたのです。③1つは耳飾りをした少女をフェルメールの家の使用人として描写し，彼女がどのようにして肖像画のモデルになるかを述べています。④もう1つは，フェルメールの絵画の所有者の人生についての短編集です。⑤この2つの小説はたいへん高く賞賛されているので，あなたもそれらの話が本当であると信じてしまうかもしれません！

# Lecture 2　Summary

**Listening**　チャートを見ながら講義をもう一度聴き，Lecture Notesを完成させよう。(答えは右ページ)　CD 13

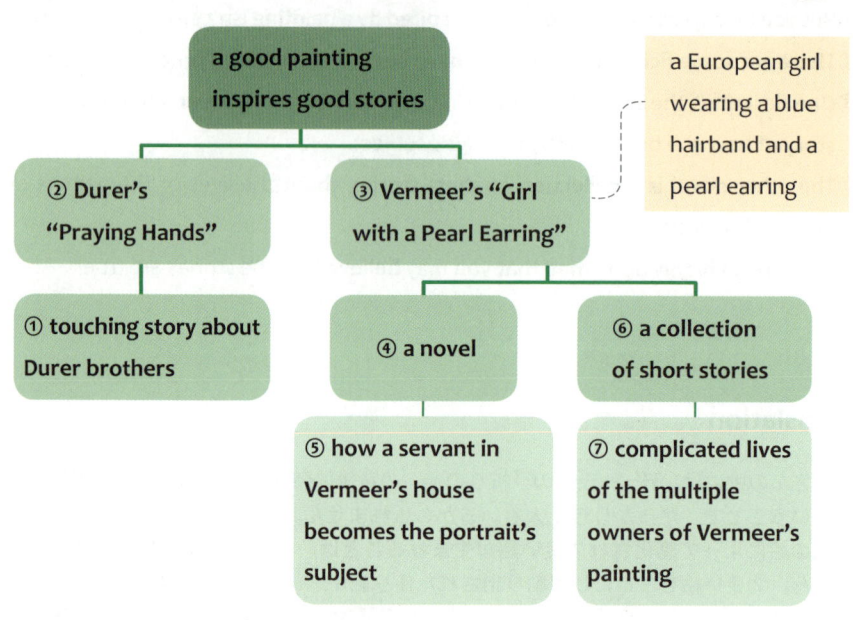

```
          a good painting
        inspires good stories
        /                  \
② Durer's            ③ Vermeer's "Girl     ┄┄ a European girl
"Praying Hands"       with a Pearl Earring"    wearing a blue
       |                /        \             hairband and a
① touching story    ④ a novel   ⑥ a collection  pearl earring
  about Durer                    of short stories
  brothers           |              |
                  ⑤ how a servant  ⑦ complicated lives
                   in Vermeer's     of the multiple
                   house becomes    owners of Vermeer's
                   the portrait's   painting
                   subject
```

### Lecture Notes

TOPIC
名画から生まれた物語

PURPOSE
（　A　）が書き手を刺激し（　B　）が生まれることがよくあることを示すこと

MAIN ARGUMENT
主　張：（　A　）に刺激されて（　B　）が生まれる。
例示①：デューラーの「祈りの手」に触発され，デューラー兄弟の感動的な話が生み出された。
例示②：フェルメールの「真珠の耳飾りの少女」に触発され，２つの小説が作られた。

**Speaking**　チャートを見ながら講義を要約し，声に出して言ってみよう。

Unit 2　Praying Hands

☞ 要約文(サンプル)を聴いてみよう。

## Summary

They say that **a good painting inspires good stories**. One example is **Durer's *Praying Hands***. Someone who was impressed by the great piece of art created the **touching story about the Durer brothers**. In a similar way, **Vermeer's *Girl with a Pearl Earring***, portraying **a European girl wearing a blue hairband and a pearl earring**, inspired two novelists to create intriguing stories. **One novel** tells the story of **how a servant in Vermeer's house becomes the portrait's subject**. Another one is **a collection of short stories** about the **complicated lives of the multiple owners of Vermeer's painting**.

## Translation

素晴らしい絵画は素晴らしい物語を生むと言われている。その一例がデューラーの「祈りの手」だ。この絵画の傑作に感銘を受けた人物がデューラー兄弟の感動的な話を創りだした。同様に、青いターバンと真珠の耳飾りを身につけたヨーロッパの少女を描いたフェルメールの「真珠の耳飾りの少女」に触発され、2人の小説家は面白い物語を創作した。1つの小説はフェルメール家の召使いの少女がどのようにして肖像画のモデルとなるのかについての物語で、もう1つはフェルメールの絵画の所有者たちの複雑な人生についての短編集となっている。

### Integrated Task

Do you agree or disagree with the following statement?

Great art inspires great stories.

Use specific reasons and examples to support your answer.

☞ Lecture Notesの答え　A 絵画　B 物語

## Grammar Notes

①Great works of art inspire great stories, and Albrecht Durer's "Praying Hands" **is no exception**.

▶ A is no exception は「Aも決して例外ではない」という意味の慣用表現です。noは,「まったく〜でない」「〜からは程遠い」という強い否定の意味を加える語で,そこから「むしろ逆である」という意味が生じることがあります。例えばHe is no gentleman. と言えば,「彼は,実に粗野で失礼な男だ」と解釈されます。したがって,ここでは「アルブレヒト・デューラーの『祈りの手』は,まさにその好例である」という意味合いになります。

②According to one legend, two brothers, Albrecht and Albert Durer, lived in a tiny village near Nuremberg, **each dreaming** about becoming an artist.

▶ each dreaming ...は分詞構文の一種で, and each of them was dreaming ...と書き換えることができます。eachという語が置かれているのは,兄弟が「それぞれに,2人とも」画家になる夢を抱いていた,ということを明確にするためです。

③However, the family did **not** have the money to send **either** of them to Nuremberg to study art.

▶ notとeitherが組み合わさることで「(2人のうち)どちらも…ない」という全否定の意味が生じることに注意しましょう。家族にはお金が十分になかったため「2人いる息子のどちらの息子も勉強させてやれなかった」という趣旨を読み取ることが大切です。

④After many discussions the boys decided to toss a coin to choose **the one** who would first work at the nearby mine to **help the other study** art at the Academy.

▶ the one と the otherが対応している点に注目しましょう。コインを投げて決めようとしたのは,「先に炭鉱で働く方(＝the one)」で,その目的は「もう一方(＝the other)が美術学校で勉強できるようにするため」です。じゃんけんで言えば,「負け」を決めようとしたわけです。

▶ help は「Aが…するのを助ける」という意味で用いる場合, help A do という形になります。目的語に続く補語が動詞の原形(＝原形不定詞)である点に注意しましょう。

⑤Albrecht got the chance to study first and became a successful painter **by the time** he finished his studies at the Academy.

▶ by the timeは接続詞の一種で, by the time S Vで,「SがVするころには(もう／すでに)」という意味の副詞節を導きます。

⑥It was **then** Albert's turn to study art, but it was too late because his hands were damaged by the four years of hard work, and his right hand was suffering from arthritis.

▶ thenは，物事の順序を明示すると同時に，ここでは，「そうなのだから」「したがって」という結論を示す意味合いもあります。「アルブレヒトが学校で学び，成功した」→「次はアルベルトの番だ」というつながりを，単に順序としてではなく「アルブレヒトが成功したのだから，さて今度はアルベルトの番だ」とつないでいます。

⑦To pay homage to Albert for **all that he had sacrificed**, Albrecht carefully drew his brother's abused hands **with palms together and thin fingers stretched skyward**.

▶ all that he had sacrificedは「彼が犠牲にしたすべてのこと」という意味です。all「すべてのこと」という名詞が，関係代名詞that以下によって修飾されている構造です。またallは，「すべて」であるだけでなく，量的に「多大」であることを示唆しています。

▶ 前置詞withには〈with＋A＋状態の表現〉の形で，「Aがある状態で」という意味を示す用法があります。ここでは１つのwithに対して，〈A＋状態の表現〉が〈palms＋together〉，〈thin fingers＋stretched skyward〉と２つ並んだ構造になっていて，「手のひらを合わせた状態」と「細い指が天に向かって伸びている状態」を表しています。

## Paraphrase Notes

①**Terrific** pieces of art **engender** terrific tales, and "Praying Hands", by Albrecht Durer, **does, too.**

- ▶オリジナル①と比べて，great→terrific, inspire→engenderなど，語句レベルでの言い換えが行われています。
- ▶ does は engender terrific tales の代用です。"Praying Hands" ... does , too で「『祈りの手』もまた素晴らしい物語を生み出す」という意味です。オリジナル①の no exception を用いた表現と比較してみましょう。

②**One such story describes** Albrecht and his brother Albert **residing in** a **hamlet** near Nuremberg and **aspiring to be** artists.

- ▶「そのような物語の1つは…を描く」という英語らしい発想に基づく書き方です。オリジナル②の According to one legend という，副詞句を用いた書き方と比較してみましょう。
- ▶語句レベルでは，live in→reside in, tiny village→hamlet, dream about becoming→aspire to be といった言い換えが見られます。

③**Alas**, the Durer family was **too** poor **to** send **either** boy off to Nuremberg to train.

- ▶ Alas は，「残念なことに」「悲しいかな」という意味を表す文語的な表現です。語り口調で，時におどけた調子でよく用いられ，「しかし惜しむらくは…」といったニュアンスで，聞き手や読み手の同情を促します。
- ▶ too ~ to do から生じる否定的な意味と，either が組み合わさって，「貧しさのあまり，どちらの息子も勉強させてやれない」という全否定の意味が生じています。

④**Following** much discussion, the brothers **chose to** flip a coin to determine which one would **start off working** in a local mine and support the other going to study at art school.

- ▶オリジナル④と見比べて，After→Following, decide to do→choose to do, first work→start off working などの表現の変化を確認しましょう。

⑤Albrecht had the initial opportunity to train, and he was a successful artist **even before** leaving the Academy.

- ▶オリジナル⑤では，接続詞の by the time を用いて「卒業するころには」という意味を表していましたが，こちらでは even before leaving「卒業する以前でさえも」と表現しています。卒業の時点ですでに画家として成功していたことが，より明確に表現されています。

⑥Albert's time to study had **now** arrived, but it was not soon enough**:** four years of difficult labor had injured his hands, **plus** his right hand was arthritic.

▶nowが過去時制の枠組みの中で用いられると,「そのとき」「さて今度は」という意味になります。オリジナル⑥のthenの働きに当たります。ここでは,had arrivedという過去完了とともに用いられることで「アルブレヒトが成功した今,さあ,アルバートの番が来た」という臨場感のある表現になっています。

▶コロン (:) の働きに注目しましょう。オリジナル⑥では,接続詞becauseを用いて明確に理由として述べていた内容を,コロンだけで前の文とつないでいます。英語では,「理由・根拠」や「言い換え・説明」などが,「ピリオドで切るだけだとわかりにくいが,接続表現を用いると冗長だ」と感じられる場合には,そのつながりをコロンで表すことがあります。感覚的には"接続表現＞コロン＞ピリオド"の順に,つながりの明示度が下がると考えてください。

▶ここでのplusは,やや口語的な表現で,and moreoverに相当します。

⑦**To acknowledge Albert's huge sacrifice on his behalf**, Albrecht painstakingly sketched the mangled hands of his brother, showing his palms pressed together and his thin fingers pointing to heaven.

▶下線部は,オリジナル⑦のTo pay homage to Albert for all that he had sacrificedに当たります。pay homage toがacknowledge ... on his behalfに,all that he had sacrificedがAlbert's huge sacrificeにパラフレーズされています。allが表していた「多大な犠牲」という意味合いが,hugeという形容詞で明確に示されている点に注目しましょう。

▶その他, carefully→painstakingly, abused→mangled, stretched skyward→pointing to heavenなどの言い換えが見られます。

## Expressions and Phrases

ヒントを手がかりにして，日本語に対応する英語表現を言ってみよう。

| 日本語 | ヒント | 英語 |
|---|---|---|
| □ 地元の伝承 | lo___ le___ | local legend |
| □ 感動的な話 | to___ st___ | touching story |
| □ 架空の物語 | fi___ ta___ | fictional tale |
| □ 好奇心を掻き立てられる小説 | in___ no___ | intriguing novel |
| □ 素晴らしい小説家 | te___ no___ | terrific novelist |
| □ 高く評価されている作家 | ac___ au___ | acclaimed author |
| □ 芸術的才能 | ar___ ta___ | artistic talent |
| □ 肖像画のモデル | po___ su___ | portrait's subject |
| □ 正確な描写 | ac___ po___ | accurate portrayal |
| □ 精緻な素描 | pa___ sk___ | painstaking sketch |
| □ 数回にわたる試み | mu___ at___ | multiple attempts |
| □ 特訓 | in___ tr___ | intensive training |
| □ 弟/妹 | yo___ si___ | younger sibling |
| □ 兄弟愛 | br___ lo___ | brotherly love |
| □ 開いた手のひら | op___ pa___ | open palm |
| □ 厳しい現実 | ha___ re___ | harsh reality |
| □ 金銭的援助 | fi___ su___ | financial support |
| □ 珍しい病気 | un___ di___ | uncommon disease |
| □ 幼児期 | ea___ ch___ | early childhood |
| □ 最初の機会 | in___ op___ | initial opportunity |
| □ 数少ない例外 | ra___ ex___ | rare exception |
| □ 近隣の村 | ne___ ha___ | neighboring hamlet |
| □ 近隣の鉱山 | ne___ mi___ | nearby mine |
| □ 肉体労働 | ph___ la___ | physical labor |
| □ 酷使された労働者 | ab___ wo___ | abused worker |
| □ ぼろぼろになったトロッコ | ma___ tr___ | mangled tram |
| □ 忠実な使用人 | lo___ se___ | loyal servant |
| □ 熟練の金細工職人 | sk___ go___ | skilled goldsmith |
| □ 真珠の耳飾り | pe___ ea___ | pearl earring |
| □ 集めたもの全て | en___ co___ | entire collection |

## Unit 2　Praying Hands

□ 貧民街に住む

| re___ in the po___ di_____ | reside in the poor district |
| dw___ in the sl___ | dwell in the slums |

□ 家族を養うと心に決める

| de_____ to pr___ for the fa___ | determine to provide for the family |
| se___ one's mind on su_____ the fa___ | set one's mind on supporting the family |

□ 硬貨を投げて針路を決める

| to___ a coin to de___ which pa___ to take | toss a coin to decide which path to take |
| fl___ a coin to se___ the co_____ | flip a coin to set the course |

□ 彼の努力に敬意を払う

| pa___ ho___ to his as_____ | pay homage to his aspiration |
| ho_____ his hard wo___ | honor his hard work |

□ 利他的な行為に触発される

| be in_____ by the ac___ of se___-sa_____ | be inspired by the act of self-sacrifice |
| be to_____ by the al_____ be_____ | be touched by the altruistic behavior |

□ 失敗を認めたがらない

| be re_____ to ad___ the fa___ | be reluctant to admit the failure |
| ha___ to re_____ the er___ | hate to recognize the error |

□ 鉱山労働者間での議論を生む

| en_____ di_____ among mi_____ | engender discussions among miners |
| ge_____ di_____ among mi___ workers | generate disputes among mine workers |

□ その労働者に身体の障害を与える

| do ph_____ da___ to the wo___ | do physical damage to the worker |
| ph_____ di_____ the wo___ | physically disable the worker |

□ 関節炎を患う

| su___ from ar_____ | suffer from arthritis |
| de___ an ar___ co_____ | develop an arthritic condition |

□ 有名な画家の下で学ぶ

| ap_____ with a fa___ pa_____ | apprentice with a famous painter |
| st___ under a we___-kn___ ar___ | study under a well-known artist |

# Word List

| | | | |
|---|---|---|---|
| □ abuse [əbjúːz] | 動 | …を酷使する，…を濫用する，…を虐待する | |
| □ acclaim [əkléɪm] | 動 | …を称賛する，…を認める | |
| □ according to A | | Aによれば，Aに従って | |
| □ acknowledge [əkná:lɪdʒ\|-nɔ́l-] | 動 | …を認める | |
| | 類 | admit / accept | |
| □ apprentice [əpréntɪs] | 動 | （見習いとして）修業する　名　見習い，奉公 | |
| □ arthritis [ɑːrθráɪtɪs] | 名 | 関節炎 | |
| □ artist [áːrtəst] | 名 | 芸術家 | |
| □ based on A | | Aに基づいて | |
| □ brotherly [brʌ́ðərli] | 形 | 兄弟の | |
| □ childhood [tʃáɪldhùd] | 名 | 子供時代 | |
| □ complicated [ká:mpləkèɪtɪd\|kɔ́m-] | 形 | 複雑な，難しい | |
| | 類 | complex / intricate | |
| □ damage [dǽmɪdʒ] | 動 | …を痛める，…に損害を与える，…を傷つける | |
| | 名 | 損害，損失 | |
| □ describe [dɪskráɪb] | 動 | …を描写する，…を説明する | |
| □ determine [dɪtə́ːrmən] | 動 | …を決める，…を判断する | |
| | 類 | decide / regulate | |
| | 語法 | determine that S V …「…だと判断する」 | |
| □ be disappointed that S V … | | …にがっかりする | |
| □ draw [drɔː] | 動 | …を（線で）描く，…を引き寄せる，…を引き出す，線を引く，ゆっくり移動する | |
| □ earring [íərìŋ] | 名 | イヤリング | |
| □ engender [ɪndʒéndər] | 動 | …を生じる，…を発生させる | |
| □ example [ɪgzǽmpl\|-záːm-] | 名 | 例，模範 | |
| □ exception [ɪksépʃən, ek-] | 名 | 例外，異議 | |
| | 類 | anomaly | |
| □ familiar with A | | Aを熟知している | |
| □ fictional [fíkʃənl] | 形 | 作り話の，架空の | |
| □ financially [fənǽnʃəli\|faɪ-] | 副 | 経済的に，財政的に，金銭的に | |
| □ flip [flɪp] | 動 | …を（ひょいと）投げる，…をひっくり返す，…をはじく | |
| | 名 | 軽く打つこと | |
| | 類 | throw | |

## Unit 2　Praying Hands

| | | |
|---|---|---|
| □ follow [fá:lou｜fɔ́l-] | 動 | …の結果として起こる，…の後についていく，…の言うことを理解する |
| | 語法 | It follows that S V ... 「結果として…になる」 |
| □ goldsmith [góuldsmìθ｜góul(d)-] | 名 | 金細工師 |
| □ hate [heɪt] | 動 | …をいやに思う，…を嫌う　名 憎しみ |
| □ homage [há:mɪdʒ｜hɔ́m-] | 名 | 敬意 |
| | 類 | respect　賛辞 |
| □ huge [hju:dʒ] | 形 | 巨大な |
| | 類 | enormous / vast |
| □ impress [ɪmprés] | 動 | …に感動を与える，…に印象づける |
| □ initial [ɪníʃəl] | 形 | 最初の，頭文字の　名 頭文字 |
| | 類 | beginning |
| □ injure [índʒər] | 動 | …を痛める，…を傷つける |
| □ inspire [ɪnspáɪər] | 動 | …喚起する，…を鼓舞する，…を感激させる |
| □ interestingly [íntərəstɪŋli] | 副 | 興味深いことに |
| □ intriguing [ɪntrí:gɪŋ] | 形 | 興味をそそる |
| □ labor [léɪbər] | 名 | (つらい) 労働，仕事，労働者 |
| | 動 | 努力する，働く，苦しむ |
| □ legend [lédʒənd] | 名 | 言い伝え，伝説，逸話 |
| | 類 | myth |
| □ mangle [mǽŋgl] | 動 | …を傷つける，…を台無しにする |
| | 類 | mutilate / injure |
| □ mine [maɪn] | 名 | 炭鉱，鉱山，地雷 |
| | 動 | 坑道を掘る，(場所を) 採掘する |
| □ multiple [mʌ́ltəpl] | 形 | 多数の　名 倍数 |
| □ nearby [níərbáɪ] | 形 | 近くの　副 近くに |
| □ novel [ná:vl｜nɔ́v-] | 名 | 小説　形 斬新な |
| □ on A's behalf | | Aに代わって，Aを代表して |
| □ opportunity [à:pərt(j)ú:nəti｜ɔ̀p-] | 名 | 機会，チャンス |
| | 類 | chance |
| □ painstakingly [péɪnztèɪkɪŋli] | 副 | 丹精を込めて，念入りに |
| | 類 | carefully / earnestly |
| □ palm [pɑ:lm｜pɑ:m] | 名 | 手のひら |
| □ point to A | | Aを指さす |
| □ portray [pɔ:rtréɪ] | 動 | …を描く，…を表現する |

051

|  |  |  |
|---|---|---|
| □ portrayal [pɔːtréɪəl] | 名 | 肖像画 |
| □ pray [preɪ] | 動 | 祈る，…を願う |
| □ really [ríːli\|ríəli] | 副 | 本当に，実のところ |
| □ recognize [rékəgnàɪz] | 動 | …に気づく，…を認める |
| | 語法 | recognize A as B [A to be B]「AをBとして認める」 |
| □ reside in A | | Aに住む |
| | 類 | live in A / inhabit A |
| □ sacrifice [sǽkrəfàɪs] | 名 | 犠牲，生け贄 |
| | 動 | …を犠牲にする，…を生け贄として捧げる |
| | 類 | offering |
| □ servant [sə́ːrvnt] | 名 | 召使い，使用人，奉仕者 |
| □ sibling [síblɪŋ] | 名 | (男女差なく) きょうだい，兄弟姉妹 |
| □ similar [símələr] | 形 | 同様の |
| | 語法 | similar to A「Aに似て」 |
| □ sketch [sketʃ] | 動 | …を描く，…をスケッチする，…の概略を書く |
| | 名 | スケッチ，概略 |
| □ skyward [skáɪwərd] | 副 | 天に向かって，空の方へ |
| □ stretch [stretʃ] | 動 | …を伸ばす，…を差し出す，…に及ぶ，…を誇張する，手足を伸ばす |
| | 名 | 広がり，体を伸ばすこと |
| □ subject [sʌ́bdʒekt] | 名 | テーマ，学科，被験者，臣民 |
| | 形 | (subject to Aで) Aの影響を受けやすい |
| □ suffer from A | | Aを患う，Aで苦しむ |
| □ support [səpɔ́ːrt] | 動 | …を支援する，…を扶養する |
| | 名 | 支持，援助 |
| □ survive [sərváɪv] | 動 | 生き残る，…を生き延びる，…より長生きする |
| □ tale [teɪl] | 名 | 話，物語 |
| □ talent [tǽlənt] | 名 | 才能，逸材 |
| □ terrific [tərífik] | 形 | すばらしい，ものすごい |
| | 類 | marvelous / wonderful |
| □ toss [tɔ(ː)s] | 動 | …をぽんと投げる，…を捨てる，寝返りを打つ |
| □ touched [tʌtʃt] | 形 | 感動して，心を動かされて |
| □ touching [tʌ́tʃɪŋ] | 形 | 感動的な |
| | 類 | moving |
| □ train [treɪn] | 動 | 教育を受ける，訓練する  名 列車 |
| □ turban [tə́ːrbən] | 名 | ターバン |

| | | | |
|---|---|---|---|
| □ uncommon [ʌnkɑ́ːmən \| -kɔ́m-] | 形 | まれな |
| | 類 | rare |
| □ work [wəːrk] | 名 | 作品, 仕事 |

## 参考文献

*Albrecht Dürer*. (2013, February 14). Retrieved September 10, 2015, from Barefoot's World website: http://www.barefootsworld.net/albrechtdurer.html

*Albrecht Durer Biography*. (n.d.). Retrieved September 10, 2015, from albrecht-durer.org website: http://www.albrecht-durer.org/biography.html

Donsbach, M. (n.d.). *Historical Novels about Artists Part I: Novels about European Artists through the 17th Century*. Retrieved September 10, 2015, from HistoricalNovels.info website: http://www.historicalnovels.info/Artists.html

*Girl with a Pearl Earring Summary & Study Guide*. (2015). Retrieved September 10, 2015, from BOOKRAGS website: http://www.bookrags.com/studyguide-girl-with-a-pearl-earring/#gsc.tab=0

*Girl in Hyacinth Blue, Book Summary*. (n.d.). Retrieved September 10, 2015, from BookBrowse website: https://www.bookbrowse.com/reviews/index.cfm/book_number/1768/girl-in-hyacinth-blue

# Unit 3 Mpemba Effect

## Integrated Task

Explain what the Mpemba effect is and give possible explanations for the phenomenon.

## Key Words

**counterintuitive**

▶ intuitive「直感的な」にcounter-「反対の」という接頭辞がついたもので,「直感に反した」という意味の形容詞です。そもそも「直感」とは,「論理や証拠によることなく,何かを正しいと感じること」ですが,それに反するとは,「何かがおかしい,変だ」と感じるということです。温度の異なるものを同じ温度にまで冷やす過程について,直感的に正しいと感じることは何でしょう。それが,この講義を理解する入口です。

**evaporate**

▶「蒸発する」という意味の動詞です。物質の3形態は「固体」「液体」「気体」ですが,化学では液体が気体に変化する過程を「気化」と呼び,英語ではvaporizationと言います。ちなみに,気体が液体になることを「液化」(liquefaction),液体が固体になることを「凝固」(coagulation)と呼びます。細かな仕組みはさておき,$H_2O$が「氷」⇔「水」⇔「蒸気」と形態を変えることは日常的に観察・経験され,それだけにintuitiveな理解が働きやすいのですが,講義では,それを分子レベルの現象として客観的に説明しています。

# Lecture 1　Original

**Listening**　講義を聴いてみよう。

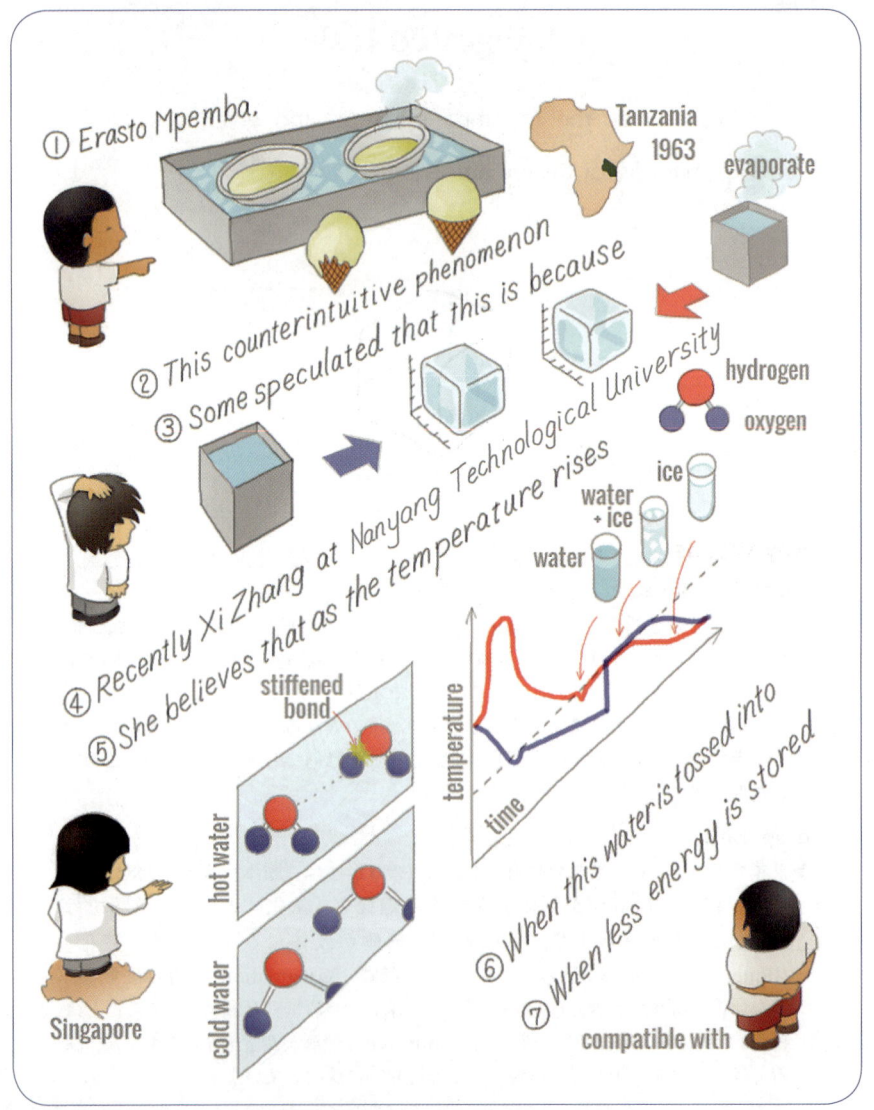

① Erasto Mpemba,
Tanzania 1963
evaporate
② This counterintuitive phenomenon
③ Some speculated that this is because
hydrogen
oxygen
④ Recently Xi Zhang at Nanyang Technological University
⑤ She believes that as the temperature rises
water
water + ice
ice
stiffened bond
hot water
cold water
Singapore
temperature
time
⑥ When this water is tossed into
⑦ When less energy is stored
compatible with

**Speaking**　イラストを見ながら講義を再現してみよう。

056

Unit 3  Mpemba Effect

## Script

①**Erasto Mpemba,** a Tanzanian high school student, discovered in cooking class in 1963 that a hot ice cream mix freezes faster than a cold mix. ②**This counterintuitive phenomenon** is called the Mpemba effect, and scientists still cannot offer a clear explanation as to why it happens. ③**Some speculated that this is because** hot water evaporates faster than cold, but they could not find any difference in the volumes of ice formed from water at different temperatures. ④**Recently Xi Zhang at Nanyang Technological University** in Singapore has taken particular note of the bond between the hydrogen and oxygen atoms that make up water. ⑤**She believes that as the temperature rises,** the water molecules store energy in the stiffened bond between hydrogen and oxygen. ⑥**When this water is tossed into** a cold environment, the stored energy is quickly released, creating additional cooling effects. ⑦**When less energy is stored,** the additional effect is smaller, resulting in slower cooling, an explanation compatible with what Mpemba found with his fast-freezing ice cream mix.

## Translation

①タンザニアの高校生，エラスト・ムペンバは，1963年調理の授業中に，熱いアイスクリームミックスが冷たいアイスクリームミックスよりも速く凍ることを発見した。②直感に反したこの現象はムペンバ効果と呼ばれ，科学者はそれがなぜ起こるのかに関して依然として明確な説明をすることができないでいる。③これは熱湯が冷水より速く蒸発するからであると推測した者もいたが，異なる温度の水から作られる氷の間に体積の違いは全く見られなかった。④最近，シンガポールの南洋理工大学のシー・チャンは水を構成する水素原子と酸素原子の結びつきに特に注目した。⑤彼女は，温度が上昇するにつれて，水の分子は水素と酸素の間の堅い結合の中にエネルギーを蓄えると考えている。⑥この水が寒い環境の中に放り出されると，蓄えられたエネルギーがすぐに放出され，さらなる冷却効果を起こす。⑦エネルギーの蓄えが少ないと，そういった付加的な効果は小さくなり，その結果，冷えるのに時間がかかることとなるのだが，これはムペンバが速く凍るアイスクリームミックスで見出したことと整合する説明である。

☞ スクリプトの文法ポイントについては，p.066～の**Grammar Notes**を参照しよう。

# Lecture 1　Paraphrase

**Listening**　別の表現を用いた講義を聴いてみよう。

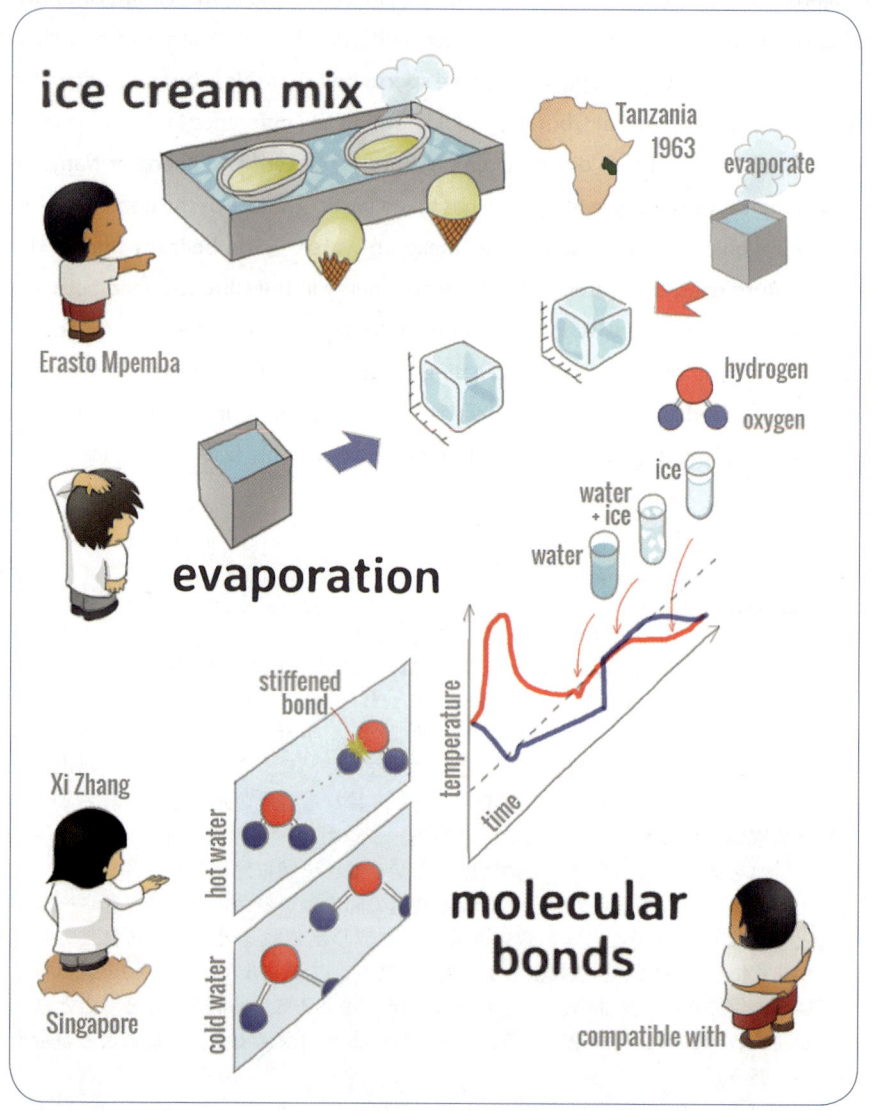

ice cream mix

Erasto Mpemba

Tanzania 1963

evaporate

hydrogen
oxygen

ice
water + ice
water

evaporation

Xi Zhang

Singapore

stiffened bond

hot water

cold water

temperature
time

molecular bonds

compatible with

**Speaking**　イラストを見ながら講義の内容を英語で説明しよう。

Unit 3　Mpemba Effect

## Script

①A high school student in Tanzania named Erasto Mpemba, in a cooking class in 1963, found out that a hot **mixture of ice cream** freezes more quickly than a cold one. ②This result, which flies in the face of logic, is known as the Mpemba effect, and it remains a mystery to scientists. ③Some surmised that it was due to the fact that hot water **evaporates** more quickly than cold, but no difference was detected in the amount of ice created by water at various temperatures. ④Not long ago, Xi Zhang of Singapore's Nanyang Technological University has focused intently on the **molecular bond** between hydrogen and oxygen, the components of water. ⑤Xi speculates that the molecules of water store energy when the hydrogen-oxygen bonds stiffen from heating. ⑥Once the water is moved into a low-temperature space, the held-in energy rapidly escapes, resulting in still more cooling. ⑦When the amount of energy held in the bonds is smaller, this added effect is more modest, meaning that the cooling time increases, which is consistent with Mpemba's ice cream mixture experience.

## Translation

①エラスト・ムペンバという名のタンザニアの高校生が，1963年調理の授業中に，熱いアイスクリームミックスのほうが，冷たいものより速く凍ることを発見した。②この結果は，理屈を無視したものであり，ムペンバ効果として知られているが，科学者には謎のままである。③それは熱湯が冷水より速く蒸発するという事実のためだと推測した者もいたが，さまざまな温度の水で作られる氷の間に量の全く違いは見出せなかった。④最近，シンガポールの南洋理工大学のシー・チャンは熱心に水素と酸素の分子結合に焦点をあてた。⑤シーは，水素と酸素の結合が熱によって強くなると，水分子はエネルギーを蓄えると考える。⑥いったん水が低温の場所に移されると，蓄えられたエネルギーが急速に漏れ出し，結果的に冷却効果がさらに高まる。⑦結合の内部に蓄えられたエネルギーの量が小さくなると，この付加的な効果はより小さなものになり，冷却時間が増えるということになるが，これは，ムペンバのアイスクリームミックスに関する経験と一致する。

☞ パラフレーズのポイントについては，p.068〜の**Paraphrase Notes**を参照しよう。

# Conversation

**Listening** 講義に関連する会話を聴いてみよう。

Student: Um, professor? There's something I don't understand about the Mpemba effect.

Professor: Go ahead, shoot.

Student: Thanks. I have never made ice cream myself, you know, because I usually buy ice cream that's already … well, ice cream! So, what is an ice cream mix and how do you make ice cream?

Professor: Ha-ha, I see your point.

Well, Let's say you want to make an old-fashioned, plain vanilla ice cream, OK? The basic ingredients are: cream, milk, sugar, and vanilla extract.

①But in some areas these ingredients might be pretty expensive, or in some cases …

②Hence the alternative of an ice cream mix that has …

Student: Uh-huh, I see. So what's the next step?

Professor: ③You mix the ingredients and heat them up in a saucepan until …

④You then pour the mixture into a bowl, cover it, and place it …

⑤This cooling process requires an hour or two, depending on …

Student: So that's when this Tanzanian student noticed the difference in the cooling speeds! Thanks!

**Speaking** 上の会話文を見ながら音声を聴き，教授のパートを再現してみよう。

Unit 3　Mpemba Effect

## Script

①**But in some areas these ingredients might be pretty expensive, or in some cases** not even available.
②**Hence the alternative of an ice cream mix that has** everything you need premixed and ready to go.
③**You mix the ingredients and heat them up in a saucepan until** the sugar is completely dissolved.
④**You then pour the mixture into a bowl, cover it, and place it** in the refrigerator to cool down.
⑤**This cooling process requires an hour or two, depending on** the type and volume of the ice cream.

## Translation

学生：あのー，先生？　ムペンバ効果についてわからないことがあるんです。
教授：どうぞ，言ってごらん。
学生：すみません。僕，自分でアイスクリームを作ったことがないんです。その，というのもアイスクリームって普通，買うものでしょ，だからそれはすでに…そう，アイスクリームになってますよね！　だから，アイスクリームミックスって何なのですか，そしてアイスクリームって，どうやって作るのですか。
教授：ハハ，あなたの言っていることはよくわかるわ。えーと，例えば，あなたが昔ながらのふつうのバニラアイスクリームを作りたいとするわね。いい？　主な材料は，クリーム，牛乳，砂糖，バニラエッセンスなの。①でも，場所によっては，これらの材料はとても高価だったり，場合によっては，手に入らないこともあるのよ。②だから，必要なすべての材料があらかじめ混ぜてあって，すぐに使えるアイスクリームミックスがその代わりになるのね。
学生：へえ，わかりました。それで，次にどうするんですか？
教授：③材料を混ぜて，砂糖が完全に溶けるまで，シチュー鍋でそれを温めるの。④それから，その混ぜたものをボウルの中に入れ，蓋をして，冷蔵庫に入れて冷やすわけ。⑤熱を冷ますのに，アイスクリームの種類や量によって1，2時間は必要よ。
学生：ということは，そのときこのタンザニアの生徒が冷却速度の違いに気づいたということですね。ありがとうございました。

# Lecture 2　Original

**Listening**　新たな講義を聴いてみよう。

Okay, the theory of molecular bonding between hydrogen and oxygen, postulated by Xi Zhang of Singapore to explain Mpemba effect, is not widely accepted by the scientific community, because the new theory lacks predictive power.

①In fact, some argue that the effect does not exist at all and is possibly a product of …

②They believe it impossible to control a large number of …

Others have offered different explanations for the phenomenon.

③Recently, a chemist from Croatia suggested that …

④According to his theory, convection currents flowing in warm water cause …

⑤Still, it is plausible that several different mechanisms, such as …

If you can explain it successfully, maybe someday you will have your name etched in history!

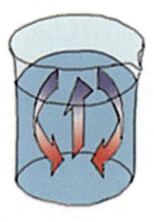

**Speaking**　吹き出しを見ながら足りない語を補い，講義を再現してみよう。

Unit 3　Mpemba Effect

## Script

①**In fact, some argue that the effect does not exist at all and is possibly a product of** imperfect experimental procedure.
②**They believe it impossible to control a large number of** extraneous variables.
③**Recently, a chemist from Croatia suggested that** convection might be responsible.
④**According to his theory, convection currents flowing in warm water cause** it to cool more rapidly.
⑤**Still, it is plausible that several different mechanisms, such as** insulating frost and dissolved gases, may cause or contribute to a Mpemba effect.

## Translation

　さて，水素と酸素の分子結合の理論は，ムペンバ効果を説明するために，シンガポールのシー・チャンによって仮説として出されたのですが，その新しい理論が予測力を欠いているため科学界では広く受け入れられていないのです。
　①実のところ，一部の人たちはそのような現象は全く存在せず，不完全な実験手順の産物である可能性があると主張しています。②たくさんの剰余変数を統制することは不可能だと彼らは考えます。
　また一部の人たちは，その現象に対して違った説明をしてきました。③最近，クロアチア出身の化学者が熱の対流が原因だと示唆しています。④彼の理論によれば，湯の中に流れている対流が湯をより急速に冷やすということです。⑤しかし今もなお，霜の断熱効果や溶存ガスなどいくつか違ったメカニズムがムペンバ効果を引き起こしたり，その一因となっているとも考えられます。もし，皆さんがそれをうまく説明できれば，ひょっとすると，いつか，あなたの名前が歴史に刻まれるかもしれませんよ！

063

# Lecture 2　Summary

**Listening**　チャートを見ながら講義をもう一度聴き，Lecture Notesを完成させよう。(答えは右ページ) CD20

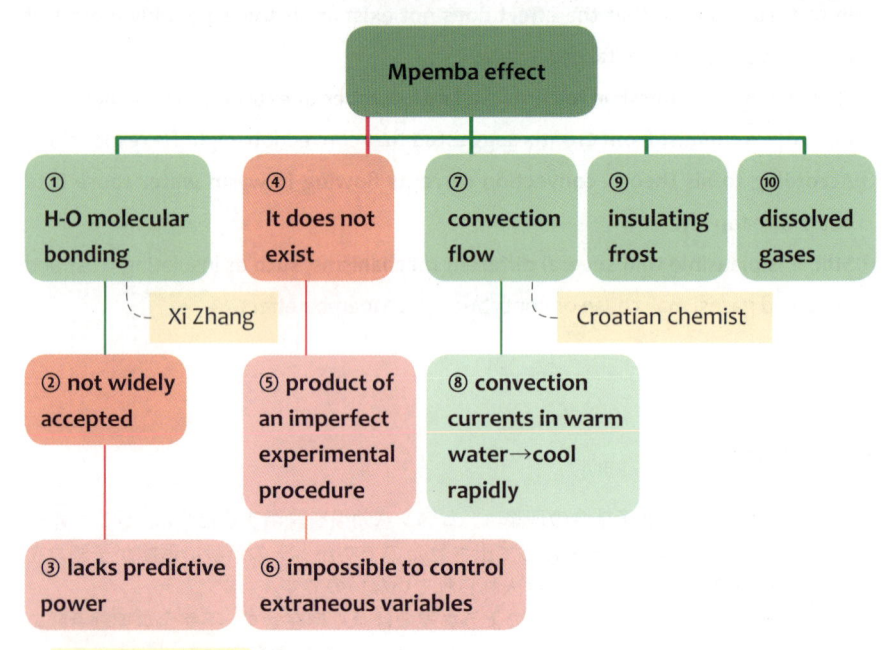

```
                    Mpemba effect
    ┌──────┬──────┼──────┬──────┐
    ①      ④      ⑦      ⑨      ⑩
  H-O    It does convection insulating dissolved
molecular not    flow    frost    gases
bonding  exist
    ┊              ┊
  Xi Zhang      Croatian chemist

  ② not widely    ⑤ product of   ⑧ convection
    accepted       an imperfect    currents in warm
                   experimental    water→cool
                   procedure       rapidly

  ③ lacks predictive  ⑥ impossible to control
    power              extraneous variables
```

### Lecture Notes

TOPIC
ムペンバ効果の（　A　）

PURPOSE
ムペンバ効果の（　A　）には諸説ありいまだに解明されていないことを示すこと

MAIN ARGUMENT
主　張：ムペンバ効果については諸説ある。
例示①：ムペンバ効果は水素と酸素の結合が関係しているという説は科学界ではあまり受け入れられていないし，ムペンバ効果自体そもそも存在しないという見方もある。
例示②：対流や（　B　）や溶存ガスが関係しているという説もある。

**Speaking**　チャートを見ながら講義を要約し，声に出して言ってみよう。

## Summary

Some people do not believe that **the Mpemba effect exists**. They claim it is **a product of an imperfect experimental procedure,** saying there is no way to pin down the phenomenon because it is almost **impossible to control extraneous variables**. **Xi Zhang**'s theory of **Hydrogen-Oxygen molecular bonding** is also **not widely accepted** by the scientific community because it **lacks predictive power**. There are other theories such as **insulating frost and dissolved gases**. A **Croatian chemist** claims that **convection flow** is responsible for the phenomenon. He believes that **convection currents in warm water** help the water **cool rapidly**.

## Translation

ムペンバ効果が存在しないと考える人たちがいる。ムペンバ効果は不完全な実験手順の産物であり，余剰変数の制御はほぼ不能のためこの現象を解明することはできないとしている。シー・チャンの水素と酸素の分子結合説も，予測能力を欠くという理由で科学界で広く受け入れらるということはない。異説としては断熱効果を持つ霜や溶存ガスなどもある。あるクロアチアの化学者はこの現象の原因は対流であると主張している。温水の対流の動きが水を素早く冷却すると考えている。

### Integrated Task

Explain what the Mpemba effect is and give possible explanations for the phenomenon.

Lecture Notesの答え　A 原因　B 霜

## Grammar Notes

①Erasto Mpemba, a Tanzanian high school student, **discovered** in cooking class in 1963 **that** a hot ice cream mix freezes faster than a cold mix.

▶ discover that ...で「…ということを発見する」という意味ですが、ここではdiscoverとthat節の間に in cooking class in 1963 という副詞句が置かれているため、discover (V) that ... (O) という構造が見えにくくなっています。これは、「どこで、いつ発見したのか」という情報を discover の近くに置くことによって修飾関係を明確にすることが優先されたためです。discover「発見する」の後ろに「何を？」に当たる情報が続くことを予期しながら、先に副詞句の情報を処理するよう心掛けましょう。

②This counterintuitive phenomenon **is called the Mpemba effect**, and scientists still cannot offer a clear explanation as to why it happens.

▶ call O C「OをCと呼ぶ」の受動態は、O is called C「OはCと呼ばれる」となります。したがって、この文の the Mpemba effect は、能動態の時の補語（C）に当たります。We call this counterintuitive phenomenon the Mpemba effect が元となる能動態です。

▶ as to A は「Aに関して」という意味です。ここではAに why it happens「なぜそれが起きるのか」という名詞節が置かれています。

③Some speculated that **this is because** hot water evaporates faster than cold, but they could not find any difference in the volumes of ice **formed** from water at different temperatures.

▶ すでに述べられた事柄について、その理由を後から別の文で示す場合は、It [This / That] is because ... という形を用いるのが一般的です。ここでは、①②で示された Mpemba effect と呼ばれる現象について、その理由説明に当たる内容を「一部の人々の推測では…」に続いて示しています。

▶ formed は過去分詞で、formed from water at different temperatures 全体は、直前の ice を修飾しています。

④**Recently** Xi Zhang at Nanyang Technological University in Singapore **has taken particular note of** the bond between the hydrogen and oxygen atoms that make up water.

▶「最近」という意味の副詞 recently は、原則として過去形や現在完了形とともに用います。

▶ take particular note of は、take note of A「Aに注目する」を応用した表現で、note に particular「特別な」という形容詞が付くことによって、「Aに特に注目する」という意味になります。

Unit 3　Mpemba Effect

⑤She believes that **as the temperature rises, the water molecules store energy in the stiffened bond between hydrogen and oxygen**.

▶ここでは，接続詞thatの処理について確認しましょう。thatは接続詞ですので，その右側には「文」として自立した形，文法構造的に「文」として完成したものが続きます。したがって，その「文頭」，つまりthatの直後に，副詞句や副詞節が続き，その後に（that節内の）SVが続くこともあります。ここでは，下線部を「文」として普通に見てください。As ...., S V ～「…するにつれて～」という〈副詞節＋主節〉の構造ですね。「彼女は信じている」→「何を？」→「[下線部の内容]を」という具合に，thatの直後で「リセットされた」という意識を持つようにすると，英語の語順のまま理解しやすくなります。

⑥When this water is tossed into a cold environment, the stored energy is quickly released, **creating additional cooling effects**.

▶creating以下は分詞構文で，and this creates additional cooling effectsと書き換えることができます。this「このこと」とは，the stored energy is quickly releasedの内容全体，つまり「蓄えられたエネルギーが素早く放出されること」を指していて，「それが結果的にさらなる冷却効果を生む」と述べています。

⑦When less energy is stored, the additional effect is smaller, resulting in slower cooling, **an explanation compatible with what Mpemba found with his fast-freezing ice cream mix**.

▶下線部全体は，「Mpembaが発見したことと一致する説明」という名詞句です。compatible以降がan explanationを後ろから修飾していることに気をつけましょう。この名詞句は，その前までに述べられている内容に対して，コメントを付け加える働きをしています。わかりにくい場合は，…, and this is an explanationと書き換えてもかまいません。「たまったエネルギーが少ないと，追加的な冷却効果も小さくなり，冷却が遅くなるが，このことはMpembaが発見したことと整合する説明となる」というつながり方です。

## Paraphrase Notes

①A high school student in Tanzania named Erasto Mpemba, in a cooking class in 1963, **found out** that a hot mixture of ice cream freezes more quickly than a cold one.

▶「発見する」という表現として，オリジナル①のdiscoverに代わって，find outを用いています。どちらも「それまでわからなかったことを，何らかの努力をして明るみに出す」という意味合いです。find outの代わりにfindを用いると，単に「わかる」「知る」という意味合いになります。

②This result, which **flies in the face of** logic, is known as the Mpemba effect, and it **remains a mystery to** scientists.

▶fly in the face of Aは「A（常識など）を無視した振る舞いをする」という意味の慣用表現です。権威あるものの目の前を，何かが平気で飛んでいるイメージに由来する表現です。Aにlogic「論理，理屈」を置くことで，意味の上でオリジナル②のcounterintuitiveに相当する表現となります。

▶オリジナル②のcannot offer a clear explanationは「人」を主語とした表現でしたが，こちらではremain a mystery「謎のままである」という「物・事」を主語とした表現にパラフレーズされています。

③Some **surmised** that it was **due to the fact that** hot water evaporates more quickly than cold, but no difference was detected in the **amount** of ice created by water at various temperatures.

▶speculate→surmise，because→due to the fact that，volume→amountといった，オリジナル③で用いられた表現からの言い換えを確認しましょう。

④**Not long ago**, Xi Zhang of Singapore's Nanyang Technological University has **focused intently on** the molecular bond between hydrogen and oxygen**, the components of water**.

▶オリジナル④と比べると，Recentlyの代わりにNot long agoが，take particular note ofの代わりにfocus intently onが用いられています。

▶the components of water「水の構成要素」は，直前のhydrogen and oxygenを追加的に説明しています。わかりにくい場合は，hydrogen and oxygen, which are the components of waterと補ってみましょう。オリジナル④のthat make up water「水を構成する」に対応する表現です。

⑤Xi speculates that the molecules of water store energy when the hydrogen-oxygen bonds **stiffen from heating**.

▶オリジナル⑤では，as the temperature rises「温度が上昇するにつれて」と表現していた「原子結合の強さと温度との間にある比例関係」を，こちらでは「高温になることで強固になる」と，シンプルに表現しています。

⑥**Once** the water is moved into a **low-temperature space**, the **held-in** energy rapidly **escapes**, resulting in **still more** cooling.

▶ Once は「いったん…すると」「…するとすぐに」という意味の接続詞です。オリジナル⑥の When に相当します。

▶ その他，cold environment → low-temperature space，stored → held-in，be released → escape，additional → still more などの語句の変化に注目しましょう。

⑦When the amount of energy held in the bonds is smaller, this added effect is more modest, meaning that the cooling time increases, **which is consistent with** Mpemba's ice cream mixture experience.

▶ which は，その前で述べられた内容全体を先行詞とし，それに対して追加的な説明を加える働きをしています。and this is consistent with ... と書き換えることが可能です。オリジナル⑦の an explanation ... という名詞句を続ける説明の仕方と比較してみましょう。

## Expressions and Phrases

ヒントを手がかりにして，日本語に対応する英語表現を言ってみよう。

| 日本語 | ヒント | 英語 |
|---|---|---|
| □ 氷の生成 | ic___ fo_____ | ice formation |
| □ アイスクリームの素 | ic__ cr___ mi__ | ice cream mix |
| □ バニラ抽出物 | va____ ex_____ | vanilla extract |
| □ 大きな深鍋 | la___ sa_____ | large saucepan |
| □ 基本材料 | ba___ in_____ | basic ingredient |
| □ 冷凍冷蔵庫 | fr____-fr_____ | fridge-freezer |
| □ 科学界 | sc_____ co_____ | scientific community |
| □ 優秀な化学者 | br_____ ch_____ | brilliant chemist |
| □ 一般的な見解 | wi____ ac_____ vi__ | widely accepted view |
| □ 代替理論 | al_____ th_____ | alternative theory |
| □ 直感と相いれない考え | co_____ id__ | counterintuitive idea |
| □ 矛盾のない説明 | co_____ ex_____ | compatible explanation |
| □ 妥当な分析 | pl_____ an_____ | plausible analysis |
| □ 実験手順 | ex_____ pr_____ | experimental procedure |
| □ 昔からの方法 | ol_-fa_____ me____ | old-fashioned method |
| □ 複雑なメカニズム | co_____ me_____ | complicated mechanism |
| □ 不完全な状態 | im_____ co_____ | imperfect condition |
| □ 適度の効果 | mo____ ef____ | modest effect |
| □ 重大な発見 | re_____ di_____ | remarkable discovery |
| □ 予測力 | pr_____ po____ | predictive power |
| □ 温度上昇 | te_____ ri___ | temperature rise |
| □ 体積変化 | vo_____ ch_____ | volume change |
| □ 溶け込んだ気体 | di_____ ga__ | dissolved gas |
| □ 対流 | co_____ cu_____ | convection current |
| □ 不十分な断熱 | po__ in_____ | poor insulation |
| □ 化学成分 | ch_____ co_____ | chemical component |
| □ 水分子 | wa___ mo_____ | water molecule |
| □ 酸素原子 | ox____ at___ | oxygen atom |
| □ 水素結合 | hy_____ bo_____ | hydrogen bonding |
| □ 分子結合 | mo_____ bo___ | molecular bond |

## Unit 3　Mpemba Effect

□ 科学者にとって謎のままである

| re___ a my___ to sc_____ | remain a mystery to scientists |
| ha___ not been so___ by sc___ | have not been solved by scientists |

□ 歴史に名を残す

| ha___ your na___ et___ in hi_____ | have your name etched in history |
| ea___ your pl___ in hi___ | earn your place in history |

□ 情報を利用可能にする

| ma___ in_____ av_____ | make information available |
| al___ ac____ to in_____ | allow access to information |

□ 常識に反する

| fl___ in the fa___ of co___ se___ | fly in the face of common sense |
| be in_____ with wh___ we kn___ | be inconsistent with what we know |

□ 矛盾に注目する

| ta___ no___ of the in_____ | take note of the inconsistency |
| pa___ at_____ to the co_____ | pay attention to the contradiction |

□ 注意深い観察を必要とする

| re___ ca___ ob_____ | require careful observation |
| ne___ to be ob_____ ca___ | need to be observed carefully |

□ 無関係の要素を除外する

| ex___ ir_____ fa___ | exclude irrelevant factors |
| co___ ex_____ va_____ | control extraneous variables |

□ 温度降下の理由を説明する

| of___ an ex_____ for co____ | offer an explanation for cooling |
| gi___ an ac____ of te_____ dr___ | give an account of temperature drop |

□ 霜が原因だと推測する

| sp_____ that it is du___ to the fr___ | speculate that it is due to the frost |
| su_____ that the fr___ is re_____ | surmise that the frost is responsible |

□ より速い蒸発を引き起こす

| re___ in qu____ ev_____ | result in quicker evaporation |
| le___ to fa_____ va_____ | lead to faster vaporization |

# Word List

| | |
|---|---|
| □ a large number of A | たくさんのA |
| □ accept [əksépt, æk-] | 動 …を受け入れる，…を容認する<br>語法 accept O as C「OをCだと認める」 |
| □ additional [ədíʃnəl] | 形 付加の，追加の |
| □ alternative [ɔːltə́ːrnətɪv] | 名 代用品，(他の)選択肢<br>形 別の，それに代わる，新しい |
| □ argue that S V | …だと主張する，…だと論じる<br>類 contend / assert |
| □ as to A | Aに関して<br>類 about A / as for A |
| □ atom [ǽtəm] | 名 原子，少量 |
| □ available [əvéɪləbl] | 形 入手できる，利用できる |
| □ bond [bɑːnd \| bɔnd] | 名 結合，結束，きずな　動 結合する<br>類 tie / contact |
| □ cause A to *do* | Aに…させる，Aが…する原因となる |
| □ chemist [kémɪst] | 名 化学者 |
| □ claim that S V | …だと主張する |
| □ compatible with A | Aに整合する，Aと互換性がある |
| □ completely [kəmplíːtli] | 副 完全に，すっかり |
| □ component [kəmpóʊnənt] | 名 構成要素，部品，成分 |
| □ consistent with A | Aと一致する |
| □ contribute to A | Aに貢献する，Aの一因となる |
| □ convection [kənvékʃən] | 名 対流 |
| □ counterintuitive [kàʊntərɪnt(j)úːətɪv] | 形 直感に反した |
| □ create [kriéɪt] | 動 …を作り出す，…を創造する，…を引き起こす |
| □ current [kə́ːrənt \| kʌ́r-] | 名 流れ，電流　形 現在の |
| □ depending on A | A次第で |
| □ detect [dɪtékt] | 動 …を見出す，…を検知する<br>類 find / discover |
| □ difference [dífərəns] | 名 違い，相違 |
| □ dissolve [dɪzɑ́ːlv \| -zɔ́lv] | 動 …を溶かす，…を解散させる，…を弱める，溶ける<br>類 melt |
| □ effect [ɪfékt] | 名 効果，結果，影響，効力<br>動 …を成就する，…に影響を与える |

|  |  |  |
|---|---|---|
| □ environment [ɪnváɪrənmənt] | 名 | 環境，周囲の状況 |
|  | 類 | surroundings |
| □ escape [ɪskéɪp, es-] | 動 | 漏れ出す，逃げ出す　名 逃亡，脱出 |
| □ etch [etʃ] | 動 | （金属板などに）…を刻む |
| □ evaporate [ɪvǽpərèɪt] | 動 | 蒸発する，…徐々に消える，…を蒸発させる |
| □ expensive [ɪkspénsɪv, eks-] | 形 | 値段が高い，高くつく |
| □ experimental [ɪkspèrəméntl, eks-] | 形 | 実験の，実験的な |
| □ explanation [èksplənéɪʃən] | 名 | 説明，釈明，理由 |
|  | 類 | account |
| □ extract [ékstrækt] | 名 | エッセンス，抜粋，抽出物 |
| □ focus on A |  | Aに焦点を当てる |
| □ form [fɔːrm] | 名 | 形，形態，用紙 |
|  | 動 | …を形成する，…を構成する |
| □ freeze [fríːz] | 動 | 凍る，氷が張る，動かなくなる，…を凍らせる |
| □ hence [hens] | 副 | それゆえ，したがって |
| □ hydrogen [háɪdrədʒən] | 名 | 水素 |
| □ increase [ɪnkríːs] | 動 | 増える，増加する，…を増やす |
| □ ingredient [ɪnɡríːdiənt] | 名 | 材料，原料 |
|  | 類 | component，要因 |
| □ insulate [ínsəlèɪt|-sju-] | 動 | …を絶縁［断熱・防音］する |
| □ intently [ɪnténtli] | 副 | 熱心に，一心に |
|  | 類 | attentively |
| □ lack [læk] | 動 | …が欠けている，不足している　名 不足 |
| □ logic [lɑ́ːdʒɪk|lɔ́dʒ-] | 名 | 論理，理屈 |
| □ mechanism [mékənìzm] | 名 | メカニズム，仕組み |
| □ mixture [míkstʃər] | 名 | 混合物，混ぜた物 |
| □ modest [mɑ́dəst|mɔ́dɪst] | 形 | 小さな，適度の，控えめな |
|  | 類 | moderate |
| □ molecular [məlékjələr] | 形 | 分子の |
| □ molecule [mɑ́ːləkjùːl|mɔ́l-] | 名 | 分子，微量 |
| □ mystery [místəri] | 名 | 謎，秘密，神秘 |
| □ notice [nóʊtəs] | 動 | …に気づく |
| □ offer [ɔ́ːfər|ɔ́fə] | 動 | …を与える，…を提供する　名 申し出 |
|  | 類 | provide |

| | | |
|---|---|---|
| □ old-fashioned [óuldfǽʃənd] | 形 | 昔ながらの |
| □ oxygen [á:ksɪdʒən\|ɔ́ks-] | 名 | 酸素 |
| □ particular [pərtíkjələr] | 形 | 特別な，特定の，特有の　名 項目，詳細 |
| | 語法 | particular to A「Aに特有の」 |
| □ plain [pleɪn] | 形 | シンプルな，ふつうの，明白な　名 平原 |
| □ plausible [plɔ́:zəbl] | 形 | 真実味のある，もっともらしい |
| | 類 | reasonable |
| □ postulate [pá:stʃəlèɪt\|pɔ́stjə-] | 動 | …を主張する，…を前提とする，…だと仮定する |
| | 類 | propose / put forward / hypothesize |
| □ predictive [prɪdíktɪv] | 形 | 予測の，予測通りの |
| □ premix [pri:míks] | 動 | …を前もって混ぜる |
| □ pretty [príti] | 副 | かなり　形 かわいい |
| □ procedure [prəsí:dʒər] | 名 | 手順，手続き |
| □ product [prá:dəkt\|prɔ́d-] | 名 | 製品，成果 |
| □ rapidly [rǽpɪdli] | 副 | 急速に |
| □ recently [rí:sntli] | 副 | 最近 |
| □ refrigerator [rɪfrídʒərèɪtər] | 名 | 冷蔵庫 |
| □ release [rɪlí:s] | 動 | …を放出する，…を解放する　名 解放 |
| □ responsible for A | | Aの原因である，Aの責任がある |
| □ result in A | | Aを引き起こす，Aという結果になる |
| □ saucepan [sɔ́:spæn] | 名 | （取っ手の付いた）深鍋 |
| □ scientific community | | 科学界 |
| □ speculate that S V … | | …だと考える，推測する |
| □ stiffen [stífn] | 動 | …を固くする，固くなる |
| □ store [stɔ:r] | 動 | …を蓄える，…をとっておく　名 店，蓄え |
| | 類 | save / keep in reserve |
| □ suggest [səgdʒést] | 動 | …を示唆する，…を提案する |
| □ surmise that S V … | | …だと推測する |
| □ take note of A | | Aに気づく，Aに注意する |
| □ temperature [témpərtʃər] | 名 | 温度，体温 |
| □ theory [θí:əri\|θíə-] | 名 | 理論，学説 |
| □ variable [véəriəbl] | 名 | 不確定要素，変数 |
| | 形 | 変わりやすい，変えられる |

| □ various [véəriəs] | 形 | さまざまな，多彩な |
| □ volume [vá:ljəm \| vɔ́lju:m] | 名 | 体積，容量，音量，一巻 |

## 参考文献

*How to Make Ice Cream.* (n.d.). Retrieved September 10, 2015, from wikiHow website: http://www.wikihow.com/Make-Ice-Cream

Gray, R. (2013, November 1). *Have scientists worked out why hot water freezes faster than cold water?* Retrieved September 10, 2015, from The Telegraph website: http://www.telegraph.co.uk/news/science/science-news/10420496/Have-scientists-worked-out-why-hot-water-freezes-faster-than-cold-water.html

# Unit 4 Planetary Habitability

## Integrated Task

Explain the factors that prove or disprove an existence of extra-terrestrial life on a planet called Kepler-186f.

## Key Words

**extra-terrestrial**

▶「地球外の」という意味の形容詞です。terrestrial「地球上の」という形容詞に, extra-「外側の」という意味の接頭辞が添えられてできた語です。頭文字をならべた"E.T."が,「地球外の知的生命体」「宇宙人」という意味で広く用いられていることは, みなさんもご存じでしょう。類義語にalienという語がありますが, こちらは元来「異質な」という意味の形容詞で, 生命体であるという共通点よりも,「人類とは異なる」という点が強調される語になります。

**star / planet**

▶日常的には「星」という語でくくってしまうことの多い語ですが, 今回は明確にstarとplanetを区別しなければなりません。starとは自ら強いエネルギーを発し, 光を放つ「恒星」(fixed star) のことです。私たちの太陽系 (solar system) における唯一の恒星がthe sun「太陽」になります。一方, planetは, 恒星を中心とした軌道を周回する「惑星」のことで, この軌道のことを公転軌道と呼びます。the Earth「地球」は, 太陽を親星 (parent star) とする惑星ということになります。なお, 講義に登場するM dwarf star「M型矮星」とは, 恒星の一種で, エネルギーの比較的弱いものを指します。恒星であるからには, 何らかの惑星を持つのでしょうか。

# Lecture 1　Original

**Listening**　講義を聴いてみよう。

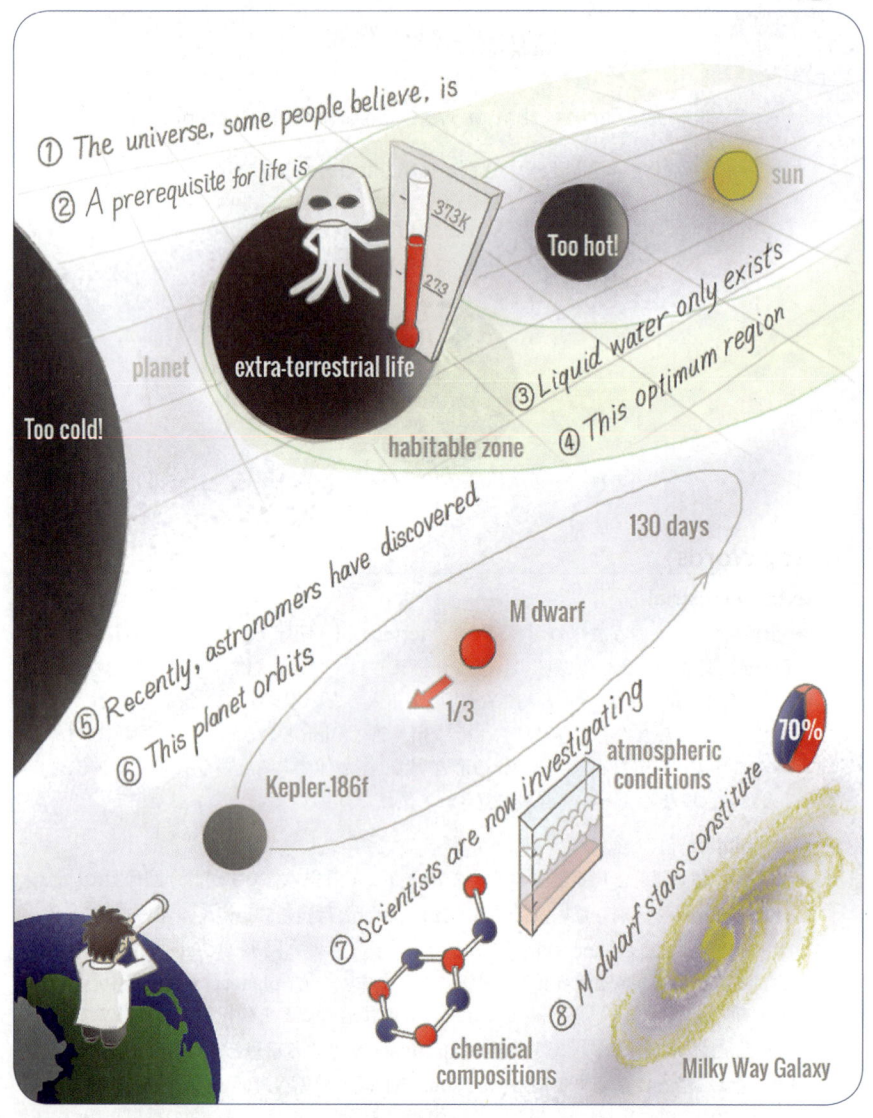

① The universe, some people believe, is
② A prerequisite for life is
③ Liquid water only exists
④ This optimum region
⑤ Recently, astronomers have discovered
⑥ This planet orbits
⑦ Scientists are now investigating
⑧ M dwarf stars constitute

sun
Too hot!
Too cold!
planet
extra-terrestrial life
373K
273
habitable zone
130 days
M dwarf
1/3
Kepler-186f
atmospheric conditions
70%
chemical compositions
Milky Way Galaxy

**Speaking**　イラストを見ながら講義を再現してみよう。

# Script

①**The universe, some people believe, is** vast enough to have some form of extra-terrestrial life. ②**A prerequisite for life is** liquid water on the surface of a planet. ③**Liquid water only exists** at temperatures between 273K and 373K, and the temperature of a planet can be predicted by measuring the planet's distance from its sun. ④**This optimum region** of space surrounding a sun-like star is called the habitable zone. ⑤**Recently, astronomers have discovered** the first Earth-size planet, Kepler-186f, orbiting in the "habitable zone" of an M dwarf star. ⑥**This planet orbits** its parent M dwarf star once in 130 days and receives one-third the energy that Earth gets from the sun. ⑦**Scientists are now investigating** the chemical compositions and atmospheric conditions of the planet. ⑧**M dwarf stars constitute** 70 percent of the stars in the Milky Way Galaxy, and planets in the habitable zone of each star are waiting to be explored.

# Translation

①宇宙はあまりに広大なので、なんらかの形態の地球外生命体がいると一部の人々は信じている。②生命が存在するための前提条件は、惑星の表面に液体の水があることである。③液体の水は273ケルビンから373ケルビンの間の温度でしか存在せず、また惑星の温度は、その惑星の太陽からの距離を測定することによって予測することができる。④宇宙の中で太陽に類似する恒星の周囲にあるこの最適領域はハビタブルゾーン（生命居住可能領域）と呼ばれる。⑤最近、天文学者たちは、M型矮星のハビタブルゾーンを周回する地球サイズの惑星「ケプラー186f」を初めて発見した。⑥この惑星は、親星であるM型矮星の周りを130日で一周し、地球が太陽から受けるエネルギーの3分の1のエネルギーを受けている。⑦現在、科学者たちはこの惑星の化学的組成と大気の状態を調査している。⑧M型矮星は天の川銀河の恒星の70パーセントを構成していて、それぞれの恒星のハビタブルゾーンに存在する惑星は、この先の探索を待つばかりである。

スクリプトの文法ポイントについては、p.088～のGrammar Notesを参照しよう。

# Lecture 1　Paraphrase

**Listening**　別の表現を用いた講義を聴いてみよう。

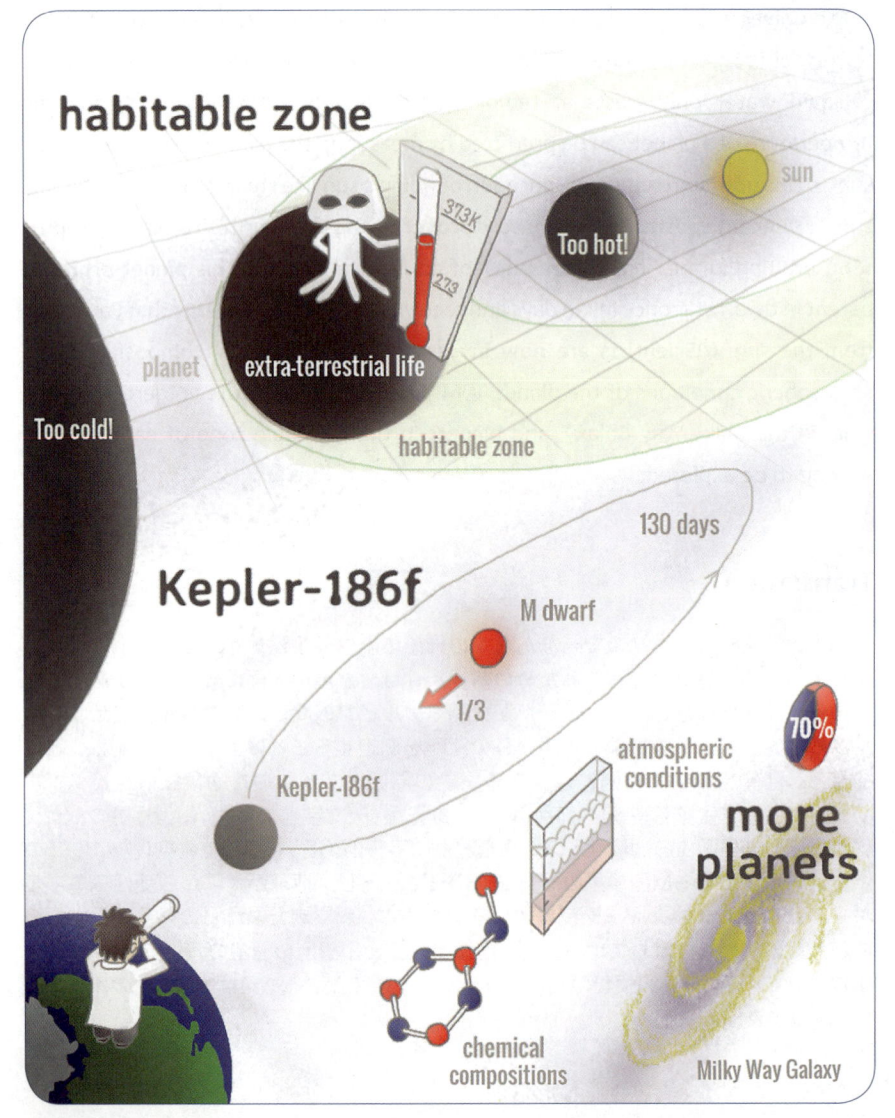

**Speaking**　イラストを見ながら講義の内容を英語で説明しよう。

Unit 4　Planetary Habitability

## Script

①It is argued that the universe is so large that there must exist extra-terrestrial life of some form or another. ②One thing life on a planetary surface needs is water in liquid form. ③This is only possible in the temperature range of 273K to 373K, and a planet's temperature is predictable once you know how far it is from its sun. ④Scientists named the area of space that is suitable for life the **"habitable zone."** ⑤Astronomers announced that they have found **Kepler-186f**, a planet the size of our Earth, that is in a "habitable zone" orbit around an M dwarf star. ⑥Kepler-186f circles its M dwarf star every 130 days and the amount of energy delivered to it from the star is one-third of that which we get from our sun. ⑦Now being studied by researchers is what chemicals and atmospheric conditions exist on Kepler-186f. ⑧70% of the stars in our Milky Way Galaxy are M dwarf stars, and their **habitable zone planets** are wonderful subjects for future research.

## Translation

①宇宙はあまりに広大なので、なんらかの形態の地球外生命体が存在しているにちがいないと主張されている。②惑星の表面に生命が存在するのに必要なものの１つは、液体の水である。③これは、273ケルビン〜373ケルビンの範囲の温度域でしか可能ではなく、また惑星の温度は、その惑星が太陽からどのぐらいの距離にあるのかがわかってしまえば、予測することができる。④科学者らは、生命が存在するのに適した宇宙空間領域を「ハビタブルゾーン（生命居住可能領域）」と名付けた。⑤天文学者らは、あるM型矮星の「ハビタブルゾーン」内にある軌道を周回し、地球と同じ大きさの惑星であるケプラー186fを発見したと発表した。⑥ケプラー186fは親星であるM型矮星を130日で一周し、親星からケプラー186fに与えられるエネルギー量は、私たちが太陽から受けるエネルギー量の３分の１である。⑦現在、研究者たちによって調査されているのは、どのような化学物質や大気の状態がケプラー186fに存在するか、ということである。⑧天の川銀河の恒星の70パーセントはM型矮星であり、そのハビタブルゾーンにある惑星は、将来のすばらしい研究テーマである。

☞ パラフレーズのポイントについては、p.090〜の**Paraphrase Notes**を参照しよう。

# Conversation

**Listening**  講義に関連する会話を聴いてみよう。

Student A: Let's prepare for our astronomy test next week.

Student B: ①**I bet we will be tested on habitable zones because our professor …**

Student A: Right. According to my notes, the definition of a habitable zone is "… where a planet can have surface temperatures that are suitable for liquid water." Does that sound right?

Student B: ②**Almost. You are missing "…" part.**

Student A: You mean, the distance from the Sun?

Student B: In our solar system, yes. But there are other sun-like stars, remember?
③**In the case of Kepler-186f, it is …**

Student A: Oh yeah! Kepler-186f orbits an M dwarf star and receives energy from it, like the Earth does from the Sun.

Student B: ④**Mm-hmm. And Kepler-186f is in the right location to …**
⑤**Umm … in other words, within …**

Student A: So, is liquid water the only prerequisite for extra-terrestrial life?

Student B: No, liquid water is just one.
⑥**The professor mentioned two others: the chemicals and …**

Student A: Got it. Thanks!

**Speaking**  上の会話文を見ながら音声を聴き，学生 B のパートを再現してみよう。

Unit 4　Planetary Habitability

## Script

①**I bet we will be tested on habitable zones because our professor** spent a good deal of time on it.
②**Almost. You are missing "the range of distances around a star"** part.
③**In the case of Kepler-186f, it is** … let's see here … an M dwarf star.
④**Mm-hmm. And Kepler-186f is in the right location to** possibly have liquid water.
⑤**Umm … in other words, within** the habitable zone of an M dwarf star.
⑥**The professor mentioned two others: the chemicals and** atmospheric conditions of the planet.

## Translation

学生Ａ：来週の天文学のテスト対策をしよう。
学生Ｂ：①絶対ハビタブルゾーンがテストに出ると思うわ。だって教授はそれにかなり時間をかけていたからね。
学生Ａ：そうだね。僕のノートだと，ハビタブルゾーンの定義は，「惑星が液体の水に適した表面温度でありうるところ」となっているんだけど，それで合っている？
学生Ｂ：②だいたい合っているけど。「恒星を中心とした距離範囲」が抜けているわ。
学生Ａ：太陽からの距離っていうこと？
学生Ｂ：私たちの太陽系なら，そういうことね。でもほかにも太陽に似た恒星があるって覚えてる？　③ケプラー186fの場合は…えっと…，あ，これだわ，M型矮星ね。
学生Ａ：そうだったね！　ケプラー186fはM型矮星の周りを回っていて，そこからエネルギーを受け取っているんだよね。地球と太陽みたいなものだね。
学生Ｂ：④そうね。さらにケプラー186fは液体の水が存在しうる位置にあるのよね。⑤えっと…つまりM型矮星のハビタブルゾーンの範囲内にあるということね。
学生Ａ：ということは，地球外生命体の前提条件になるのは，液体の水だけなの？
学生Ｂ：違うわよ，液体の水はその１つに過ぎないわ。⑥教授は他に２つのこと，つまりその惑星の化学物質と大気の状態について言及していたわ。
学生Ａ：わかった。ありがとう。

# Lecture 2　Original

**Listening**　新たな講義を聴いてみよう。　CD 27

The recent discovery of Kepler-186f has given many scientists hope that other life forms out there in the universe may be found. But other scientists remain skeptical on the issue. One question they raise is, "Is a planet in the habitable zone necessarily habitable?" Their answer is "no." Why not?

Well, they use Mars as an example. Mars is within the habitable zone around the Sun,
①**but even after decades of research, scientists have not been able to find** …
②**So just because a planet is in a habitable zone does not mean** …

Another issue scientists claim to be a problem is the notion of tidal locking.
③**This means that one half of a planet** …
Think of our moon. It always shows us the same "face," right?
④**This is because our moon is** …
⑤**When a planet is tidally locked, the bright side stays** …
Some scientists believe that Kepler-186f is tidally locked with its M dwarf star.
⑥**If it is, the conditions may not be** …

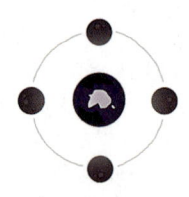

**Speaking**　吹き出しを見ながら足りない語を補い，講義を再現してみよう。

Unit 4　Planetary Habitability

## Script

①**but even after decades of research, scientists have not been able to find** concrete evidence of life.
②**So just because a planet is in a habitable zone does not mean** there's life on it.
③**This means that one half of a planet** always faces the star, while the opposite side always faces away.
④**This is because our moon is** tidally locked with the Earth.
⑤**When a planet is tidally locked, the bright side stays** extremely hot and the dark side is always freezing.
⑥**If it is, the conditions may not be** very favorable for life.

## Translation

　ケプラー186fの最近の発見は，多くの科学者に宇宙に他の生命体が発見されるかもしれないという希望を与えました。しかし，この問題についてまだ懐疑的な科学者もいます。彼らが提起している1つの問題点は，「ハビタブルゾーンにある惑星は必ず住むのに適しているのか」。彼らの答えは，「ノー」です。どうして住むのに必ずしも適さないのでしょうか。
　そこで，彼らは火星を一例に挙げます。火星は太陽の周りのハビタブルゾーンの内側にありますが，①何十年にもわたって研究したものの，科学者は生命に関する具体的な証拠を発見することができませんでした。②だから，ある惑星がハビタブルゾーン内にあるからといって，その惑星に生命が存在していることを意味しないのです。
　科学者が問題としているもう1つの争点は，潮汐固定（自転と公転の同期）という考えです。③これはつまり，ある惑星のどちらか半分の面が常に恒星に面していて，反対面は常に逆の方向を向いているということです。私たちの月を考えてみてください。月はいつも同じ「顔」を私たちに向けていますね。④これは月が地球に対して潮汐固定されているからです。⑤ある惑星が潮汐固定されている場合は，明るい側が極端に高温のままで，暗い側は常に凍りそうに寒いということです。一部の科学者は，ケプラー186fはM型矮星と潮汐固定の状態にあると考えています。⑥もしそうであれば，状況は生命にとってそれほど好ましくないかもしれません。

085

# Lecture 2　Summary

**Listening**　チャートを見ながら講義をもう一度聴き, Lecture Notesを完成させよう。(答えは右ページ)

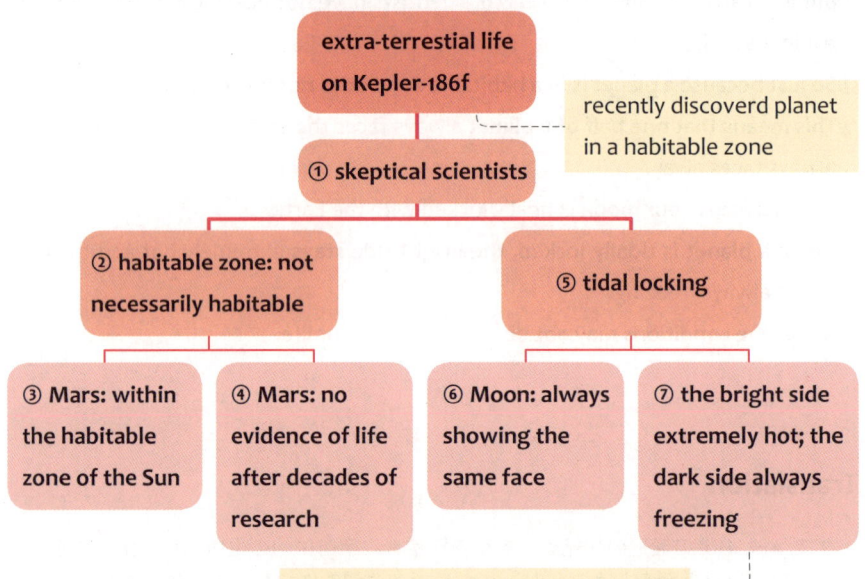

```
extra-terrestial life on Kepler-186f  ---- recently discoverd planet in a habitable zone
        │
    ① skeptical scientists
    ┌───┴───┐
② habitable zone:     ⑤ tidal locking
 not necessarily
   habitable
  ┌────┴────┐         ┌────┴────┐
③ Mars:      ④ Mars: no   ⑥ Moon:       ⑦ the bright side
within the   evidence of  always        extremely hot; the
habitable    life after   showing the   dark side always
zone of      decades of   same face     freezing
the Sun      research
```

not very favorable conditions for life

### Lecture Notes

**TOPIC**
ケプラー186fにおける地球外生命体の探査

**PURPOSE**
ケプラー186fに地球外生命体が存在する可能性が（　A　）ことを示すこと

**MAIN ARGUMENT**
主　張：ケプラー186fに地球外生命体が存在すると期待する声もあるが, 一定数の科学者はそれに懐疑的である。
理由①：（　B　）に位置していることが, 必ずしも生命体の存在を含意しない。
理由②：ケプラー186fには（　C　）がみられる。

**Speaking**　チャートを見ながら講義を要約し, 声に出して言ってみよう。

086

## Summary

There might be **extra-terrestrial life on Kepler-186f**, a **recently discovered planet in the habitable zone** of a star. However, **some scientists are skeptical**. Firstly, a **planet in the habitable zone is not necessarily habitable.** This is easy to see from the example of **Mars**. Although Mars is located **within the habitable zone of the Sun, decades of research** has found **no evidence of life** on the planet. Secondly, Kepler-186f **is tidally locked.** Similar to the Moon, the planet **always shows the same face** to the star, making **the bright side extremely hot,** and **the dark side always freezing** cold, not an ideal environment for life.

## Translation

ある恒星のハビタブルゾーンで最近発見されたケプラー186fに地球外生命体が存在するかもしれないが、それに懐疑的な科学者もいる。第1に、惑星がハビタブルゾーンに位置していることが、必ずしも生命体の存在を含意しない。これは火星の例を見れば簡単に理解できる。火星は太陽系におけるハビタブルゾーンに位置するが、数十年にわたる研究で、火星に生命体の存在を示す証拠は得られていない。第2に、ケプラー186fには潮汐固定（自転と公転の同期）がみられる。月同様、この惑星の半面が常に恒星に面している。その結果、明るい面は非常に高温である一方で、暗い面は常に凍りつくほど冷たい。生命体が存在するのに理想的とは言えない環境である。

### Integrated Task

Explain the factors that prove or disprove an existence of extra-terrestrial life on a planet called Kepler-186f.

Lecture Notesの答え　A 低い　B ハビタブルゾーン　C 潮汐固定

## Grammar Notes

①The universe, **some people believe**, is vast enough to have some form of extra-terrestrial life.

▶通常の語順であればSome people believe (that) the universe is vast enough ...となります。英語では，I think ...「私が思うに…だ」，it seems ...「どうやら…のようだ」，the study shows ...「その研究によると…ということだ」など，述べられる事柄についての「判断主」や「推量」，「情報源」などを示すSVが，主語や，文頭の副詞句・節の直後に挿入される形で示されることがあります。

②**A prerequisite for life** is **liquid water** on the surface of a planet.

▶prerequisite for A は「Aが成り立つための前提条件」という意味です。liquid waterは「液体の水」のことで，気体（gas）や固体（solid）ではない状態の"$H_2O$"ということです。

③Liquid water only exists at temperatures between 273K and 373K, and the temperature of a planet can be predicted **by measuring** the planet's distance from its sun.

▶by *doing*「〜することによって」は「意図的な手段や方法」を表すときに用います。ここでは惑星の温度が「惑星の太陽からの距離を測定する」という方法によって予測されると述べられています。

④This optimum region of space **surrounding a sun-like star is called the habitable zone**.

▶surrounding a sun-like starは，直前の名詞spaceを後ろから修飾しています。
▶is called the habitable zoneは，call O C「OをCと呼ぶ」の受動態を用いた表現で「ハビタブルゾーンと呼ばれる」という意味です。They called him a saint.「彼らは彼を聖人と呼んだ」の受動態がHe was called a saint.「彼は聖人と呼ばれた」となるように，〈be動詞＋過去分詞〉の直後に能動態のときの補語（C）が残っている点に注意しましょう。

⑤Recently, astronomers have discovered **the first Earth-size planet, Kepler-186f**, orbiting in the "habitable zone" of an M dwarf star.

▶the first Earth-size planetという普通の名詞句と，その固有名称である"Kepler-186f"が，カンマ（,）のみで並べられています。このような名詞句相互の関係を「同格」と呼びます。日本語の「最初に発見された地球大の惑星であるケプラー186f」などに相当します。今回の例のように"[一般表現]，[固有名称]"という順で並ぶこともあれば，"[固有名称]，[一般表現]"の順で並ぶこともあります。

Unit 4　Planetary Habitability

⑥This planet **orbits** its parent M dwarf star once in 130 days **and receives one third** the energy that Earth gets from the sun.

- ▶主語This planetに対して，述部がorbits ... and receives ...と２つに枝分かれした構造になっています。
- ▶ one thirdは「３分の１」という意味です。序数Xthには「Ｘ分の１」という意味があり，third「３分の１」，fourth「４分の１」，fifth「５分の１」…などとなります。また，例えば「５分の２」ならばtwo-fifthsとなるように，「Ｘ分の１」がいくつあるかによって分子を表します。したがって，分子が２以上ならば，分母は複数形になります。

⑦Scientists are now investigating the **chemical compositions and atmospheric conditions** of the planet.

- ▶ andは，chemical compositionsとatmospheric conditionsという２つの名詞句を結び付けています。注意したいのは，両者がthe と of the planetを共有している点です。つまり"the [①chemical compositions and ②atmospheric conditions] of the planet"という構造で，the と of the planetは①②の両方と結びついているという点です。

⑧M dwarf stars constitute 70 percent of the stars in the Milky Way Galaxy, and planets in the habitable zone of each star **are waiting to be explored**.

- ▶ waitという動詞は，「物・事」を主語として進行形で用いると「準備が整っている」という意味合いになります。たとえば，"Dinner is waiting for you."ならば「夕食ができていますよ」という意味，これは，「あとはあなたが食べるだけだ」という意味につながります。ここでの"are waiting to be explored"はこの意味合いで，「あとはハビタブルゾーンにある膨大な数の惑星を探査するばかりだ」と，地球外生命体を発見する可能性があることを，期待を込めて示唆しています。

## Paraphrase Notes

①**It is argued that** the universe is **so large that** there must exist extra-terrestrial life of some form or another.

▶オリジナル①ではsome people believeの挿入で表されていた「一部の人の考えでは」という意味が，ここではIt is argued that ...「…だと主張されている」という表現になっています。挿入を用いて，"The universe, **it is argued**, is so large that ..." と書くこともできます。

▶オリジナル①では，"～ enough to *do*" という表現を用いてis vast enough to have some form of ...と書かれていましたが，こちらでは "so ～ that ...." という表現でパラフレーズされています。

②**One thing life on a planetary surface needs is** water in liquid form.

▶オリジナル②のA prerequisite for life is ...が，One thing life on a planetary surface needs is ...「惑星の表面上の生命体が必要とするものの1つは…だ」という表現で置き換えられています。One thingの直後に関係代名詞のwhichが省略されていることに注意しましょう。

③**This** is only possible in the temperature range of 273K to 373K, and a planet's temperature is predictable **once you know how far it is from its sun**.

▶Thisは②のwater in liquid form「液体の水」を受けています。

▶once you know how far it is from its sun「太陽からどのくらい離れているかがわかれば」はオリジナル③のby measuring the planet's distance from its sunに相当します。once S V ...は「ひとたび…すれば」という意味の副詞節です。

④**Scientists named** the area of space that is suitable for life the "habitable zone."

▶オリジナル④の「…はハビタブルゾーンと呼ばれる」という受動態を用いた表現から，「科学者は…をハビタブルゾーンと名付けた」という能動態を用いた表現にパラフレーズされています。

▶name O Cで「OをCと名付ける」という意味ですが，ここではthe area of space that is suitable for lifeがO，the "habitable zone"がCに当たります。

⑤Astronomers announced that they have found **Kepler-186f, a planet the size of our Earth**, that is in a "habitable zone" orbit around an M dwarf star.

▶オリジナル⑤とは逆に"[固有名称]，[一般表現]"という並びで同格関係になっています。

⑥Kepler-186f circles its M dwarf star **every 130 days** and the amount of energy **delivered** to it from the star is one-third of **that which** we get from our sun.

▶オリジナル⑥の once in 130 days「130日に一度」が every 130 days「130日ごとに」で置き換えられています。

▶delivered は過去分詞で，delivered to it from the star は直前の the amount of energy を修飾しています。

▶that which ... は the amount of energy which ... の代用表現です。

⑦**Now being studied by researchers is what chemicals and atmospheric conditions exist on Kepler-186f.**

▶A is being *done* by B「AはBによって〜されているところだ」（受動態の進行形）の being *done* by Bが文頭に移動した結果，Being *done* by B is A「Bによって〜されているのはAだ」という倒置の生じた語順になっています。主語Aが比較的長い場合などにこのような倒置が起きることがあります。この文では what chemicals and atmospheric conditions exist on Kepler-186f「ケプラー186fにどのような化学物質や大気状態が存在するか」がAに当たります。

⑧**70% of the stars in our Milky Way Galaxy are M dwarf stars**, and their habitable zone planets **are wonderful subjects for future research**.

▶オリジナル⑧では，M dwarf stars constitute 70 percent of the stars「M型矮星は恒星の70％を占める」という表現が用いられていましたが，こちらでは「恒星の70％がM型矮星だ」という言い方でパラフレーズされています。

▶オリジナル⑧で，are waiting to be explored という微妙な表現で示唆していた「将来の探査への期待感」を，こちらでは「将来の探査の素晴らしい対象だ」と，ずっとストレートな表現で伝えています。

# Expressions and Phrases

ヒントを手がかりにして，日本語に対応する英語表現を言ってみよう。

| 日本語 | ヒント | 英語 |
|---|---|---|
| □ 銀河天文学 | ga___ as___ | galactic astronomy |
| □ 理論天文学者 | th___ as___ | theoretical astronomer |
| □ 天文学的探査 | as___ pr___ | astronomical probe |
| □ 広大な宇宙 | va___ un___ | vast universe |
| □ 太陽系 | so___ sy___ | solar system |
| □ 天の川銀河 | Mi___ Wa___ Ga___ | Milky Way Galaxy |
| □ 火星軌道 | Ma___ or___ | Mars orbit |
| □ 地球大の惑星 | Ea___-si___ pl___ | Earth-size planet |
| □ 矮星（半径と光度の小さい星） | dw___ st___ | dwarf star |
| □ 生命体 | li___ fo___ | life form |
| □ 地球外生物 | ex___-te___ li___ | extra-terrestrial life |
| □ 最近の発見 | re___ di___ | recent discovery |
| □ 具体的証拠 | co___ ev___ | concrete evidence |
| □ 予測される結果 | pr___ ou___ | predictable outcome |
| □ 一般に広まっている概念 | pr___ no___ | prevalent notion |
| □ 一般的定義 | ge___ de___ | general definition |
| □ 居住可能地域 | ha___ zo___ | habitable zone |
| □ 好ましい状態 | fa___ co___ | favorable condition |
| □ 適した場所 | su___ lo___ | suitable location |
| □ 最適領域 | op___ re___ | optimum region |
| □ 理想的な環境 | id___ en___ | ideal environment |
| □ 惑星表面 | pl___ su___ | planetary surface |
| □ 明るい面 | br___ si___ | bright side |
| □ 反対側 | op___ si___ | opposite side |
| □ 十分なエネルギー | su___ en___ | sufficient energy |
| □ 氷結温度 | fr___ te___ | freezing temperature |
| □ 液体水 | li___ wa___ | liquid water |
| □ 化学組成 | ch___ co___ | chemical composition |
| □ 潮汐力 | ti___ fo___ | tidal force |
| □ 引力 | gr___ pu___ | gravitational pull |

## Unit 4　Planetary Habitability

□ 宇宙空間を探査する

| ex____ ou____ sp____ | explore outer space |
| pr___ the co____ sp____ | probe the cosmic space |

□ 地球外生物についての説を否定する

| di____ a th____ on ex____-te_____ life | disprove a theory on extra-terrestrial life |
| ne____ a hy_____ about al____ | negate a hypothesis about aliens |

□ 生命存在の証拠がない

| la____ ev____ of life | lack evidence of life |
| fi___ no ev_____ that li___ may ex____ | find no evidence that life may exist |

□ 生命の必須条件と考えられている

| be co_____ as a pr_____ for life | be considered as a prerequisite for life |
| be se____ as an es_____ co_____ for life | be seen as an essential condition for life |

□ その惑星が居住可能だと主張する

| cl____ the pl____ to be ha_____ | claim the planet to be habitable |
| in____ that the pl____ can su____ life | insist that the planet can support life |

□ 表面の温度を予測する

| pr____ the su____ te_____ | predict the surface temperature |
| es____ the te_____ on the su____ | estimate the temperature on the surface |

□ 大気成分を調査する

| in_____ at_____ co_____ | investigate atmospheric composition |
| ex____ at_____ co_____ | examine atmospheric components |

□ 大気の80パーセントを占める

| ac____ for 80 pe____ of the ai____ | account for 80 percent of the air |
| co_____ 80 pe____ of the at_____ | constitute 80 percent of the atmosphere |

□ 研究にかなりの時間を費やす

| pu____ in a go____ de____ of time on re_____ | put in a good deal of time on research |
| sp____ co_____ time on re_____ | spend considerable time on research |

□ 未来への大きな希望を与える

| gi____ great ho____ for the fu____ | give great hope for the future |
| of____ im_____ ho____ for the fu____ | offer immense hope for the future |

# Word List

| | | |
|---|---|---|
| □ a good deal of A | | たくさんのA<br>類 much A / a lot of A |
| □ announce [ənáuns] | | 動 …を発表する，…を知らせる<br>類 make public / report |
| □ astronomer [əstrá:nəmər\|-trɔ́n-] | | 名 天文学者 |
| □ astronomy [əstrá:nəmi\|-trɔ́n-] | | 名 天文学 |
| □ atmospheric [ætməsférɪk] | | 形 大気の |
| □ bet (that) S V | | …だと断言する |
| □ chemical [kémɪkl] | | 形 化学の　名 化学製品，化学物質 |
| □ circle [sə́:rkl] | | 動 …の周りを回る，…を丸で囲む<br>名 円，循環 |
| □ composition [kɑ̀:mpəzíʃən\|kɔ̀m-] | | 名 組成，構成，(詩・曲などの) 作品 |
| □ concrete [kɑ:nkrí:t] | | 形 明確な，具体的な，コンクリート製の<br>名 固形物 |
| □ condition [kəndíʃən] | | 名 状態，状況，条件，(長期的な) 病気<br>類 state<br>動 …を条件づける，…を左右する |
| □ decade [dékeɪd, dɪkéɪd] | | 名 10年間 |
| □ definition [dèfəníʃən] | | 名 定義，明確さ |
| □ deliver [dɪlívər] | | 動 …を与える，…を実行する，…を配達する，…を出産する |
| □ distance [dístəns] | | 名 距離，遠距離，相違 |
| □ dwarf [dwɔːrf] | | 形 標準より小さい　名 小人 (こびと) |
| □ exist [ɪgzíst] | | 動 存在する，生存する |
| □ explore [ɪksplɔ́:r, eks-] | | 動 …を探険する，…を探査する，…を調査する |
| □ extra-terrestrial [èkstrətəréstriəl] | | 形 地球外の |
| □ favorable [féɪvərəbl] | | 形 好都合な，有利な，好意的な |
| □ habitable [hǽbətəbl] | | 形 住むのに適した |
| □ ideal [aɪdíːəl\|-díəl] | | 形 理想的な　名 理想 |
| □ investigate [ɪnvéstəgèɪt] | | 動 …を調査する，研究する<br>類 look into / probe |
| □ location [loukéɪʃən] | | 名 位置，場所 |
| □ measure [méʒər] | | 動 …を測定する，…を評価する，…の寸法がある<br>類 calculate<br>名 対策，基準，程度，寸法 |
| □ mention [ménʃən] | | 動 …について述べる，…に言及する |

| | | |
|---|---|---|
| □ necessarily [nèsəsérəli] | 副 | 必ず，必然的に |
| □ note [nout] | 名<br>動 | メモ 注釈，(楽器などの) 音，紙幣，注目<br>…に注意を払う，…に言及する，<br>…を書き留める |
| □ opposite [á:pəzɪt] | 形<br>名<br>前 | 反対の，反対側の<br>正反対の人（もの）<br>…の向かい側に |
| □ optimum [á:ptəməm\|óp-] | 形 最適の，最善の 名 最適の度合い |
| □ orbit [ɔ́:rbət] | 動<br>名 | …の軌道を回る，軌道に乗る<br>軌道，範囲 |
| □ planetary [plǽnətèri] | 形 | 惑星の，地球上の |
| □ planet [plǽnət] | 名 | 惑星，(the ～で) 地球，世界全体 |
| □ possibly [pá:səbli\|pɔ́s-] | 副 | ひょっとしたら，もしかしたら |
| □ predict [prɪdíkt] | 動<br>類 | …を予測する，…を予言する<br>forecast / foretell |
| □ predictable [prɪdíktəbl] | 形 | 予測可能な |
| □ prepare for A | Aに備える |
| □ prerequisite [prìːrékwəzɪt] | 名<br>類<br>形 | 前提条件<br>requirement<br>不可欠の |
| □ raise [reɪz] | 動<br><br>名 | …を提起する，…を上げる，…を育てる，<br>(資金など) を集める<br>昇給 |
| □ range [réɪndʒ] | 名 範囲，領域 動 (ある範囲に) およぶ，渡る |
| □ recent [ríːsnt] | 形 | 最近の |
| □ region [ríːdʒən] | 名<br>類 | 領域，地域<br>district / province |
| □ skeptical [sképtɪkl] | 形 | 懐疑的な |
| □ solar system | 太陽系 |
| □ sound [saund] | 動 …のように聞こえる，…を鳴らす 名 音 |
| □ star [stɑːr] | 名 | 恒星，星，人気者 |
| □ suitable for A | Aに適切である |
| □ surround [səráund] | 動 | …を取り囲む，…に結びつく |
| □ tidally [táɪdli] | 副 | 潮の作用によって |
| □ universe [júːnəvə̀ːrs] | 名 | 宇宙，森羅万象，領域 |
| □ vast [væst\|vɑːst] | 形 | 広大な，莫大な |

## 参考文献

Walter, F. M. (n.d.). *AST 248 : Search for Life in the Universe Fall 2014, AST 248 Chapter 10 HW Problems*. Retrieved September 5, 2015, from Astronomy Program, Dept. of Physics and Astronomy, Stony Brook University website: http://www.astro.sunysb.edu/fwalter/AST 248/hw_ch10.pdf

*Habitable Zones*. (n.d.). Retrieved September 5, 2015, from The Universe Around Us. An Introduction to Astrobiology website: http://phillips.seti.org/kids/habitable-zones.html#

# Unit 5 Da Vinci's Bird Sketches

## Integrated Task

Explain some early developments in aerodynamics contributed by great thinkers of the past such as Aristotle, Archimedes, and Leonardo Da Vinci.

## Key Words

**Leonardo Da Vinci**

▶イタリアのルネサンス期を代表する芸術家，そして博学者であるレオナルド・ダ・ヴィンチは，絵画のみならず，彫刻，建築，科学，工学，音楽などあらゆる芸術・学問の分野にわたって，卓越した技量と洞察を発揮しました。「万能の人」（*uomo universale*）と呼ばれるゆえんです。「最後の晩餐」，「モナ・リザ」などの絵画の代表作を見たことがない方はいないでしょう。彼の作品の特徴は，その描き方に解剖学や光学の知識が反映されていることで，その根底にあった作業が，精緻な観察（observation）だと言われています。講義では，自然物を対象とした彼の観察の一端が紹介されます。

**aerodynamics**

▶dynamics「力学」という語にaero-「空気の」という接頭辞が付いてできた語です。「空気力学」と訳し，空気の流れが，その流れの中にある物体へどのような影響を及ぼすかを解明しようとする学問を指します。たとえば，飛行機のような重い物体が空に浮かぶ仕組みを説明しようとすると，空気力学の理解が必要になります。ところで，ライト兄弟にとって初めての本格有人飛行が試みられたのは1903年，一方，ダ・ヴィンチが活躍したのは，1400年代後半から1500年代初頭にかけてです。この4世紀もの「時間差」を念頭におくと，講義が大いに興味深く感じられるはずです。

# Lecture 1　Original

**Listening**　講義を聴いてみよう。　CD 30

① Dreaming of flying

larks

Leonardo Da Vinci

② He left many drawings

③ His drawings clearly show

The Codex on the Flight of Birds

principles of aerodynamics

angle and speed

a ↑ lift

④ Firstly, the angle and speed

⑤ This is easy to test

Shape: upper curved surface

change the angle

⑥ The shape of the wing

⑦ You can easily confirm this

⑧ As the flowing air

reduce air pressure

**Speaking**　イラストを見ながら講義を再現してみよう。

Unit 5　Da Vinci's Bird Sketches

## Script

①**Dreaming of flying,** Leonardo Da Vinci made careful observations of larks and other birds common to the Italian countryside. ②**He left many drawings** of flying birds with lines of air passing under and over each wing, in his private notebook called *Codex on the Flight of Birds*. ③**His drawings clearly show** that he had begun to understand important principles of aerodynamics. ④**Firstly, the angle and speed** of the wing are crucial in determining the lift it can create. ⑤**This is easy to test** in real life by holding your arm out of a car window and changing the angle of your hand. ⑥**The shape of the wing** is also important; the curved upper surface, for example, adds additional lift. ⑦**You can easily confirm this** by blowing the curved top surface of a piece of paper placed in front of you. ⑧**As the flowing air** from your breath reduces the air pressure above the page, the paper rises from below.

## Translation

①飛ぶことを夢見て，レオナルド・ダ・ヴィンチはイタリアの田舎でよく見かけられるヒバリなどの鳥を注意深く観察した。②彼は「鳥の飛翔についての手稿」と呼ばれている自分専用のノートに，飛んでいる鳥のスケッチを数多く残したが，そのスケッチには両翼の上下を流れる空気の線が描かれていた。③彼のスケッチは，彼が空気力学の重要な原理を理解し始めていたということをはっきり示している。④まず，翼の角度と速さはそれが生み出すことのできる揚力を決めるうえで大変重要である。⑤このことは車の窓の外へ腕を出して手の角度を変えてみることで，実生活の中でも簡単に試すことができる。⑥翼の形もまた大変重要であり，例えば翼の上面が湾曲していれば，さらに揚力が得られる。⑦このことは目の前に置かれた湾曲した紙の上面に息を吹きかけることで，簡単に確かめることができる。⑧息をすることで流れ出る空気が，その１枚の紙の上にある空気圧を減らすので，紙は下から上に持ち上がるのである。

　　スクリプトの文法ポイントについては，p.108〜の**Grammar Notes**を参照しよう。

## Lecture 1　Paraphrase

**Listening**　別の表現を用いた講義を聴いてみよう。

CD 31

larks

Leonardo Da Vinci

**notebook**

The Codex on the Flight of Birds

principles of aerodynamics

angle and speed

a ↑ lift

**angle and speed**

shape: upper curved surface

change the angle

**shape of the wing**

reduce air pressure

**Speaking**　イラストを見ながら講義の内容を英語で説明しよう。

100

Unit 5　Da Vinci's Bird Sketches

## Script

①Leonardo Da Vinci aspired to fly, and he closely studied larks and other birds one can easily find in rural Italy. ②*Codex on the Flight of Birds* was the name of a personal **notebook** he kept, and in it he drew numerous pictures of birds in flight, indicating with lines the flow of air above and below every wing. ③What is clear from these drawings is that Da Vinci was beginning to comprehend the fundamental laws of aerodynamics. ④One of these laws is that the amount of lift a wing can produce is very dependent on the **angle and speed** of the wing. ⑤You can readily test this yourself by extending your arm out the window of a fast-moving car and altering your hand's angle. ⑥Also critical is the **shape of the wing**; the curve in the upper surface, for instance, increases lift. ⑦This, too, can be proven very simply: blow across the top surface of a curved sheet of paper that is close to you. ⑧The air flow from your mouth decreases the air pressure over the sheet and the sheet lifts up.

## Translation

①レオナルド・ダ・ヴィンチは空を飛ぶことを切望し，イタリアの田舎で簡単に見つけることができるヒバリなどの鳥について綿密に研究した。②「鳥の飛翔に関する手稿」は彼が記録していた自分専用のノートの名前であり，その中に彼は膨大な数の飛んでいる鳥の絵を描き，すべての翼の上下に空気の流れを線で示した。③これらのスケッチから明らかなことは，ダ・ヴィンチは空気力学の基本的な法則を理解し始めていたということである。④これらの法則のうちの1つは，翼が生み出すことのできる揚力の総量は，翼の角度と速さによって大きく変わるということである。⑤このことは，高速で走っている車の窓から腕を外へ伸ばして，手の角度を変えることで，自分ですぐに検証することができる。⑥また，翼の形もきわめて重要である。例えば，翼の上面の湾曲は揚力を上げるのである。⑦これもまた，とても簡単に証明できる。すぐそばにある湾曲した紙の上面に息を吹きかければよい。⑧口から出る空気流が紙の真上の気圧を下げ，紙は持ち上がるのである。

☞ パラフレーズのポイントについては，p.110〜の**Paraphrase Notes**を参照しよう。

## Conversation

**Listening** 講義に関連する会話を聴いてみよう。

Student A: Did you know that Leonardo Da Vinci was well-versed in physics?
Student B: I thought he was a renowned painter and sculptor.
Student A: Of course.
　　　　　①**He started out as an apprentice of art but later developed a passion for mechanical designs, especially for …**
　　　　　②**He envisioned developing a telescope 100 years before …**
Student B: So he was talented in both drawing and designing?
Student A: To say the least.
　　　　　③**Da Vinci was also interested in anatomy, particularly …**
　　　　　④**So it's not surprising that he was able to capture …**
Student B: Right, he really understood the principles of flying.
Student A: ⑤**What's really interesting is that his drawings were usually accompanied by …**
　　　　　I could spend hours just looking at his illustrations!

**Speaking** 上の会話文を見ながら音声を聴き，学生Aのパートを再現してみよう。

Unit 5  Da Vinci's Bird Sketches

## Script

①**He started out as an apprentice of art but later developed a passion for mechanical designs, especially for** things like weapons and scientific devices.
②**He envisioned developing a telescope 100 years before** one was invented.
③**Da Vinci was also interested in anatomy, particularly** the structure of limbs and their dependence on nerves and joints.
④**So it's not surprising that he was able to capture** the motion of flight in his drawings of birds' wings.
⑤**What's really interesting is that his drawings were usually accompanied by** detailed explanatory notes.

## Translation

学生Ａ：レオナルド・ダ・ヴィンチが物理学に精通していたことを知っていたかい？
学生Ｂ：彼は画家や彫刻家として有名なんだと思っていたわ。
学生Ａ：もちろん，①彼は芸術家として修業を始めたんだけど，後に機械設計，とりわけ兵器や科学装置に強い思いを抱くようになったんだ。②彼は望遠鏡が発明される100年前からその開発を心に思い描いていたんだよ。
学生Ｂ：ということは，彼は素描と設計の両方で才能があったのね。
学生Ａ：控えめにいってもそういうことだね。③ダ・ヴィンチはまた解剖学，とりわけ腕や脚の構造や，それが神経と関節に依存していることに興味があったんだ。④だから，彼が鳥の翼の素描において飛ぶ動きを捉えることができていたのは驚くことではないんだね。
学生Ｂ：そうね，飛行の原理を本当に理解していたのね。
学生Ａ：⑤実に興味深いことに，彼の素描にはたいてい詳細な注釈が付けられているんだ。彼のイラストをただ見るだけで何時間も過ごせるよ。

# Lecture 2　Original

**Listening**　新たな講義を聴いてみよう。

Leonardo Da Vinci was not the first to contribute to the development of aerodynamics. In fact, ancient Greek philosophers that most of you are familiar with had already contemplated the concept. Let me give you two examples.

①Aristotle was the first to conceive of the idea that …,
②and that resistance is created when …
③This was an important concept in understanding the relationship between gaseous fluids and …

The next contribution came from Archimedes a hundred years after Aristotle. He, too, understood that an object moving through fluids, such as air, is subject to pressure.
④And in order for the object to move in a certain direction, he said, the pressure …
⑤This idea was instrumental in designing devices on airplanes that …

**Speaking**　吹き出しを見ながら足りない語を補い，講義を再現してみよう。

## Script

①**Aristotle was the first to conceive of the idea that** air has weight,
②**and that resistance is created when** an object moves through air.
③**This was an important concept in understanding the relationship between gaseous fluids and** upward forces in regards to flying.
④**And in order for the object to move in a certain direction, he said, the pressure** must be properly controlled.
⑤**This idea was instrumental in designing devices on airplanes that** increase and decrease pressure during flight.

## Translation

　　レオナルド・ダ・ヴィンチが最初に空気力学の発達に貢献したわけではありません。実のところ，皆さんのほとんどがよく知っている古代ギリシャの哲学者がすでにその概念を熟考していました。２つの例を挙げてみましょう。
　　①アリストテレスは空気には重さがあるという考えを思いついた最初の人で，②物体が空気中を通って運動するとき抵抗が生じるということもわかっていました。③これは，飛行に関してガス状流体と押し上げ力との間の関係を理解する点で重要な概念でした。
　　次の貢献はアリストテレスの100年後にアルキメデスがもたらしたものです。彼も，空気のような流体を通って運動する物体は圧力を受けやすいということを理解していました。④そして，物体が一定の方向に運動するためには，圧力が適切に制御されなければならない，と彼は言ったのです。⑤この考えは，飛行中の圧力を増加させたり減少させたりする，飛行機に取り付けられる装置を設計するのに役立ちました。

# Lecture 2　Summary

**Listening**　チャートを見ながら講義をもう一度聴き，Lecture Notesを完成させよう。(答えは右ページ)　CD 34

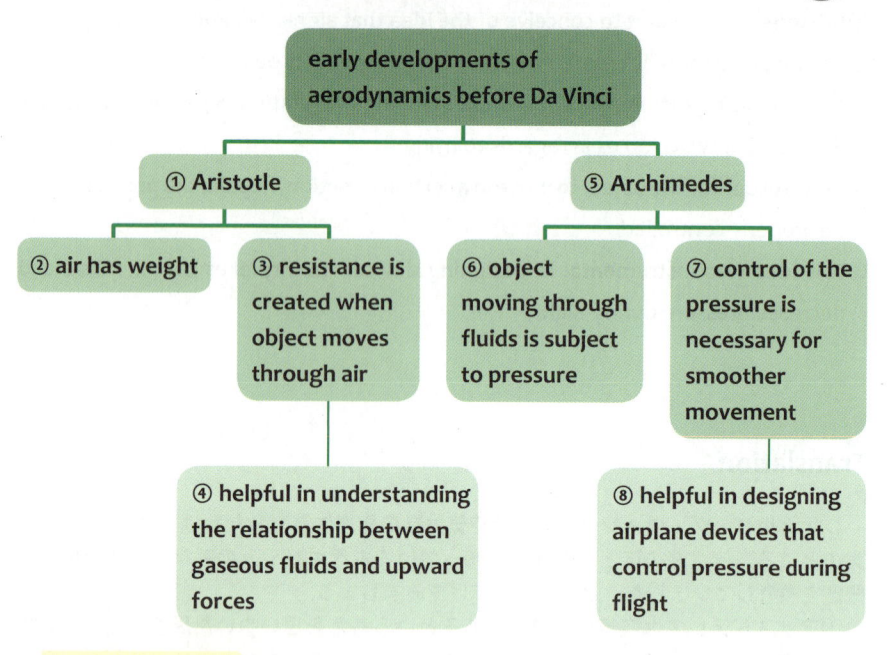

```
            early developments of
          aerodynamics before Da Vinci
           ┌──────────────┴──────────────┐
        ① Aristotle                   ⑤ Archimedes
      ┌─────┴─────┐                 ┌─────┴─────┐
② air has      ③ resistance is    ⑥ object      ⑦ control of the
  weight         created when       moving through  pressure is
                 object moves       fluids is       necessary for
                 through air        subject to      smoother
                                    pressure        movement
                      │                                  │
                ④ helpful in                      ⑧ helpful in designing
                understanding the                 airplane devices that
                relationship between              control pressure during
                gaseous fluids and                flight
                upward forces
```

## Lecture Notes

**TOPIC**
空気力学の初期の発展

**PURPOSE**
ダ・ヴィンチ以前の空気力学の発展を紹介すること

**MAIN ARGUMENT**
主　張：空気力学への貢献はダ・ヴィンチが最初ではない。
例示①：アリストテレスは空気に重さがあり，物が空気中を動くとき（　A　）が生まれることを発見した。
例示②：アルキメデスは流体の中で物が動くとき（　B　）の影響を受けることを発見した。

**Speaking**　チャートを見ながら講義を要約し，声に出して言ってみよう。

Unit 5　Da Vinci's Bird Sketches

☞ 要約文（サンプル）を聴いてみよう。

## Summary

**Prior to Da Vinci**, two Greek philosophers contributed to **the early developments of aerodynamics**. The first one was **Aristotle**. He was considered the first to point out that **air has weight** and that **resistance is created when an object moves through air**. This finding is **helpful in understanding the relationship between gaseous fluids and upward forces**. The other was **Archimedes**. He found that an **object moving through fluids is subject to pressure**, and that **control of the pressure is necessary for smoother movement**. The discovery is now **helpful in designing airplane devices that control pressure during flight**.

## Translation

ダ・ヴィンチより前に，2人のギリシャの哲学者が初期の空気力学の発展に貢献している。1人目はアリストテレスである。彼は空気に重さがあること，そして物が空気中を動くとき抵抗が生まれることを指摘した最初の人と考えられている。この発見は，ガス状流体と上向きの力の関係を理解するうえで助けとなっている。もう1人はアルキメデスである。彼は流体の中で物が動くとき圧力の影響を受けること，そして滑らかな動きのために圧力を制御することが必要であることを発見した。この発見は現在，飛行中に圧力を制御する飛行機の装置を設計する際に助けとなっている。

---

## Integrated Task

Explain some early developments in aerodynamics contributed by great thinkers of the past such as Aristotle, Archimedes, and Leonardo Da Vinci.

---

☞ Lecture Notesの答え　A 抵抗　B 圧力

## Grammar Notes

①**Dreaming of flying**, Leonardo Da Vinci made careful observations of larks and other birds **common to the Italian countryside**.

▶ Dreaming of flying は分詞構文です。Leonardo Da Vinci <u>dreamed of flying and</u> made careful observations ... と and を用いて書き換えても大きな意味の違いはありませんが，and で結んだ場合は「夢見た」→「観察した」という順序や，理由と結果の関係が強く感じられます。一方，分詞構文を用いると，「夢見た」と「観察した」が同時に成立するように感じられます。

▶ common to the Italian countryside は，直前の other birds を修飾しています。わかりにくい場合は，larks and other birds <u>which are</u> common to ... と，〈関係代名詞＋be動詞〉を補ってみましょう。

②He left many drawings of flying birds with lines of air **passing under and over each wing**, in his private notebook **called** *Codex on the Flight of Birds*.

▶ passing は現在分詞で，直前の名詞 air を説明しています。and がつかないでいる under と over は，passing と each wing を共有していることに注意しましょう。つまり，<u>passing under each wing</u> <u>and</u> passing <u>over each wing</u> の重複部分を取り除いた結果，下線部だけが残った形になっています。「それぞれの翼の下と上とを流れる（空気）」という意味です。

③**His drawings clearly show** that he **had begun** to understand important principles of aerodynamics.

▶ ⓐ show that ... は「ⓐ は…ということを示す」，つまり「ⓐ によって…ということがわかる」という意味です。「情報源」を表す語（＝ⓐ）を主語において，「それが何かを示す／伝える／教える…」という表現は，英語の特徴の1つです。

▶ had begun は過去完了形です。ダ・ヴィンチが鳥のスケッチを描いた時点を基準にして，「<u>その時点ですでに理解し始めていた（ことを彼のスケッチは示している）</u>」という意味合いを表します。

④**Firstly**, the angle and speed of the wing are crucial in determining the lift **it can create**.

▶ Firstly は，「まず第一に」という意味で，列挙の始まりを示しています。⑥の also との連動に注目しましょう。

▶ it can create は，直前の the lift を修飾しています。わかりにくい場合は，the lift <u>which</u> it can create と，関係代名詞を補ってみましょう。

⑤**This is easy to test** in real life by holding your arm out of a car window and changing the angle of your hand.

▶ This is easy to test は「これを試すのは簡単だ」という意味で，It is easy to test this と書き換えることができます。test と this が，意味の上でVとOの関係にあることに注意しましょう。This が受けているのは，④の「翼の角度と速さが揚力の決定に極めて重要だ」という内容で，test this とは「そのことを試す」という意味です。

⑥The shape of the wing is **also** important; the curved upper surface, **for example**, adds additional lift.

▶ also は④のFirstly と連動しています。④ではFirstly に続いて，揚力の決定に重要な要素である「翼のangle と speed」が挙げられました。ここでは，also によって，別の重要な要素が挙げられることが明示されます。

▶ for example は，The shape of the wing の具体例が示されることを明示しています。主語の直後に挿入される形で置かれています。for example, the curved upper surface adds additional lift と先頭においても同じことです。

⑦You can easily **confirm** this by blowing the curved top surface of a piece of paper **placed** in front of you.

▶ confirm は⑤のtest「～を試す」の類義語で，「～を確認する，裏付ける」という意味です。by *doing*「～することによって」という表現を用いて手段を表している点も⑤と類似しています。

▶ placed は過去分詞で，placed in front of you 全体で直前の a piece of paper を修飾しています。place は「～を（ある場所に）置く」という意味ですから，全体で「目の前に置かれた1枚の紙」という意味になります。

⑧**As the flowing air from your breath reduces the air pressure above the page**, the paper rises from below.

▶ 接続詞 as の基本的な働きは，主節で表される事柄と同時に成立している状況を示すことです。⑧の下線部は，主節の「紙が持ち上がる」という事柄と同時に，「空気の流れによって紙の上方の気圧が下がる」という現象が成立していることを表しています。「…なので」と理由だと解釈してもよいですし，「…して」と単に時を表していると解釈してもかまいません。

## Paraphrase Notes

①Leonardo Da Vinci aspired to fly, **and** he closely studied larks and other birds **one can easily find in rural Italy**.

- ▶分詞構文を用いたオリジナル①とは異なり，andで2つのセンテンスをつないでいます。
- ▶ one can easily find in rural Italyは，直前のother birdsを修飾しています。other birds <u>which</u> one can ... と補うことができます。オリジナル①のcommon to the Italian countrysideの言い換えです。

②*Codex on the Flight of Birds* was the name of a personal notebook he kept, and **in it** he drew numerous pictures of birds in flight, indicating **with lines** the flow of air above and below every wing.

- ▶ in itは，in the personal notebook (named Codex on the Flight of Birds) という意味です。「彼は…という名のノートに多くのスケッチを残した」というオリジナル②の書き方から，「…がノートの名であり，彼はそこに多くのスケッチを描いた」という書き方に変わっています。
- ▶ with linesは「線を用いて」という意味の副詞句で，indicate (V) the flow (O) というVOの間に割り込む形で置かれています。

③**What is clear from these drawings is that** Da Vinci **was beginning** to comprehend the fundamental laws of aerodynamics.

- ▶ What is clear from these drawings is that ...は，「これらのスケッチから明らかなのは…ということだ」という意味です。オリジナル③のHis drawings clearly show that ...という表現と比べてみましょう。
- ▶ was beginning to comprehend ...という過去進行形は，「(スケッチを描いた時点で) 理解し始めていた」という意味合いです。すでに「理解し始める」というプロセスは始まっていたわけですから，結果的にはオリジナル③の過去完了形と同じ事実を述べていることに注意しましょう。

④One of these laws is that the amount of lift a wing can produce **is very dependent on** the angle and speed of the wing.

- ▶ A is dependent on Bという表現に注目しましょう。「AはBに依存する」「AはB次第である」という意味で，「Bが変わればAも変わる」という関係が成り立ちます。これを，オリジナル④で用いられた表現に置き換えると，B is crucial in determining A「Aの決定においてBは重要である」となります。

⑤You can **readily** test this **yourself** by **extending** your arm out the window of a fast-moving car and **altering** your hand's angle.

▶ yourselfは「(他の誰でもなく)あなた自身で」という意味合いを添えています。「ひとりで」「独力で」という意味ではない点に注意しましょう。

▶ readilyは「容易に」という意味で，オリジナル⑤の This is <u>easy</u> to test の意味を言い換えたものです。

▶ その他，hold→extend，change→alter といった言い換えを確認しましょう。

⑥Also **critical is the shape of the wing**; the curve in the upper surface, for instance, increases lift.

▶ 下線部は critical (C) is (V) the shape of the wing (S) という CVS の語順になっています。④で挙げられた the angle と speed of the wing に加えて，「もう1つ重要なのは…」と補語(C)から述べ始めたため，後続する SV が，VS の語順になったものです。

⑦This, too, can **be proven** very **simply**: **blow** across the top surface of a curved sheet of paper that is **close to** you.

▶ blow ...は命令文の形になっています。説明文などで用いられる命令文は，「〜してみよう」「〜してください」というニュアンスになります。

▶ オリジナル⑦と見比べて，confirm→prove，easily→simply，in front of→close to などの言い換えを確認しましょう。

⑧The air flow from your mouth **decreases** the air pressure over the sheet **and** the sheet **lifts up**.

▶ オリジナル⑧では，接続詞 as を用いて結び付けていた内容を，ここではシンプルに and でつないでいます。

▶ その他，reduce→decrease，rise from below→lift up などの言い換えが行われています。

## Expressions and Phrases

ヒントを手がかりにして，日本語に対応する英語表現を言ってみよう。

| 日本語 | ヒント | 英語 |
|---|---|---|
| □ 流体物理学 | fl___ ph___ | fluid physics |
| □ 空気力学の原理 | ae_____ pr_____ | aerodynamics principle |
| □ 気流 | fl___ ai___ | flowing air |
| □ 空気抵抗 | ai_ re_____ | air resistance |
| □ ガス状流体 | ga_____ fl___ | gaseous fluid |
| □ 移動物体 | mo_____ ob___ | moving object |
| □ 水平飛行 | le__ fl___ | level flight |
| □ 上部の表面 | up___ su___ | upper surface |
| □ 曲がった上面 | cu___ to_ | curved top |
| □ 適切な角度 | su_____ an___ | suitable angle |
| □ 推定重量 | es_____ we___ | estimated weight |
| □ 傾いたシート | ti___ sh___ | tilted sheet |
| □ 機械設計 | me_____ de___ | mechanical design |
| □ 科学装置 | sc_____ de_____ | scientific devices |
| □ 解剖学的構造 | an_____ st_____ | anatomical structure |
| □ 滑らかな関節 | sm___ jo___ | smooth joint |
| □ 伸ばされた手足 | ex___ li___ | extended limbs |
| □ 知覚神経 | se_____ ne___ | sensory nerves |
| □ 決定的な貢献 | cr_____ co_____ | critical contribution |
| □ 古代の哲学者 | an_____ ph_____ | ancient philosopher |
| □ 詳細説明 | de_____ il_____ | detailed illustration |
| □ なじみのある概念 | fa_____ co_____ | familiar concept |
| □ 裏付けとなる証拠 | co_____ ev_____ | confirming evidence |
| □ 管理された環境 | co_____ en_____ | controlled environment |
| □ 農村地帯 | ru___ ar___ | rural area |
| □ 才能のある見習い | ta_____ ap_____ | talented apprentice |
| □ 私的なノート | pr_____ no_____ | private notebook |
| □ よくある彫刻 | co_____ sc_____ | common sculpture |
| □ 有名な彫刻家 | re_____ sc_____ | renowned sculptor |
| □ 多くの線画 | nu_____ dr_____ | numerous drawings |

## Unit 5  Da Vinci's Bird Sketches

□ 飛ぶ鳥の観察をする

| make ob_____ of fl____ birds | make observations of flying birds |
| ob_____ birds in fl____ | observe birds in flight |

□ 羽の動きを捉える

| ca_____ the mo____ of the wi____ | capture the motion of the wings |
| gr____ the wi____ mo_____ | grasp the wing movement |

□ 注釈が添えられている

| ac_____ by ex_____ no____ | accompanied by explanatory notes |
| pr_____ with br____ ex_____ | presented with brief explanations |

□ 飛行機に情熱を持つようになる

| de_____ a pa_____ for ai_____ | develop a passion for airplanes |
| be____ pa_____ about ai_____ | become passionate about aircraft |

□ そのテーマについて熟考する

| co_____ the su_____ | contemplate the subject |
| po____ over the su_____ | ponder over the subject |

□ 圧力の影響下にある

| be su____ to pr____ | be subject to pressure |
| be un____ the in_____ of pr_____ | be under the influence of pressure |

□ 基本法則を理解する

| co_____ the fu_____ la____ | comprehend the fundamental laws |
| un_____ the ba____ pr_____ | understand the basic principles |

□ 兵器類に精通している

| be we____ ve____ in we_____ | be well versed in weaponry |
| have ex_____ fa_____ with we_____ | have extensive familiarity with weapons |

□ 問題の原因を突き止める

| de_____ the ca____ of the pr_____ | determine the cause of the problem |
| de____ the so____ of the tr_____ | detect the source of the trouble |

□ 解剖学の研究をすることを熱望する

| as____ to st____ an_____ | aspire to study anatomy |
| dr____ of pu_____ an____ sc_____ | dream of pursuing anatomical science |

# Word List

| | | | |
|---|---|---|---|
| □accompany [əkʌ́mpəni] | 動 | …を伴う，…に同行する | |
| □aerodynamics [èəroudainǽmiks] | 名 | 空気力学 | |
| □alter [ɔ́:ltər] | 動 | …を変える，…を作り替える，変わる | |
| | 類 | change | |
| □anatomy [ənǽtəmi] | 名 | 解剖学 | |
| □angle [ǽŋgl] | 名 | 角度，（物を眺める）位置 | |
| □aspire to *do* | | …することを切望する | |
| | 類 | desire to *do* / yearn for *doing* | |
| □blow [blou] | 動 | …に息を吹きかける，…を爆破する，息を吐く，（風が）吹く | |
| | 名 | 一吹き，一撃 | |
| □breath [breθ] | 名 | 息，呼吸 | |
| □capture [kǽptʃər] | 動 | …を捉える，…を獲得する | |
| | 名 | 逮捕，捕獲物 | |
| □certain [sə́:rtn] | 形 | （明言を避けて）ある…，例の…（人を主語にして）確信している | |
| □closely [klóusli] | 副 | 綿密に，密接に，近く | |
| □common [kɑ́:mən｜kɔ́m-] | 形 | よくある，普通の，ありふれた，(common to A で) A に共通の | |
| □conceive [kənsí:v] | 動 | …（考えなど）を思いつく，…を理解する，…だと想像する | |
| □confirm [kənfə́:rm] | 動 | …を確かめる，…を確認する | |
| | 類 | verify / corroborate | |
| □consider [kənsídər] | 動 | …をよく考える | |
| | 語法 | consider *doing*「…しようかと検討する」consider O (to be [as]) C「OをCと考える」 | |
| □contemplate [kɑ́:ntəmplèit, -tem-｜kɔ́n-] | 動 | …をじっくり考える，…を想定する，沈思する | |
| □contribution [kɑ̀:ntrəbjú:ʃən｜kɔ̀n-] | 名 | 貢献，寄付，積立金 | |
| □countryside [kʌ́ntrisàid] | 名 | 田舎，田園地帯 | |
| □critical [krítikl] | 形 | 重要な，批評の，あら探しをする | |
| | 類 | crucial / vital / essential | |
| □crucial [krú:ʃəl] | 形 | 極めて重要な，決定的な | |
| □curved [kə:rvd] | 形 | 湾曲している，カーブしている | |
| □dependence on A | | Aへの依存，Aの上に成り立っていること | |

Unit 5　Da Vinci's Bird Sketches

| | | |
|---|---|---|
| □ dependent on A | | Aによって変わる，Aに頼っている |
| □ detailed [díːteɪld, dɪtéɪld] | 形 | 詳細な |
| □ device [dɪváɪs] | 名 | 装置，工夫 |
| □ direction [dərékʃən] | 名 | 方向 |
| □ drawing [drɔ́ːɪŋ] | 名 | スケッチ，デッサン，素描 |
| □ envision [ɪnvíʒən] | 動 類 | …を心に描く<br>conceive |
| □ especially [ɪspéʃəli, es-] | 副 | 特に |
| □ explanatory [ɪksplǽnətɔ̀ːri, eks-] | 形 | 説明的な |
| □ extend [ɪksténd, eks-] | 動 類 | …を拡大する，…を伸ばす<br>expand / enlarge |
| □ flow [floʊ] | 名 動 | 流れ　流れる |
| □ fluid [flúːɪd] | 名 形 | 液体　流動的な |
| □ fundamental [fʌ̀ndəméntl] | 形 名 | 基本的な，重要な　基本，根本 |
| □ gaseous [gǽsiəs] | 形 | ガス状の |
| □ Greek [gríːk] | 名 形 | ギリシャ人，ギリシャ語<br>ギリシャの |
| □ illustration [ìləstréɪʃən] | 名 | 説明図，イラスト，解説 |
| □ in regard to A | 類 | Aに関して (= with regard to A)<br>regarding A / concerning A |
| □ indicate [índəkèɪt] | 動 | …を示す，…をほのめかす |
| □ instrumental [ìnstrəméntl] | 形 | 役に立つ，楽器だけの |
| □ interested in A | | Aに興味がある |
| □ invent [ɪnvént] | 動 | …を発明する，…を捏造する |
| □ joint [dʒɔɪnt] | 名 動 | 関節，継ぎ目　形　共同の<br>…をつなぎ合わせる |
| □ lark [lɑːrk] | 名 | ヒバリ |
| □ law [lɔː] | 名 | 法則，法律，法学 |
| □ lift [lɪft] | 名 動 | 揚力，持ち上げること<br>…を持ち上げる，持ち上がる |
| □ limb [lɪm] | 名 | 手足 |
| □ motion [móʊʃən] | 名 | 動き |
| □ nerve [nəːrv] | 名 | 神経，緊張 |
| □ numerous [n(j)úːmərəs] | 形 類 | 非常にたくさんの，数多くの<br>countless / innumerable |

115

|  |  |  |
|---|---|---|
| □ observation [à:bzərvéɪʃən] | 名 | 観察, 情報, 意見 |
| □ passion [pǽʃən] | 名 | 情熱, 激情, 感情 |
| □ philosopher [fəlá:səfər] | 名 | 哲学者 |
| □ physics [fízɪks] | 名 | 物理学 |
| □ place [pleɪs] | 動 | …を置く  名 場所 |
| □ point out that S V … | | …だと指摘する |
| □ pressure [préʃər] | 名 動 類 | 圧力, 圧迫, 押すこと / …に圧力をかける / stress |
| □ principle [prínsəpl] | 名 | 原理, 主義, 道義 |
| □ prior to A | | Aに先だって |
| □ produce [prəd(j)ú:s] | 動 | …を生み出す, …を引き起こす, …を製造する, …を取り出す |
| □ properly [prá:pərli \| prɔ́pəli] | 副 | 適切に |
| □ prove [pru:v] | 動 類 | …を証明する / verify, substantiate |
| □ readily [rédəli] | 副 類 | 簡単に, すぐに / easily / without difficulty |
| □ relationship [rɪléɪʃənʃìp] | 名 | 関係, 交際 |
| □ renowned [rɪnáʊnd] | 形 | 有名な, 高名な |
| □ resistance [rɪzístəns] | 名 | 抵抗, 耐性 |
| □ rural [rúərəl] | 形 | 田舎の, 田舎風の |
| □ sculptor [skʌ́lptər] | 名 | 彫刻家 |
| □ simply [símpli] | 副 | 簡単に, 単に, まったく |
| □ smooth [smú:ð] | 形 動 | なめらかな, 順調な / …を(伸ばして)平らにする, …を取り除く |
| □ spend A *doing* | | …してA(時間など)を過ごす |
| □ structure [strʌ́ktʃər] | 名 | 構造, 機構, 建造物 |
| □ talented [tǽləntɪd] | 形 | 才能のある |
| □ telescope [téləskòup] | 名 | 望遠鏡 |
| □ upward [ʌ́pwərd] | 形 副 | 上方への / 上の方に |
| □ weapon [wépən] | 名 | 武器 |

Unit 5 Da Vinci's Bird Sketches

☐ weight [weɪt]
　名　重さ，重いもの，負担，重要性
　動　…を圧迫する，…におもりをつける

☐ well-versed in (on) A
　Aに詳しい
　類　familiar with A

## 参考文献

Johnston, D. (n.d.). *Early Developments in Aerodynamics*. Retrieved September 8, 2015, from U.S. Centennial of Flight Commission website: http://www.centennialofflight.net/essay/Theories_of_Flight/early_aero/TH3.htm

This Month in Physics History April 15, 1452: The Birth of a Visionary — Leonardo da Vinci. (2004, April). *APS NEWS, 13*(4), 2. Retrieved from http://www.aps.org/publications/apsnews/200404/history.cfm

# Unit 6 Dinosaur Metabolism

## Integrated Task

Some people believe dinosaurs were cold-blooded, and others don't. Explain some competing theories on the issue of dinosaur metabolism.

## Key Words

**paleontologist**

▶ paleontology「古生物学」にたずさわる研究者のことです。古生物学とは，かつて地球上に生きていた生物について，おもに化石の調査研究によって，その生態を明らかにしようとする学問です。化石（fossil）は，さまざまな時代に属する地層から発見されるので，古生物学は，おのずと過去における生物の進化に目を向けることになります。今回の講義では，dinosaur「恐竜」の生態に迫ります。元来「恐ろしいトカゲ」という意味を持つdinosaurですが，彼らは本当に「トカゲ」だったのでしょうか。

**warm-blooded / cold-blooded**

▶ それぞれ「温血の」，「冷血の」という意味の形容詞です。体温変化に注目をして動物を分類するときの名称で，warm-blooded animalは，体温が比較的高く，1日あるいは1年を通じて安定しています。そのため「恒温動物」とも呼ばれます。一方，cold-blooded animalは，比較的体温が低く，時間帯や季節によって体温が大きく変化する動物で，「変温動物」とも呼ばれます。mammal「哺乳類」は前者に，reptile「爬虫類」は後者に属します。一般に，warm-blooded animalの方が活動的で，動きも俊敏だとされていますが，dinosaurはどうでしょうか。皆さんが映画や図鑑などから得た恐竜のイメージを思い浮かべながら，講義の内容を理解しましょう。

# Lecture 1　Original

**Listening**　講義を聴いてみよう。

CD 37

① For years, paleontologists
② As researchers found more complete bones
③ Their arguments were based mainly on

sluggish
cold-blooded

warm-blooded
more active
smarter
faster

④ New methods such as bone histology
⑤ Since there is a positive correlation
⑥ This means dinosaurs might
⑦ Findings such as this

growth rate
metabolism

**Speaking**　イラストを見ながら講義を再現してみよう。

## Script

①**For years, paleontologists** believed that dinosaurs could be compared to sluggish cold-blooded lizards. ②**As researchers found more complete bones** of dinosaurs, some started to contend that dinosaurs were warm-blooded creatures, which are generally more active, smarter and faster. ③**Their arguments were based mainly on** the anatomical structures of dinosaurs, but this method was fiercely questioned. ④**New methods such as bone histology** have made it possible to measure the growth rates of dinosaurs. ⑤**Since there is a positive correlation** between growth rate and metabolism, they reached the conclusion that dinosaurs fell right between cold-blooded animals and warm-blooded animals. ⑥**This means dinosaurs might** have eaten more than cold-blooded reptiles do, but they might not have had to eat much to maintain a high body temperature like warm-blooded mammals do. ⑦**Findings such as this** offer valuable clues into different aspects of their lives, such as how they hunted and why they grew so large.

## Translation

①長年の間，古生物学者たちは恐竜が動きの緩慢な冷血動物であるトカゲと同じようなものだ，と信じていた。②研究者たちが恐竜の完全な化石をより多く発見するにつれて，恐竜は冷血動物よりも全般的に活発で，賢く，動きの速い温血動物だったと主張する研究者も出てきた。③彼らの主張は主に恐竜の解剖学上の構造に基づいていたが，この方法は激しい批判にさらされた。④骨組織学などの新しい手法のおかげで，恐竜の成長率を測定することができるようになった。⑤成長率と新陳代謝の間には正の相関関係があるので，学者たちは恐竜が冷血動物と温血動物のちょうど中間に属するという結論に至った。⑥つまり，恐竜は冷血動物である爬虫類よりは多くの量を食べていたかもしれないが，温血動物である哺乳類ほどには，高い体温を保つためにたくさん食べる必要もなかったかもしれないということである。⑦こういった発見は，どのようにして恐竜は獲物を狩っていたか，どうして恐竜はこれほどまで大きく成長したのか，といった恐竜の生態に関するさまざまな側面に対して貴重な手がかりを提供している。

　　スクリプトの文法ポイントについては，p.130〜の**Grammar Notes**を参照しよう。

# Lecture 1　Paraphrase

**Listening**　別の表現を用いた講義を聴いてみよう。

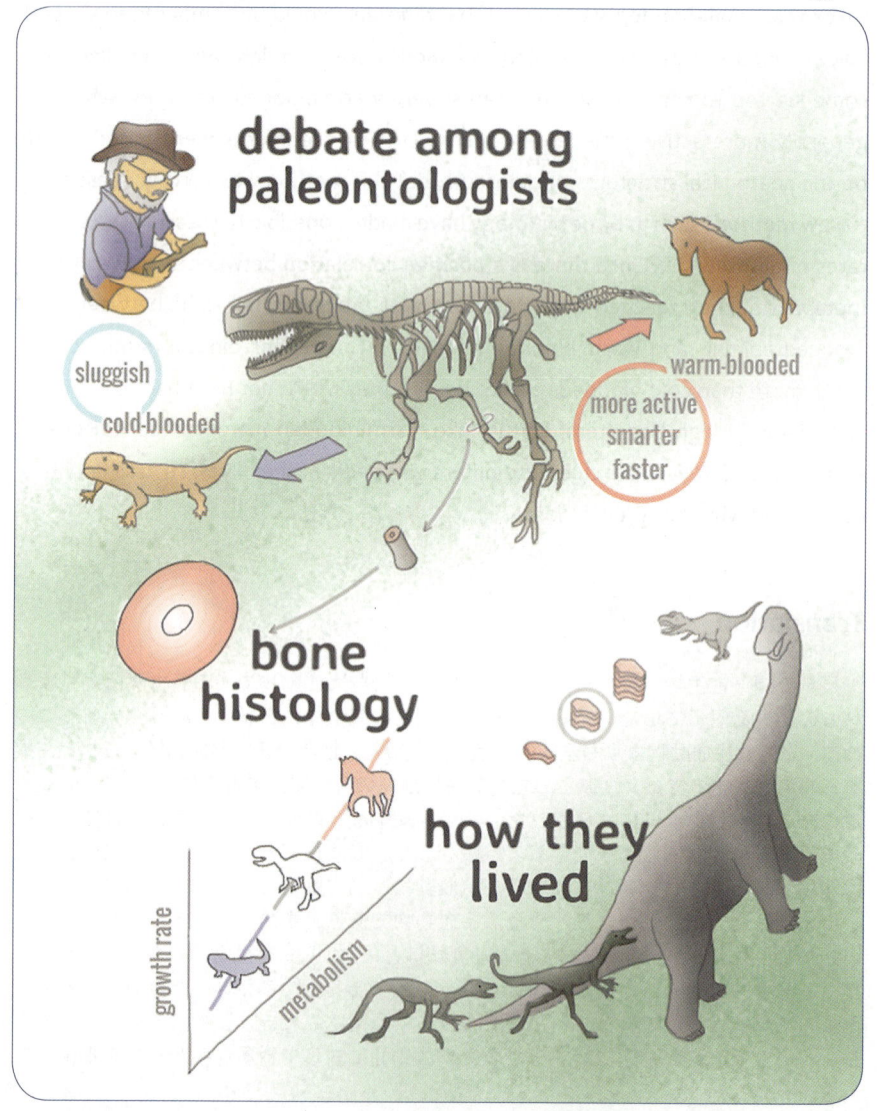

**Speaking**　イラストを見ながら講義の内容を英語で説明しよう。

## Script

①Paleontologists have long maintained that dinosaurs were similar to slow-moving, **cold-blooded** lizards. ②Following the discovery of more intact skeletal parts, however, some scientists began arguing that dinosaurs were, in fact, **warm-blooded** animals, which are usually more energetic, intelligent and quick. ③This claim was largely founded on the structural components of a dinosaur's body, but this approach was hotly debated. ④New techniques like **bone histology** are now allowing researchers to measure the speed of growth of dinosaurs. ⑤The rate of a creature's growth and its metabolic rate are directly connected, and the determination is that dinosaurs functioned in some middle ground between cold- and warm-bloodedness. ⑥Perhaps they ingested more than cold-blooded reptiles do, but it may not have been necessary for them to eat the quantities that warm-blooded mammals need to sustain an elevated body temperature.

## Translation

①考古学者たちは，恐竜がゆっくりと動く冷血動物であるトカゲに似た存在だと，長い間主張してきた。②しかしながら，完全な骨格がより多く発見されたあとで，一部の科学者は，実のところ恐竜は，一般にもっと活発で，賢く，動きが速いとされている温血動物であったのではないかと主張し始めた。③この主張は，主に恐竜の体の構造上の要素に基づいていたが，この研究方法は白熱した議論の的となった。④骨組織学のような新しい技術によって，今，研究者たちは恐竜の成長速度を測定することができるようになりつつある。⑤生物の成長率と新陳代謝率は直接関係していて，結論は，恐竜が温血動物と冷血動物の中間で活動していたというものである。⑥ひょっとすると，恐竜は冷血動物である爬虫類よりも多くの量を摂取していたのかもしれないが，温血動物である哺乳類が高い体温を保つために必要なほどの量を食べる必要はなかったのかもしれない。

☞ パラフレーズのポイントについては，p.132〜の**Paraphrase Notes**を参照しよう。

## Conversation

**Listening** 講義に関連する会話を聴いてみよう。

Student A: Hey Richard.
I heard you visited the Museum of Natural History in Washington D.C. Anything interesting?
Student B: As a matter of fact, yes. I saw this very interesting exhibit about dinosaurs.
**①Some paleontologists now think that dinosaurs were …**
Student A: Huh? So what does that make them?
Student B: **②The exhibit used the term *mesothermic*, which means …**
There are only a few mesothermic species in existence today, such as great white sharks.
Student A: But I learned that dinosaurs have long been considered cold-blooded, just like modern reptiles.
Student B: That's what I thought, too. But what the paleontologists did was to look at the growth rates and metabolism of dinosaurs.
**③You know, how fast …**
**④The *archaeopteryx*, known as the ancestor of modern birds, apparently took …**
But a modern hawk of the same size takes only six weeks to do so.
**⑤Paleontologists also found out that the dinosaurs grew …**
Student A: So dinosaurs grew more slowly than mammals but faster than modern reptiles?
Student B: Yes, and as such these findings place the dinosaurs in-between warm-blooded and cold-blooded animals.

**Speaking** 上の会話文を見ながら音声を聴き，学生Bのパートを再現してみよう。

Unit 6　Dinosaur Metabolism

## Script

①**Some paleontologists now think that dinosaurs were** neither cold-blooded nor warm-blooded.

②**The exhibit used the term *mesothermic*, which means** a medium range blood temperature or in-between warm-blooded and cold-blooded.

③**You know, how fast** they probably grew and how much they ate.

④**The *archaeopteryx*, known as the ancestor of modern birds, apparently took** two years to reach full maturity.

⑤**Paleontologists also found out that the dinosaurs grew** much faster than modern reptiles, which are cold-blooded.

## Translation

学生Ａ：ねえ，リチャード。聞いたわよ，ワシントンD.C.にある自然史博物館を訪れたんだって。何かおもしろいものあった？

学生Ｂ：それがね，あったんだよ。恐竜についての非常に興味深い展示を見たんだ。①一部の古生物学者たちは，恐竜は冷血動物でも温血動物でもなかった，と今は考えているんだ。

学生Ａ：えっ？　じゃあ，恐竜は何動物になるの？

学生Ｂ：②その展示では「中温性」という用語を使っていて，それは中間範囲の血液温度，つまり温血動物と冷血動物の中間にあることを意味するんだ。現存している中温性種はほんのわずかしかいないんだ，例えばホオジロザメとかね。

学生Ａ：でも，恐竜は今の爬虫類と全く同じで，長い間冷血動物だと考えられてきたって，教わったよ。

学生Ｂ：僕もそう思っていたよ。でも，古生物学者たちが何をしたかというと，恐竜の成長率と新陳代謝率を調べたんだ。③ほら，恐竜がおそらくどのくらいの速さで成長したか，そしてどのくらいの量を食べたかってことさ。④現生の鳥類の祖先として知られている始祖鳥は，完全な成体になるのにどうやら２年かかったようだ。でも，それと同じ大きさの今のタカは，そうなるのに６週間しかかからないんだ。⑤古生物学者たちは，また恐竜は冷血動物である今の爬虫類よりずっと速く成長したことを発見したんだ。

学生Ａ：つまり，恐竜は哺乳類に比べて成長が遅かったけど，今の爬虫類よりは成長が速かったということね。

学生Ｂ：そういうことだね。それで，これらの発見をもとに，恐竜を温血動物と冷血動物の中間に位置づけたんだよ。

# Lecture 2　Original

**Listening**　新たな講義を聴いてみよう。

While there are new discoveries each year in science, sometimes re-evaluating previous studies may lead scientists to new findings as well. Dr. Michael D'Emic reanalyzed a previous study that had classified dinosaurs as mesothermic, which led him to conclude that the dinosaurs were warm-blooded. Interesting, but how? You may ask.

Well, Dr. D'Emic claimed that the previous study underestimated the dinosaurs' growth rates.
①You see, wild animals do not grow …
②Growth typically tends to slow down or even pause when …
③And this uneven growth is evident in …

④But the previous study did not account for the uneven growth when …
Also, by statistically analyzing the dinosaurs in relation to modern birds, which are descendants of Mesozoic dinosaurs,
⑤Dr. D'Emic concluded that the dinosaurs were …

**Speaking**　吹き出しを見ながら足りない語を補い，講義を再現してみよう。

## Script

①**You see, wild animals do not grow** at constant rates.

②**Growth typically tends to slow down or even pause when** the climate is harsh and food is scarce.

③**And this uneven growth is evident in** the rings in dinosaurs' bones, like tree rings.

④**But the previous study did not account for the uneven growth when** classifying the dinosaurs as mesothermic.

⑤**Dr. D'Emic concluded that the dinosaurs were** not an intermediate species but warm-blooded animals.

## Translation

　科学においては毎年新しい発見がありますが，時にこれまでの諸研究を再評価することで，また科学者たちを新たな発見へと導くことがあるかもしれません。マイケル・デミック博士は恐竜を中温性として分類した，ある以前の研究を再度分析し，その結果，博士は，恐竜は温血動物だったという結論に至りました。「おもしろい話だけど，でもどうして？」とお尋ねになるかもしれませんね。

　実は，デミック博士は以前の研究は恐竜の成長率を過小評価していると主張したのです。①ほら，野生動物は一定の割合では成長しませんよね。②一般に成長は，気候が厳しかったり，食料が不足したりすると遅くなるか，一時的に止まることさえあります。③そしてこの一様でない成長は，木の年輪同様，恐竜の骨の年輪においてもはっきりわかります。

　④しかし，以前の研究は恐竜を中温性と分類したときに，一様でない成長を説明しませんでした。また，中生代の恐竜の子孫である現代の鳥類との関係で恐竜を統計的に分析することによって，⑤デミック博士は，恐竜は中間種ではなく，温血動物だと結論づけたのです。

# Lecture 2　Summary

**Listening**　チャートを見ながら講義をもう一度聴き，Lecture Notesを完成させよう。(答えは右ページ)　CD 41

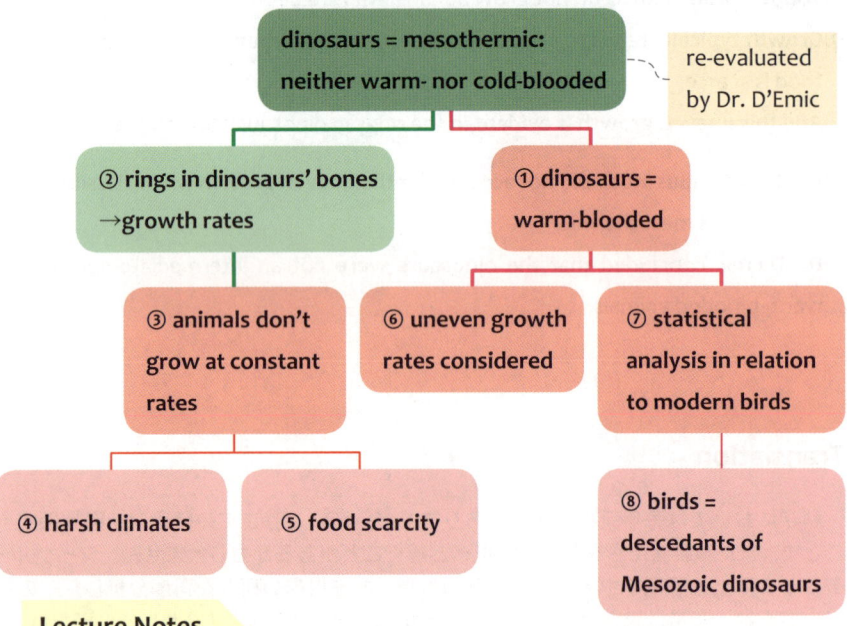

```
                dinosaurs = mesothermic:              re-evaluated
                neither warm- nor cold-blooded        by Dr. D'Emic

      ② rings in dinosaurs' bones          ① dinosaurs =
         →growth rates                        warm-blooded

      ③ animals don't       ⑥ uneven growth      ⑦ statistical
         grow at constant      rates considered     analysis in relation
         rates                                      to modern birds

                                                 ⑧ birds =
      ④ harsh climates    ⑤ food scarcity          descendants of
                                                    Mesozoic dinosaurs
```

### Lecture Notes

TOPIC
恐竜の代謝

PURPOSE
恐竜が（　A　）動物であるとする説を見直す研究を紹介すること

MAIN ARGUMENT
主　張：デミック博士は，先行研究を見直して恐竜は（　B　）動物であると結論付けている。
理由①：先行研究は，生き物は一定速度で成長するという誤った前提をもとにしている。
理由②：デミック博士の研究では，一定ではない成長速度も考慮され，現代の（　C　）と比較する形で統計的分析が行われている。

**Speaking**　チャートを見ながら講義を要約し，声に出して言ってみよう。

Unit 6　Dinosaur Metabolism

☞ 要約文（サンプル）を聴いてみよう。

## Summary

One study on the issue of dinosaur metabolism claims that dinosaurs were **mesothermic, neither warm- nor cold-blooded**, showing the **growth rate** calculated from the **rings in dinosaurs' bones**. This conclusion was **re-evaluated by Dr. D'Emic**, who says that the study ignores the fact that **animals don't grow at constant rates** because they are subject to **harsh climates and food scarcity**. Dr. D'Emic rather claims that **dinosaurs were warm-blooded**. In his study, he **considered** the **uneven growth rates** and did **statistical analysis in relation to modern birds**. This analysis was appropriate because **birds** are **descendants of Mesozoic dinosaurs**.

## Translation

恐竜の代謝について，骨の年輪から算出した成長速度を示し，恐竜は温血でも冷血でもない中温動物であるとしている研究がある。デミック博士はこの結論を疑い，厳しい気候や食糧不足の影響下にある動物は一定の速度では成長しないという事実をこの研究は無視していると言っている。デミック博士は，むしろ恐竜は温血動物であったと主張している。彼の研究では一定ではない成長速度が考慮され，現代の鳥類との比較における統計分析が行われた。鳥が中生代の恐竜の子孫であることを考えるとこの分析は妥当であった。

### Integrated Task

Some people believe dinosaurs were cold-blooded, and others don't. Explain some competing theories on the issue of dinosaur metabolism.

☞ Lecture Notesの答え　A 中温　B 温血　C 鳥類

# Grammar Notes

①For years, paleontologists believed that dinosaurs could **be compared to** sluggish cold-blooded lizards.

▶ be compared to A「Aに例えられる」「Aと同等とみなされる」という意味です。この表現は，類似していることを示すために用いられることが多く，ここでは，「恐竜は，動きの緩慢な冷血動物であるトカゲみたいなものだ」といった意味合いです。

②As researchers found more complete bones of dinosaurs, some started to contend that dinosaurs were warm-blooded creatures, **which are generally more active, smarter and faster**.

▶ which以下は，warm-blooded creaturesについての説明です。すべての温血動物に当てはまる説明ですので，関係代名詞whichの前にカンマが付けられています。このような関係詞の用法を非制限用法と言います。一部の研究者が「恐竜は温血動物だ」と主張し始めたのですが，冷血動物ではなく温血動物であるということは，すなわちどういうことなのかを，①のsluggishと対比的なmore active, smarter and fasterという特徴を挙げて説明しているのです。

③**Their arguments** were based mainly on the anatomical structures of dinosaurs, but **this method** was fiercely questioned.

▶ Their argumentsとは，②で述べられたdinosaurs were warm-blooded creatures「恐竜は温血動物だ」という主張のことです。また，this methodとは直前で述べられているwere based mainly on the anatomical structures of dinosaurs「おもに恐竜の解剖学的構造に基づいて」という手法のことです。このように，指示内容を持つ表現によって，文と文とが内容的に連結されている点に注目しましょう。

④New methods **such as** bone histology **have made it possible to** measure the growth rates of dinosaurs.

▶ such asは具体例を導く表現で，A such as Bは「（たとえば）BのようなA」という意味です。ここでは，「新しい調査方法」の例としてbone histology（骨組織学）が挙げられています。"bone histology"のような専門的な用語は，たとえそれ自体の意味が不明だったとしても，「新しい調査方法の一例だ」ということがわかれば十分に文意をとることができます。

▶ S make it possible to do ...は，S make O C「SはOをCにする」を基本とした表現で，「Sは～することを可能にする」という意味です。Oの位置に置かれたitは形式目的語と呼ばれ，その具体的な内容はto do ...になります。

⑤**Since** there is a positive correlation between growth rate and metabolism, they **reached the conclusion that** dinosaurs **fell right between cold-blooded animals and warm-blooded animals.**

▶ Since は接続詞で，ここでは理由を表す副詞節を導いています。理由を表す接続詞には because がありますが，since は because とは異なり，「因果関係」を示すことに重点があるのではなく，主節で述べられることの前提となる事実を「(おわかりの通り)…なのだから」という意味合いで添える働きです。

▶ reach the conclusion that ... は「…という結論に達する」という意味です。この that は接続詞で，that 節は直前の名詞句 the conclusion の内容を説明しています。

▶ fall right between A and B は「A と B のちょうど真ん中に当たる」という意味です。動詞 fall には，「(部類，範囲など) に入る，属する」という意味を表す用法があります。また，ここでの right は強意の副詞で between に「ちょうど (真ん中だ)」という意味を添えています。

⑥**This means** dinosaurs might have eaten more than cold-blooded reptiles do, but they might not have had to eat much to maintain a high body temperature **like** warm-blooded mammals **do**.

▶ This means (that) ... は「これは…ということを意味する」「これはつまり…ということだ」という意味で，直前の内容から導かれる結論や考察を提示する表現です。ここでの This は⑤で述べられた「恐竜が冷血動物と温血動物の中間に当たる」という内容を受けています。

▶ ここでの like は，後ろに S V をともなって「…のように」という意味を表しています。正式には as [in the way] warm-blooded mammals do と書きます。like は前置詞であり，後ろには名詞句が続くのが原則ですが，くだけた表現では as や in the way と同様に用いられることがあります。

▶ do は (have to) eat much to maintain a high body temperature に相当する内容を受けています。前出の動詞句の反復を避けるために，このように do が用いられることがあります。

⑦Findings **such as this** offer valuable clues into different aspects of their lives, such as how they hunted and why they grew so large.

▶ Findings such as this で「このような発見」という意味です。this は④～⑥の内容，特に⑥で述べられた「恐竜の食べる食物の量」についてわかったことを受けています。This finding と言うよりも，「この発見に限らず，このような恐竜の生態を明らかにする発見」という，より一般論化した言い方となっている点が大切です。

## Paraphrase Notes

①Paleontologists have long maintained that dinosaurs **were similar to slow-moving**, cold-blooded lizards.

▶オリジナル①のbe compared toという類似点を示す表現が，より直接的なbe similar toに置き換えられています。また，sluggishもslow-movingという平易な表現に変わっています。

②**Following** the discovery of more intact skeletal parts, **however**, some scientists began arguing that dinosaurs were, in fact, warm-blooded animals, which are usually more energetic, intelligent and quick.

▶Following 〜は「〜に続いて」「〜の後に」という意味です。オリジナル②のAs ...よりも「より多くの完全な骨の発見」→「新たな主張の開始」という前後関係を明確にした表現です。

▶however「しかしながら」は①と②の文のつながりを明示する副詞です。文頭の副詞句の後ろに挿入された形になっています。わかりにくい場合は，howeverを文頭に移動してもかまいません。howeverに相当する表現のないオリジナル②と比べて，論の展開がより伝わりやすくなっています。

③This claim was largely founded on the structural components of a dinosaur's body, but this approach was hotly debated.

▶オリジナル③からの語句レベルでの言い換えに注目しましょう。arguments→claim, be based on→be founded on, anatomical structure→structural components, method→approach, be fiercely questioned→be hotly debatedなど，重要な語彙ばかりです。

④New techniques **like** bone histology are now **allowing researchers to measure** the speed of growth of dinosaurs.

▶オリジナル④で用いられていたsuch asに代わって，likeで具体例を示しています。
▶make it possible to doの代わりに，allow O to do「Oが〜するのを可能にする」という表現を用いてパラフレーズされています。enable O to doでもほぼ同じ意味になります。

⑤**The rate of a creature's growth and its metabolic rate are directly connected,** and the determination is that dinosaurs functioned in some middle ground between cold- and warm-bloodedness.

▶下線部は，オリジナル⑤ではSinceを用いて表していた内容です。ここでは副詞節とせずに，普通に「文」として述べ，そのままand the determination is that ...「そして，確定されたのは…ということだ」とつないでいます。

Unit 6　Dinosaur Metabolism

⑥**Perhaps** they ingested more than cold-blooded reptiles do, but **it may not have been necessary for them to eat** the quantities that warm-blooded mammals need to sustain an elevated body temperature.

▶オリジナル⑥で用いられていた This means (that) ... といった，つながりを明示する表現は用いられていません。文の並びだけで「観察結果」→「それに基づく結論，考察」というつながりが十分にわかるからです。

▶オリジナル⑥では，might have eaten more「より多くの量を食べていたのかもしれない」と，助動詞 might で表していた推量の意味を，こちらでは perhaps という副詞で表しています。また，they might not have had to eat は，it is necessary for A to *do*「Aは〜する必要がある」という形式主語の構文を用いて，it may not have been necessary for them to eat にパラフレーズされています。

## Expressions and Phrases

ヒントを手がかりにして，日本語に対応する英語表現を言ってみよう。

| 日本語 | ヒント | 英語 |
|---|---|---|
| □ 有名な古生物学者 | re____ pa_____ | renowned paleontologist |
| □ 中生代の恐竜 | Me_____ di_____ | Mesozoic dinosaur |
| □ 動きの遅いトカゲ | sl_____ li____ | sluggish lizard |
| □ 冷血の爬虫類 | co____-bl____ re_____ | cold-blooded reptile |
| □ 温血の哺乳類 | wa____-bl____ ma____ | warm-blooded mammal |
| □ 中間種 | in_____ sp_____ | intermediate species |
| □ 中温動物 | me_____ sp_____ | mesothermic species |
| □ 解剖学的評価 | an_____ ev_____ | anatomical evaluation |
| □ 構造要素 | st_____ co_____ | structural component |
| □ 骨の一部 | sk____ pa____ | skeletal part |
| □ 無傷組織 | in____ ti____ | intact tissue |
| □ 骨組織学 | bo__ hi_____ | bone histology |
| □ エネルギー代謝 | en_____ me____ | energetic metabolism |
| □ 新陳代謝率 | me_____ ra____ | metabolic rate |
| □ 一定のペース | co____ pa____ | constant pace |
| □ 一定でない成長 | un____ gr____ | uneven growth |
| □ 統計分析 | st_____ an_____ | statistical analysis |
| □ 直接的関係 | di_____ co_____ | direct connection |
| □ 正の相関関係 | po_____ co_____ | positive correlation |
| □ 適切な方法 | ap_____ me____ | appropriate method |
| □ 利口なやり方 | sm____ ap_____ | smart approach |
| □ 集団狩猟 | gr____ hu_____ | group hunting |
| □ 高い知性 | hi____ in_____ | high intelligence |
| □ 違う側面 | di_____ as____ | different aspect |
| □ 遠い祖先 | re_____ an_____ | remote ancestor |
| □ 直系の子孫 | di____ de_____ | direct descendant |
| □ 厳しい気候 | ha____ cl_____ | harsh climate |
| □ 食糧不足 | fo____ sc____ | food scarcity |
| □ 年輪 | tr____ ri____ | tree rings |
| □ 特別展示 | sp_____ ex_____ | special exhibit |

## Unit 6　Dinosaur Metabolism

□ 論争を呼ぶテーマと見られている

| be re_____ as a co_____ to____ | be regarded as a controversial topic |
| be co_____ a ho____ de____ is____ | be considered a hotly debated issue |

□ 誤解に基づいている

| be fo_____ on a mi_____ | be founded on a misconception |
| be ba_____ on a mi_____ | be based on a misinterpretation |

□ 化石に容易に見ることができる

| be ea____ ob_____ in the fo_____ | be easily observed in the fossils |
| be ev_____ in the fo_____ re____ | be evident in the fossilized remains |

□ 彼らが食べていたものの貴重な手掛かりを提供する

| of____ va_____ cl_____ as to what they at____ | offer valuable clues as to what they ate |
| pr____ te_____ cl_____ about their di_____ | provide telling clues about their diet |

□ 水が不足していると主張する

| co_____ that they la____ wa____ | contend that they lack water |
| ma_____ that wa____ is sc____ | maintain that water is scarce |

□ 病気になりやすい

| te____ to ge____ a di_____ | tend to get a disease |
| be pr_____ to il_____ | be prone to illness |

□ 完全に大人になるのに時間がかかる

| ta____ a while to be_____ fully gr_____ | take a while to become fully grown |
| ta____ long to re_____ full ma_____ | take long to reach full maturity |

□ 体が大きくなった理由の説明となる

| ex_____ why they gr____ so big | explain why they grew so big |
| ac_____ for their hu____ bo____ si____ | account for their huge body size |

□ 体の大きさと強い相関関係がある

| have a st_____ co_____ with bo____ si____ | have a strong correlation with body size |
| co_____ st_____ with bo____ si____ | correlate strongly with body size |

□ 成長速度の速さを過小評価する

| un_____ the fast gr_____ ra____ | underestimate the fast growth rate |
| un_____ the ra____ pa____ of gr_____ | underrate the rapid pace of growth |

# Word List

| | | |
|---|---|---|
| ☐ account for A | | Aを説明する |
| | 類 | explain A |
| ☐ active [ǽktɪv] | 形 | 活動的な，積極的な，活動中の |
| | 類 | energetic / lively |
| ☐ allow A to *do* | | Aが…するのを可能にする，Aが…するのを許す |
| | 類 | permit A to *do* |
| ☐ analysis [ənǽləsɪs] | 名 | 分析 |
| ☐ analyze [ǽnəlàɪz] | 動 | …を分析する，…を検討する |
| ☐ anatomical [ænətάmɪkl] | 形 | 解剖学上の，解剖の，構造上の |
| ☐ apparently [əpǽrəntli] | 副 | どうも…らしい，外見上は |
| ☐ approach [əpróʊtʃ] | 名 | 研究方法，接近方法，取り組み |
| | 動 | …に着手する，…に近づく |
| ☐ argument [άːrgjəmənt\|άːgjʊ-] | 名 | 主張，議論，論争 |
| ☐ as a matter of fact | | 実を言うと |
| ☐ as well | | …もまた |
| ☐ be founded on A | | Aに基づいている |
| | 類 | be based on A |
| ☐ blood [blʌd] | 名 | 血液，血統 |
| ☐ body temperature | | 体温 |
| ☐ bone [boʊn] | 名 | 骨，骨格 |
| ☐ calculate [kǽlkjəlèɪt] | 動 | …を計算する，…を予想する |
| ☐ classify [klǽsəfàɪ] | 動 | …を分類する |
| ☐ climate [kláɪmət] | 名 | 気候，(ある気候条件の)地域，風土 |
| ☐ clue [kluː] | 名 | 手掛かり |
| | 類 | hint |
| ☐ cold-blooded [kòʊldblʌ́dɪd] | 形 | 変温の，冷血の，冷酷な |
| ☐ compare A to B | | AをBに例える，AをBと比較する |
| ☐ complete [kəmplíːt] | 形 | 完全な，全部の |
| | 類 | absolute / full / whole / thorough |
| | 動 | …を仕上げる，…を完成させる |
| ☐ conclude that S V … | | …だと結論づける |
| | 類 | decide that S V … |
| ☐ conclusion [kənklúːʒən] | 名 | 結論，終わりの部分 |
| ☐ connected [kənéktɪd] | 形 | 関係した，関連した，接続した |
| | 類 | related |
| ☐ constant [kάːnstənt\|kɔ́n-] | 形 | 絶え間ない，一定の |

Unit 6　Dinosaur Metabolism

|  |  |
|---|---|
| □ contend [kənténd] | 動 …だと主張する，戦う，議論する<br>語法 contend that S V …「…だと主張する」<br>contend with A「Aに取り組む」 |
| □ correlation [kɔ̀:rəléɪʃən \| kɔ̀r-] | 名 相関関係，相互関連 |
| □ creature [krí:tʃər] | 名 動物，生き物 |
| □ debate [dɪbéɪt] | 名 議論，討論<br>類 discussion / argument<br>動 …を討論する，議論する |
| □ descendant [dɪséndənt] | 名 子孫，末裔（えい）<br>類 offspring |
| □ determination [dɪtə̀:rmənéɪʃən] | 名 結論，決定，決心<br>類 conclusion |
| □ dinosaur [dáɪnəsɔ̀:r] | 名 恐竜 |
| □ directly [dərékt/li \| daɪ-] | 副 直接に，まっすぐに |
| □ elevated [éləvèɪtɪd] | 形 高い，高尚な |
| □ energetic [ènərdʒétɪk] | 形 活発な，精力的な<br>類 active / lively |
| □ evident [évədənt] | 形 明らかな，明白な |
| □ exhibit [égzɪbɪt] | 名 展示，展示品　動 …を展示する，…を示す |
| □ existence [ɪgzístəns] | 名 存在，生存 |
| □ fiercely [fíərsli] | 副 激しく，猛烈に |
| □ finding [fáɪndɪŋ] | 名 発見物，調査結果 |
| □ following A | Aの後で，Aに引き続いて |
| □ function [fʌ́ŋkʃən] | 動 働く，機能を果たす，作動する<br>類 work<br>名 機能，作用 |
| □ generally [dʒénərəli] | 副 大体において，一般に，通例は |
| □ growth [groʊθ] | 名 成長，発展 |
| □ growth rate | 成長率 |
| □ harsh [hɑ:rʃ] | 形 厳しい<br>類 severe / tough |
| □ histology [hɪstá:lədʒi] | 名 組織学 |
| □ hunt [hʌnt] | 動 狩りをする，探し求める，…を追跡する<br>名 追跡，狩 |
| □ ignore [ɪgnɔ́:r] | 動 …を無視する，…を怠る<br>類 disregard |

137

|  |  |
|---|---|
| □ in relation to A | Aと関連して |
| □ in-between [ìnbɪtwíːn] 形 | 中間の |
| □ ingest [ɪndʒést] 動 | …を摂取する，…を飲み込む |
| 類 | consume / swallow / take in |
| □ intact [ɪntǽkt] 形 | 完全な，無傷の |
| 類 | complete |
| □ interesting [íntərəstɪŋ] 形 | 興味深い |
| □ intermediate [ìntərmíːdiət] 形 | 中間の，中級の |
| □ issue [íʃuː] 名 | 問題，発行，出版物 |
| 動 | …を発行する，…を支給する |
| □ lead A to do | Aに…させる |
| □ lizard [lízərd] 名 | トカゲ |
| □ mainly [méɪnli] 副 | 主に，大体は |
| □ maintain [meɪntéɪn, men-] 動 | …を維持する，…を保存する，…だと主張する |
| 類 | preserve |
| 語法 | maintain that S V …「…だと主張する」 |
| □ mammal [mǽml] 名 | 哺乳動物 |
| □ maturity [mət(j)úərəti] 名 | 成熟 |
| □ medium [míːdiəm] 形 | 中間の 名 媒体，手段 |
| □ mesothermic [mesoʊθɔ́ːrmɪk] 形 | 温帯の，中温の |
| □ metabolic [mètəbɑ́ːlɪk|-bɔ́l-] 形 | 新陳代謝の，物質交代の |
| □ metabolism [mətǽbəlìzm] 名 | 新陳代謝 |
| □ middle [mídl] 形 | 中間の |
| □ modern [mɑ́ːdərn|mɔ́dn] 形 | 今の，現代の |
| □ museum [mju(ː)zíːəm] 名 | 博物館，美術館 |
| □ necessary [nésəsèri] 形 | 必要な，不可欠な |
| □ paleontologist [pèɪlɑːntɑ́ːlədʒɪst] 名 | 古生物学者 |
| □ pause [pɔːz] 動 | ちょっと止める，一時停止ボタンを押す |
| 名 | 小休止，区切り，ためらい |
| □ perhaps [pərhǽps, pərǽps] 副 | ひょっとすると，おそらく |
| 類 | maybe, possibly |
| □ positive [pɑ́ːzətɪv|pɔ́z-] 形 | 正の，明確な，積極的な，自信のある |
| 類 | affirmative |
| □ previous [príːviəs] 形 | 以前の，前の |
| □ probably [prɑ́ːbəbli, prɔ́b-] 副 | おそらく，十中八九 |

# Unit 6  Dinosaur Metabolism

| | | |
|---|---|---|
| □ quantity [kwá:ntəti \| kwɔ́n-] | 名 | 量 |
| | 類 | amount |
| □ question [kwéstʃən] | 動 | …に異議を唱える，（人を）尋問する |
| | 類 | doubt, distrust |
| □ range [reɪndʒ] | 名 | 範囲，幅　動　及んでいる，及ぶ |
| □ re-evaluate [rìːɪvǽljueɪt] | 動 | …を再評価する |
| □ reanalyze [rìːǽnəlaɪz] | 動 | …を再分析する |
| □ relation [rɪléɪʃən] | 名 | 関係，関連，親戚 |
| □ reptile [réptl \| -taɪl] | 名 | 爬虫類 |
| □ scarce [skeərs] | 形 | 乏しい，まれな |
| □ scarcity [skéərsəti] | 名 | 欠乏，不足 |
| | 類 | shortage |
| □ shark [ʃɑːrk] | 名 | サメ |
| □ similar to A | | Aに似ている，Aと同様で |
| □ skeletal [skélətl] | 形 | 骨格の |
| □ sluggish [slʌ́gɪʃ] | 形 | 緩慢な，反応の遅い，怠惰な |
| | 類 | inactive |
| □ species [spíːʃiːz] | 名 | （生物）種 |
| □ statistical [stətístɪkl] | 形 | 統計の，統計学上の |
| □ statistically [stətístɪkli] | | 統計的に，統計学上 |
| □ structural [strʌ́ktʃərəl] | 形 | 構造の，構造上の |
| □ sustain [səstéɪn] | 動 | …を保つ，…を維持する，…を持続させる |
| | 類 | preserve / keep up / maintain |
| □ tend to *do* | | …しがちである |
| □ term [təːrm] | 名 | （専門）用語，期間，学期　動　…と呼ぶ |
| □ typically [típɪkli] | 副 | 主として，典型的に |
| □ underestimate [ʌ̀ndəréstəmèɪt] | 動 | …を過小評価する　名　過小評価 |
| □ uneven [ʌníːvn] | 形 | 不規則な，平らでない |
| □ valuable [vǽljuəbl] | 形 | 貴重な，価値の高い　名　貴重品 |
| | 類 | precious |
| □ warm-blooded [wɔ̀ːrmblʌ́dɪd] | 形 | 恒温の，温血の |

## 参考文献

D'Emic, M. D. (2015, May 29). Comment on "Evidence for mesothermy in dinosaurs". *Science, 348*(6238), 982. doi:10.1126/science.1260061

*Dinosaurs Were Warm-Blooded, Scientist Suggests.* (2015, May 29). Retrieved September 7, 2015, from Sci-News.com website: http://www.sci-news.com/paleontology/science-dinosaurs-warm-blooded-02857.html

*Were Dinosaurs Cold- or Warm-Blooded? New Study Tries to Answer Longstanding Question.* (2014, June 13). Retrieved September 7, 2015, from Sci-News.com website: www.sci-news.com/paleontology/science-dinosaurs-cold-warm-blooded-01985.html

# Unit 7 Biggest Bird Nests

## Integrated Task

Do you agree or disagree with the following statement?

*It is natural for animals to behave selfishly all the time in order to survive.*

Use specific reasons and examples to support your answer.

## Key Words

**selfish**

▶「身勝手な」という意味の形容詞です。名詞 self（自己）から派生した語で，ほぼ同じ意味の語に self-centered「自己中心的な」や egoistic「利己主義的な」があります。生物にとって selfish であるとは，自己の生存を最優先するという自然な状態です。これが，今回の講義を理解するための土台となる考え方です。

**survive**

▶「生存する」という意味の動詞です。live よりも「生命を存続させる」という意味合いが強く，したがって，生物学的な意味での「個体の生存」，「種の存続」と結びつきやすい動詞です。この講義のテーマも，the sociable weaver という鳥のある特異な行動が，種の保存とどのように結びついているかということです。

**communal**

▶「共同の」という意味の形容詞です。com- という接頭辞は「共に」という意味を持ち，**com**mon，**com**municate，**com**munity などの語に見られます。「何かを共有すること」と「個体や種が生存すること」との関係が，講義を理解するカギになります。

# Lecture 1　Original

**Listening**　講義を聴いてみよう。

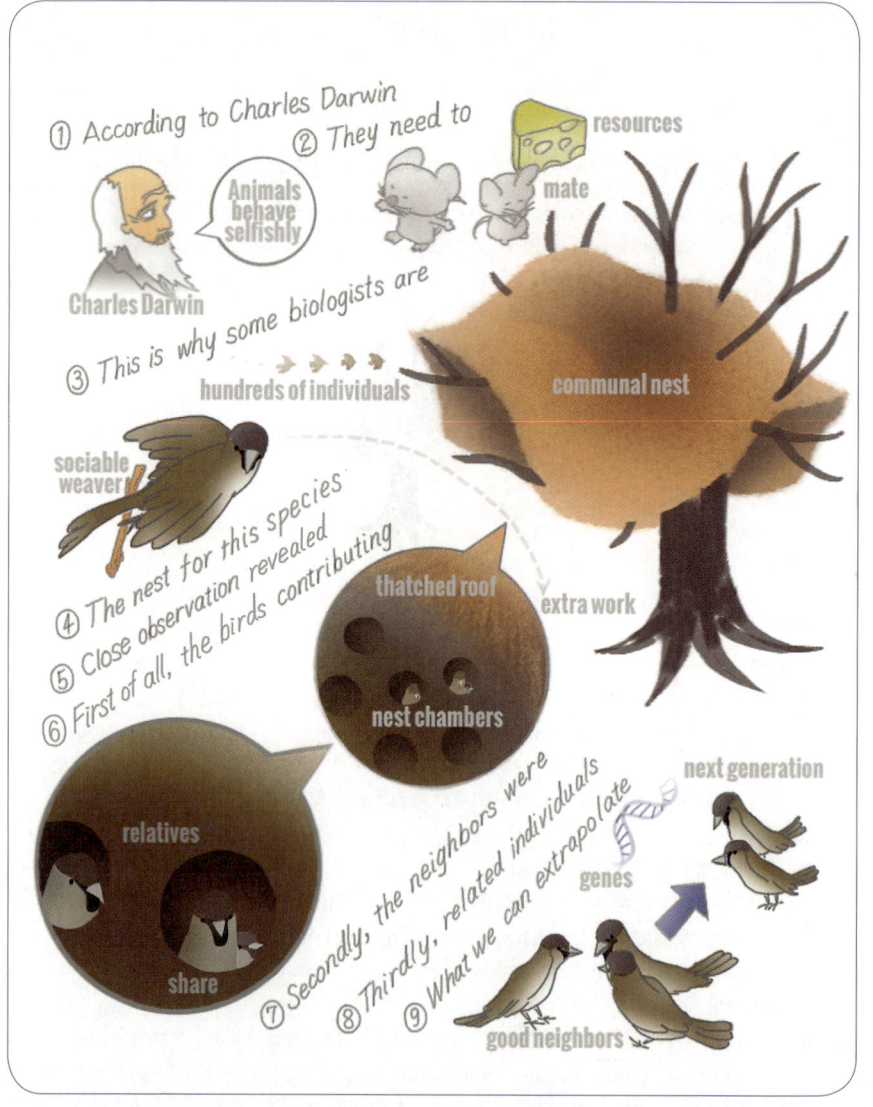

CD 44

① According to Charles Darwin
Animals behave selfishly
Charles Darwin

② They need to
resources
mate

③ This is why some biologists are
hundreds of individuals
communal nest

sociable weaver

④ The nest for this species
⑤ Close observation revealed
⑥ First of all, the birds contributing

thatched roof
extra work
nest chambers

relatives
share

⑦ Secondly, the neighbors were
⑧ Thirdly, related individuals
⑨ What we can extrapolate
genes
next generation
good neighbors

**Speaking**　イラストを見ながら講義を再現してみよう。

## Script

①**According to Charles Darwin,** it is natural that animals should behave selfishly to survive. ②**They need to** look after themselves, protect their resources, find a mate and reproduce. ③**This is why some biologists are** intrigued by the sociable weaver, which builds a communal nest housing hundreds of individuals. ④**The nest for this species** consists of individual nest chambers embedded within a communal thatched roof, the building of which requires extra work for the community. ⑤**Close observation revealed** several things. ⑥**First of all, the birds contributing** to thatch building did so above their own nest chamber. ⑦**Secondly, the neighbors were** often relatives, which suggests the thatch building might be directed towards kin. ⑧**Thirdly, related individuals** tended to share the use of nest chambers. ⑨**What we can extrapolate** from these facts is that these sociable birds benefit from having good neighbors, which indirectly helps them pass on their genes to the next generation.

## Translation

①チャールズ・ダーウィンによれば，動物が生き延びるために利己的に行動するのは当然である。②動物は自分で自分の面倒を見たり，自分たちの資源を守ったり，つがいの相手を見つけたり，生殖したりする必要がある。③だからこそ，生物学者の中には，数百羽の個体を収容する共同巣を作るシャカイハタオリに好奇心をそそられる者がいる。④この種の鳥の巣は，共同の草葺き屋根の内側に埋め込まれた個々の巣室から成っているのだが，このような屋根を作ることは，集団にとっては余計に手間がかかることだ。⑤詳しく観察すると，いくつかの事柄が明らかになった。⑥まず第1に，草葺きの屋根を作ることに貢献している鳥は，巣の中の自分たちの巣室の上に草葺きの屋根を作っていた。⑦第2に，隣接する室にいる鳥は血縁関係がある場合が多く，これは草葺きの屋根を作る行為が近親の仲間に向けられている可能性を示唆している。⑧第3に，血縁関係のある個体は巣室の使用を共有する傾向にあった。⑨これらの事実から私たちが推定できることは，この社交的な鳥は近くの仲間と良好な関係にあることから利益を得ていて，それが自分の遺伝子を次の世代に伝えるのに間接的に役に立っているということだ。

☞ スクリプトの文法ポイントについては，p.152〜の**Grammar Notes**を参照しよう。

# Lecture 1　Paraphrase

**Listening**　別の表現を用いた講義を聴いてみよう。

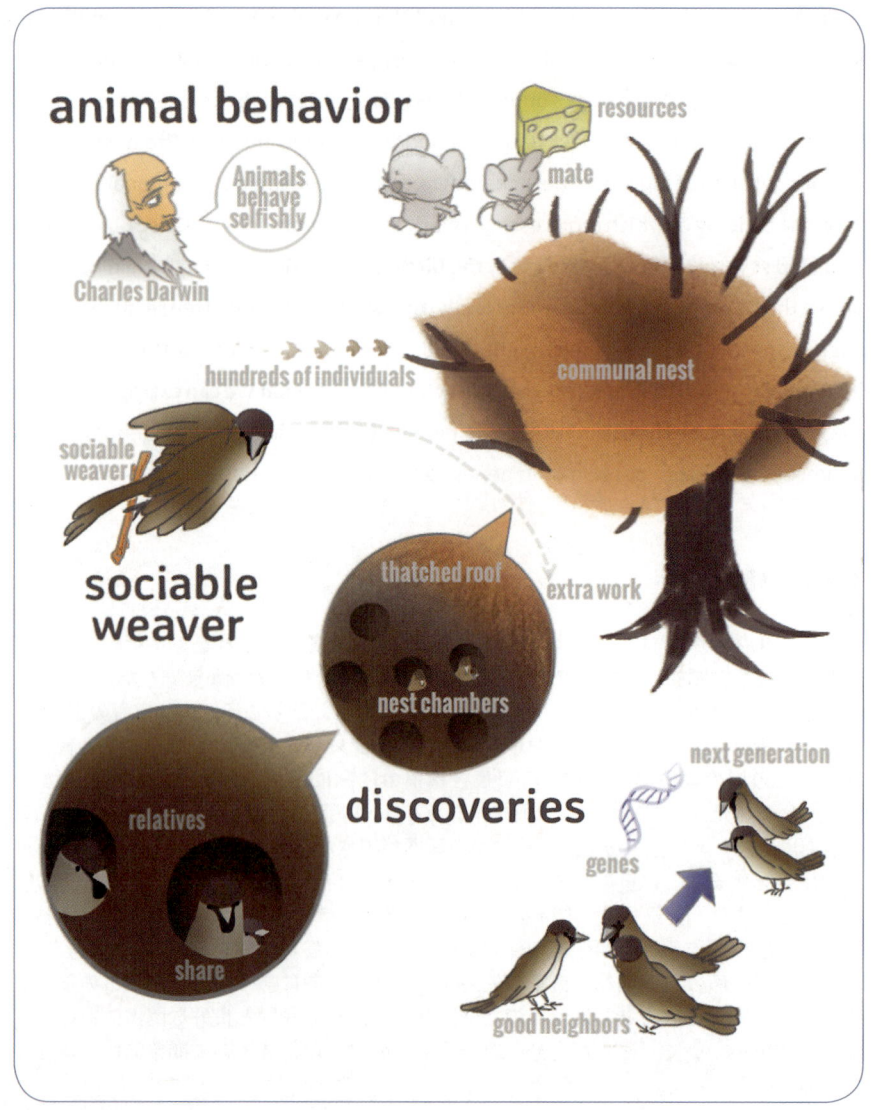

## animal behavior

Animals behave selfishly — Charles Darwin

resources　mate

hundreds of individuals

communal nest

sociable weaver

## sociable weaver

thatched roof

extra work

nest chambers

relatives

share

## discoveries

genes

next generation

good neighbors

**Speaking**　イラストを見ながら講義の内容を英語で説明しよう。

Unit 7　Biggest Bird Nests

## Script

①Charles Darwin considered it only logical that animals would behave in a selfish manner in order to survive. ②Their **behaviors** include protecting themselves, guarding resources, mating and having offspring. ③A puzzle in the field of social biology, therefore, is the **sociable weaver**, a bird which builds a group nest that accommodates several hundred of their kind. ④Separate nesting chambers are covered under one roof, the thatching of which has to be undertaken as additional labor for the entire community. ⑤By carefully studying this kind of nest, the researchers made certain **discoveries**. ⑥For one thing, when a bird helped with the roof, it did the part that covered its own chamber. ⑦For another, a bird's neighbors were frequently all related, so the thatching can be seen as a family-serving activity. ⑧Lastly, it is common that related birds share nest chambers. ⑨From the above facts it follows that good neighbors ultimately make it easier for their genes to be handed down to the succeeding generation.

## Translation

①チャールズ・ダーウィンは，動物が生き延びるために利己的なやり方で行動するのはきわめて当然であると考えていた。②動物の行動には，自分を守ったり，資源を守ったり，交尾をしたり，子を持ったりすることが含まれる。③それゆえ，社会生物学の分野における謎となっているのは，数百羽の仲間を収容する集団の巣を作る，シャカイハタオリという鳥である。④個々の巣室は１つの屋根で覆われ，その屋根の草葺きは集団全体にとっての余分の仕事として引き受けられなければならない。⑤この種の巣を注意深く調べることにより，研究者はいくつかの発見をした。⑥１つには，屋根葺きに協力するとき，鳥は自分の巣室を覆う部分を葺いた。⑦もう１つは，ある鳥の近くに住む鳥は，すべて血縁関係にあることがよくあり，だから草葺きは血族に尽くす活動と見なすことができる。⑧最後に，巣室は同じ血族の範囲内で共有されているのが一般的だ。⑨上記の事実から言えるのは，近くの仲間と仲良くすることで，最終的には自分の遺伝子を次の世代に伝えることがより容易になるということだ。

☞ パラフレーズのポイントについては，p.154〜の**Paraphrase Notes**を参照しよう。

# Conversation

**Listening**  講義に関連する会話を聴いてみよう。

Professor: So before we go on to the next chapter, I want to take a few minutes to review what we have discussed about the nesting habits of the social weaver so that you will be prepared for the quiz next week. First, what is so unique about the social weaver?

Student: ①**Well, most of all, the social weaver defies** …
②**He said that most animals behave selfishly, that they only** …
③**But in the case of the social weaver,** …

Professor: Right, so that's the bottom line – the social weaver is not selfish. Here's a key term that your text does not mention – altruism. This is the opposite of being selfish. This means giving priority to others over yourself. Okay, so what did you notice about its nesting habits?

Student: ④**That the birds build** …?

Professor: Well, just building the roof itself isn't all that special. Many other species of animals do so.

Student: Oh! Let me rephrase that.
⑤**They help build the communal thatched roof under which** …
⑥**They all live close to each other and** …

Professor: Right. So this communal living provides the birds with a more secure and more comfortable environment for breeding. I think you guys are in good shape for the quiz next week!

**Speaking**  上の会話文を見ながら音声を聴き，学生のパートを再現してみよう。

Unit 7　Biggest Bird Nests

## Script

①**Well, most of all, the social weaver defies** Darwin's theories of animal behavior.
②**He said that most animals behave selfishly, that they only** look out for themselves.
③**But in the case of the social weaver,** communal survival seems to be essential.
④**That the birds build** thatched roofs above their own chamber?
⑤**They help build the communal thatched roof under which** many of their relatives live.
⑥**They all live close to each other and** share their chambers.

## Translation

教授：では，次の章に行く前に，少し時間を取ってシャカイハタオリの巣作りの習性について議論したことを復習したいと思います。そうすると来週の小テストの準備になるでしょう。まず，シャカイハタオリについて非常に独特な点は何でしょうか？
学生：①ええと，まず何と言っても，シャカイハタオリは，動物行動についてのダーウィンの諸理論に反しています。②ダーウィンが述べていたことは，ほとんどの動物が利己的に行動し，自分のことしか考えていないということです。③しかし，シャカイハタオリの場合，共同で生存する点がきわめて重要であるように思えます。
教授：その通りですね。それが肝心な点なんです。つまり，シャカイハタオリは利己的ではありません。ここでキーワードを示しましょう。これはみなさんのテキストには言及されていません。利他主義という言葉です。これは利己主義と反対の意味の言葉です。その意味は，自己よりも他者を重視するということです。それでは，シャカイハタオリの巣作りの習性についてどんなことに気づきましたか。
学生：④草葺き屋根を自分の巣室の上に作るということですか？
教授：うーん，屋根自体を作るだけならそんなに特別なことではありませんね。他にも多くの種の動物が屋根を作ります。
学生：あっ！　言い直させてください。⑤その鳥は，血縁関係のある仲間がたくさん住む，共同の草葺き屋根を作るのを手伝います。⑥彼らは互いの近くに暮らし，巣室を共有します。
教授：その通り。だからこのような共同生活は鳥に繁殖するのにより安全で，より快適な環境を提供してくれるのです。みんな来週の小テストは良い成績が取れそうですね。

147

# Lecture 2　Original

**Listening**　新たな講義を聴いてみよう。

Okay, the sociable weaver is unique because it helps other members of its species. But if you think that the sociable weaver is the only animal that has the notion of communal survival, think again. Let me give you the example of the meerkat.

The meerkat is a small mammal that looks like a ferret or a skinny raccoon and lives in grassland areas of Africa.
①**When meerkats are in a group, one member plays the role of a sentinel, which …** ,
like hawks, snakes and hyenas, while the others are eating.
②**When the sentinel detects approaching predators, it …**
③**This brave behavior allows the others …**
… their nests underground before the predators can attack.

There is some debate as to how altruistic the sentinel meerkat is.
④**Some scientists argue that the sentinel meerkat …**
⑤**Others argue that the sentinel can easily be …**
⑥**Still, in my opinion the meerkat has a very effective communal method to ensure …**

**Speaking**　吹き出しを見ながら足りない語を補い，講義を再現してみよう。

Unit 7　Biggest Bird Nests

## Script

①**When meerkats are in a group, one member plays the role of a sentinel, which** stands guard and looks out for predators,
②**When the sentinel detects approaching predators, it** alerts the other group members to the danger with special calls.
③**This brave behavior allows the others** enough time to escape into their burrows.
④**Some scientists argue that the sentinel meerkat** has eaten before the others.
⑤**Others argue that the sentinel can easily be** the first one to escape.
⑥**Still, in my opinion the meerkat has a very effective communal method to ensure** the survival of its own members.

## Translation

　さて，シャカイハタオリが独特なのは，その鳥が同種の他の仲間の手伝いをするからです。しかし，もし皆さんが，シャカイハタオリが共同で生存するという考えを持つ唯一の生き物だと思うなら，考え直してください。ミーアキャットを例に取ってみましょう。
　ミーアキャットは，フェレットか痩せたアライグマみたいで，アフリカの草原地帯に生息する小さな哺乳動物です。①ミーアキャットが集団でいるときは，1匹が見張りの役目を果たして，他の仲間が餌を食べている間，見張りに立ち，タカやヘビやハイエナのような捕食動物を警戒します。②見張りが近づいてくる捕食動物を見つけると，他の仲間に特別な鳴き声で危険を警告します。③この勇敢な行為は，他の仲間に自分たちの巣穴，つまり地下にある住みかに，捕食動物に襲われないうちに逃げ込むのに十分な時間を与えるのです。
　見張り役のミーアキャットがどのくらい利他的なのかに関して多少議論があります。④一部の科学者は，見張り役のミーアキャットは他の仲間より先に餌を食べていると主張しています。⑤他の科学者は，見張り役のミーアキャットは，容易に一番先に逃げることができると主張しています。⑥それでもやはり，私に言わせれば，ミーアキャットは自分の仲間が生存するのを確実にする，非常に効果的な共同的手法を持っているのです。

# Lecture 2　Summary

**Listening**　チャートを見ながら講義をもう一度聴き，Lecture Notesを完成させよう。（答えは右ページ）　CD 48

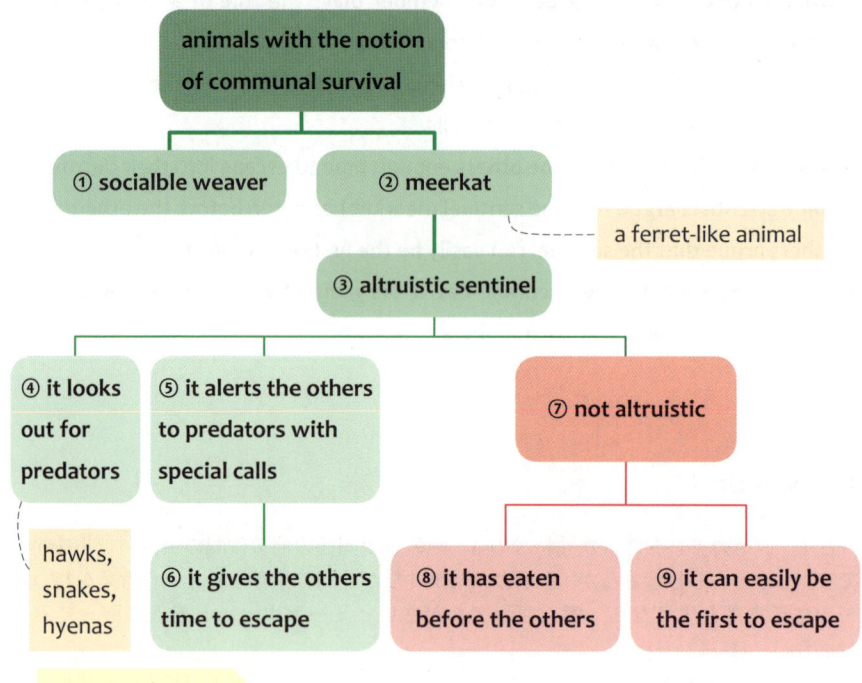

```
animals with the notion of communal survival
├─ ① socialble weaver
└─ ② meerkat ……… a ferret-like animal
       │
       ③ altruistic sentinel
       ├─ ④ it looks out for predators ……… hawks, snakes, hyenas
       ├─ ⑤ it alerts the others to predators with special calls
       ├─ ⑥ it gives the others time to escape
       └─ ⑦ not altruistic
              ├─ ⑧ it has eaten before the others
              └─ ⑨ it can easily be the first to escape
```

## Lecture Notes

**TOPIC**
利他的な行動をとる動物

**PURPOSE**
シャカイハタオリ以外の動物に見られる利他的な行動を提示すること

**MAIN ARGUMENT**
主張：シャカイハタオリ以外の動物にも利他的な行動が見られる。
例示：（　A　）には，仲間が餌を食べている間，（　B　）が来ないか見張る役割がある。
反論：見張り行為が利他的な行為であると言えるかどうかについては異論もある。

**Speaking**　チャートを見ながら講義を要約し，声に出して言ってみよう。

Unit 7　Biggest Bird Nests

☞ 要約文（サンプル）を聴いてみよう。

## Summary

The **sociable weaver** may not be the only **animal with the notion of communal survival**. The meerkat, **a ferret-like animal**, also appears to behave **altruistically**. When meerkats are eating food, one member plays the role of **sentinel**. **It looks out for predators**, such as **hawks, snakes and hyenas**. When the sentinel sees approaching predators, **it alerts them to the danger with a special call, giving them time to escape**. However, some think that it is **not necessarily an altruistic** behavior. Firstly, **the sentinel is the one who has eaten before the others**. Secondly, **it can easily be the first one to escape**.

## Translation

シャカイハタオリが共同で生存するという考えを持つ唯一の生き物ではないだろう。フェレットに似たミーアキャットもまた利他的と見える行動をとる。ミーアキャットは餌を食べている間，1匹が見張り役をする。タカやヘビやハイエナなどの天敵が来ないか警戒するのだ。見張り役は，近づいてくる天敵を見つけると，特別な鳴き声で他の仲間に危険を知らせ，彼らが逃げる時間を確保する。しかし，この行為は必ずしも利他的な行為ではないと考える人もいる。第1に，見張り役は仲間より先に食事を済ませているし，第2に，見張り役は最初に逃げ出すことが容易にできるのである。

### Integrated Task

Do you agree or disagree with the following statement?

*It is natural for animals to behave selfishly all the time in order to survive.*

Use specific reasons and examples to support your answer.

☞ Lecture Notesの答え　A　ミーアキャット　B　天敵

151

## Grammar Notes

①According to Charles Darwin, it is natural that animals **should** behave selfishly to survive.

▶It is natural that S should *do*. は「Sが〜するのは当然だ」という意味です。shouldが「…するべきだ」という意味ではない点に注意しましょう。このような，〈主観的な判断〉を表す文では，that節内の述語動詞がshould *do* となることがあります。

②They need to **look** after themselves, **protect** their resources, **find** a mate and **reproduce**.

▶need toに後続する動詞がlook, protect, find, reproduceと4つ並べられている構造に気をつけましょう。このような構造では，"A, B, C <u>and</u> D"と，並列の最後の項目がandによって導かれるのが特徴です。

③**This is why** some biologists are intrigued by the sociable weaver**, which** builds a communal nest **housing hundreds of individuals**.

▶This is why ...は，前文の内容を受けて「（まさに）これが理由となって…」と結果を導く表現です。

▶which以下はthe sociable weaverの特徴を説明しています。「共同の巣を作らないsociable weaver」と区別しているわけではないので，whichの前にカンマが置かれます。このような関係詞の用法は「非制限用法」と呼ばれます。

▶housing hundreds of individualsは，a communal nestを後ろから修飾しています。

④The nest for this species massive nest consists of individual nest chambers **embedded within a communal thatched roof**, **the building of which** requires extra work for the community.

▶embedded within a communal thatched roofは，individual nest chambersを後ろから修飾しています。

▶..., the building of **which** requires ...は，..., **and** the building of **the roof** requires ...と書き換えることができます。andでつなぐよりも関係詞を用いたほうが，情報の緊密さが増して，「それを作ることが余計な手間を要する」ということがa communal thatched roofについての重要な説明であると感じられます。ここでは，「（それを築くことが）余計な手間暇を要する<u>にもかかわらず</u>，共同の屋根の下に個々の巣が築かれる」という意味合いです。

⑤**Close observation** revealed several things.

▶Close observationはobserve closely（詳しく観察する）という動詞表現を基本とした名詞句です。文全体は，このClose observationが主語となり，それが「いくつかのことを明らかにした」と述べています。このように，英語ではよく，主語に手段や原因をおいて，「手段・原因が結果をもたらす」と発想します。

⑥**First of all**, the birds contributing to thatch building did so above their own nest chamber. ⑦**Secondly**, the neighbors were often relatives**, which** suggests the thatch building might be directed towards kin. ⑧**Thirdly**, related individuals tended to share the use of nest chambers.

▶⑤の several things「いくつかの観察結果」を具体的に列挙しています。「第1に…，第2に…，第3に…」という表現を標識として，観察結果が1つずつ挙げられています。

▶⑦の …, **which** suggests …は，…, **and this** suggests …と書き換えることができます。which は「近くの巣の鳥がしばしば血縁関係にあった」という，直前の内容を受けています。関係代名詞の which には，このように直前で述べられた「内容」を先行詞とする用法があります。これは非制限用法の一種なので，which の前にカンマを置きます。

⑨**What we can extrapolate from these facts is that** these sociable birds benefit from having good neighbors**, which** indirectly **helps them pass on** their genes to the next generation.

▶What we can extrapolate from these facts (=S) is (=V) that … (=C) という構造です。「これらの事実から推定できるのは…ということだ」という意味です。

▶which は，「これらの鳥が，近くの鳥たちと良好な関係にあることで得をする」という直前の内容を受けています。⑦の which と同様です。

▶help O *do* は「Oが〜するのに役立つ」という意味です。目的語の後ろに動詞の原形（＝原形不定詞）が続くのが特徴です。

## Paraphrase Notes

①Charles Darwin **considered it only logical that** animals would behave in a selfish manner in order to survive.

▶ A consider it only logical that S V ...は「SがVするのは論理的に過ぎない（＝どう見ても論理的だ）とAは考える」という意味で，オリジナル①の According to A, it is natural that S should ...と同じ意味合いです。「論理的である（logical）」ということは，「それ以外に考えられない」，「当然のことだ」という解釈につながります。

②**Their behaviors include** protecting themselves, guarding resources, mating and having offspring.

▶ オリジナル②では，They need to ...「彼らは…する必要がある」と表現していた内容を，「彼らの行動は…することを含む」という表現で伝えています。

③A puzzle in the field of social biology, **therefore**, is **the sociable weaver, a bird which** builds a group nest that accommodates several hundred of their kind.

▶ therefore「したがって」「このようなわけで」は，直前の文との論理的なつながりを示す接続副詞で，ここでは主語の後ろに挿入されています。オリジナル③の This is why ...と比べてみましょう。

▶ the sociable weaverの後ろに置かれたコンマは，具体的な説明となる言い換えを導きます。わかりにくい場合は，the sociable weaver, which is a bird which ...と，〈関係詞＋be動詞〉を補ってみましょう。

④Separate nesting chambers are covered under **one roof, the thatching of which** has to be undertaken as additional labor for the entire community.

▶ ... one roof, the thatching of **which** has to be undertaken ...は，... one roof, **and** the thatching of **the roof** has to be undertaken ...と書き換えることができます。オリジナル④にも同じ構造がありました。building という語がthatching という語で置き換えられています。

⑤**By carefully studying this kind of nest**, the researchers made certain discoveries.

▶ オリジナル⑤の「観察が結果を明らかにした」という表現を，「観察することによって，研究者は発見した」という別表現に置き換えています。by *doing* は「（意図・目的を伴って）〜することによって」という意味です。

⑥**For one thing**, when a bird helped with the roof, it did the part that covered its own chamber. ⑦**For another**, a bird's neighbors were frequently all related, so the thatching can be seen as a family-serving activity. ⑧**Lastly**, **it is common that** related birds share nest chambers.

▶「1つには…，また…，最後に…」という「列挙」を示す表現のバリエーションを，オリジナル⑥⑦⑧と比較しましょう。

▶⑧の it is common that ... は「…は一般的なことだ」という意味で，ある事柄が広く見られることを表します。オリジナル⑧では tend to *do*（～する傾向がある）という表現が用いられていましたが，これに対応する表現です。

⑨**From the above facts it follows that** good neighbors ultimately **make it easier for their genes to be handed down** to the succeeding generation.

▶ from A(,) it follows that S V ...は「Aという根拠から，…という結論が得られる」という意味です。オリジナル⑨の What we can extrapolate from these facts is that ...と比較しましょう。

▶ make it easier for A to be *done* は「Aが～されるのを容易にする」という意味で，オリジナル⑨の help O *do* という表現に対応しています。「～するのを容易にする」とは，「～するのを助ける，促す」と解釈することができますね。

## Expressions and Phrases

ヒントを手がかりにして，日本語に対応する英語表現を言ってみよう。

| | | |
|---|---|---|
| □ 自然現象 | na____ ph____ | natural phenomenon |
| □ 興味を引かれた生物学者 | in____ bi____ | intrigued biologist |
| □ 社会生物学 | so____ bi____ | social biology |
| □ 共同体の存続 | co____ su____ | communal survival |
| □ 共同体全体 | en____ co____ | entire community |
| □ 相互の保護 | mu____ pr____ | mutual protection |
| □ 緻密な観察 | cl____ ob____ | close observation |
| □ 近親者 | cl____ re____ | close relative |
| □ つがう可能性のある相手 | po____ ma____ | potential mate |
| □ 生殖能力 | re____ ca____ | reproductive capacity |
| □ 繁殖地 | br____ si____ | breeding site |
| □ 優性遺伝子 | do____ ge____ | dominant gene |
| □ 次の世代 | su____ ge____ | succeeding generation |
| □ 血縁個体 | re____ in____ | related individual |
| □ 巣作りの習慣 | ne____ ha____ | nesting habit |
| □ 絶滅危惧種 | th____ sp____ | threatened species |
| □ 安全な部屋 | se____ ch____ | secure chamber |
| □ 草葺き屋根 | th____ ro____ | thatched roof |
| □ 豊かな資源 | pl____ re____ | plentiful resource |
| □ 追加の労働 | ad____ la____ | additional labor |
| □ 自己中心的な行為 | se____ be____ | selfish behavior |
| □ 利他的行動 | al____ be____ | altruistic behavior |
| □ 効果的な手段 | ef____ me____ | effective means |
| □ 論理的方法 | lo____ me____ | logical method |
| □ 間接的な影響 | in____ ef____ | indirect effect |
| □ 反対方向 | op____ di____ | opposite direction |
| □ 個性的な考え | un____ no____ | unique notion |
| □ キーワード | ke____ te____ | key term |
| □ 最優先 | fi____ pr____ | first priority |
| □ 肝心な点 | bo____ li____ | bottom line |

## Unit 7　Biggest Bird Nests

□ 目前にある危険について隣人に警告する

| wa___ ne_____ about pr___ da_____ | warn neighbors about present danger |
| al___ ne_____ to the im___ ri_____ | alert neighbors to the imminent risk |

□ 共同体のため余分に働くことを求める

| re___ ex___ wo___ for the co_____ | require extra work for the community |
| de___ ad___ se___ to the co_____ | demand additional service to the colony |

□ 彼らの行動から動機を推察する

| ex_____ the mo_____ from their ac_____ | extrapolate the motives from their actions |
| in___ the in_____ from their be_____ | infer the incentives from their behavior |

□ 彼らの子孫に知恵を伝える

| pa___ on the wi_____ to their de_____ | pass on the wisdom to their descendants |
| ha___ down the wi_____ to their of_____ | hand down the wisdom to their offspring |

□ 動物行動の原理に反する

| de___ the pr_____ of an___ be_____ | defy the principles of animal behavior |
| co_____ the la___ of an___ ac_____ | contradict the laws of animal activities |

□ 巣穴を守る仕事を引き受ける

| un_____ the job of gu_____ the bu____ | undertake the job of guarding the burrow |
| ta___ the ro___ of de_____ the den | take the role of defending the den |

□ 見張りの安全を確保する

| en___ the sa____ of the se_____ | ensure the safety of the sentry |
| se___ the sa____ of the se_____ | secure the safety of the sentinel |

□ 生殖能力を優先する

| pr_____ the ab_____ to re_____ | prioritize the ability to reproduce |
| pu___ much va____ on br____ ca_____ | put much value on breeding capacity |

□ 天敵の兆候を察知する

| de___ si___ of na___ en_____ | detect signs of natural enemies |
| se___ the pr_____ of pr_____ | sense the presence of predators |

□ 利己的な性格をあらわにする

| re___ the se___ na____ | reveal the selfish nature |
| ex___ the se___-se____ in_____ | expose the self-serving inclination |

# Word List

| | | | |
|---|---|---|---|
| □ accommodate [əkɑ́:mədèɪt\|əkɔ́m-] | 動 | …を収容する，…を適応させる，…を提供する | |
| | 類 | lodge | |
| □ activity [æktívəti] | 名 | 活動，活発さ | |
| □ alert [ələ́:rt] | 動 | …に警戒態勢を取らせる | |
| | 形 | 油断のない，機敏な | |
| | 名 | 警戒警報 | |
| □ altruism [ǽltruìzm] | 名 | 利他主義 | |
| | 類 | selflessness | |
| □ altruistically [æ̀ltruístɪkəli] | 副 | 利他的に | |
| □ altruistic [æ̀ltruístɪk] | 形 | 利他主義の | |
| □ appear to *do* | | …するように見える | |
| □ behave [bɪhéɪv] | 動 | 行動する，振る舞う，行儀よくする | |
| | 類 | conduct oneself | |
| □ behavior [bɪhéɪvjər] | 名 | 振る舞い，態度 | |
| □ benefit from A | | Aから利益を得る | |
| □ biologist [baɪɑ́:lədʒɪst\|-ɔ́l-] | 名 | 生物学者 | |
| □ biology [baɪɑ́:lədʒi\|-ɔ́l-] | 名 | 生物学 | |
| □ bottom line | | 肝心な点，譲れない点 | |
| □ breeding [brí:dɪŋ] | 名 | 繁殖，血統 | |
| □ chamber [tʃéɪmbər] | 名 | 部屋，空間，会議所 | |
| | 類 | room / compartment | |
| □ chapter [tʃǽptər] | 名 | チャプター，章，一区切り | |
| □ comfortable [kʌ́mftəbl] | 形 | 快適な，居心地の良い，満足して | |
| □ communal [kəmjú:nl\|kɔ́mjʊ-] | 形 | 共同の，共有の | |
| | 類 | shared / collective | |
| □ community [kəmjú:nəti] | 名 | 集団，共同体，地域社会，動物群集 | |
| □ consist of A | | Aから成り立つ | |
| | 類 | be made up of A / be composed of A | |
| □ contribute to A | | Aに貢献する，Aに寄付する | |
| □ covered with A | | Aに覆われている | |
| □ defy [dɪfáɪ] | 動 | …を無視する，…に従わない，…を受け付けない | |
| □ direct [dərékt\|daɪ-] | 動 | …を向ける，方向づける，…を指揮する | |
| | 形 | 直接の，直行の，率直な | |
| □ embed [ɪmbéd] | 動 | …を（あるものの一部として）埋め込む | |

Unit 7　Biggest Bird Nests

|  |  |
|---|---|
| □ entire [ɪntáɪər] | 形 全体の，完全な<br>類 whole |
| □ essential [ɪsénʃəl, es-] | 形 不可欠の，きわめて重要な<br>類 indispensable, crucial |
| □ extrapolate A from B | BからAを推定する<br>類 infer / conclude |
| □ extra [ékstrə] | 形 余計な，必要以上の，特別の<br>類 additional<br>名 割り増し，余分なもの |
| □ family-serving | 血族に尽くす，家族で行う |
| □ frequently [fríːkwəntli] | 副 しばしば，頻繁に |
| □ gene [dʒiːn] | 名 遺伝子 |
| □ generation [dʒènəréɪʃən] | 名 世代 |
| □ go on to A | （別のことに続けて）Aに取りかかる，Aにうつる |
| □ guard [gɑːrd] | 動 …を守る，用心する<br>名 護衛者，見張り，保護物 |
| □ hand down | …を（後の世代に）伝える<br>類 pass down |
| □ house [haʊz] | 動 …を収容する，…に住宅を与える<br>類 accommodate |
| □ include [ɪnklúːd] | 動 …を含む，…を含める |
| □ indirectly [ìndəréktli, ìndaɪréktli] | 副 間接的に，副次的に |
| □ infect [ɪnfékt] | 動 …を感染させる，…に影響を与える |
| □ intrigue [ɪntríːg] | 動 …の好奇心をそそる |
| □ key [kiː] | 名 （解決につながる）鍵，重要なもの |
| □ kin [kɪn] | 名 血縁，親族 |
| □ logical [lɑ́dʒɪkl｜lɔ́dʒ-] | 形 当然の，論理的な |
| □ look after A | Aの面倒を見る，Aの世話をする<br>類 take care of A, attend A |
| □ mate [meɪt] | 名 つがいの片方，友人，仲間<br>動 つがう，…をつがわせる |
| □ neighbor [néɪbər] | 名 隣人，仲間 |
| □ nest [nest] | 名 巣，住みか |
| □ notion [nóʊʃən] | 名 観念，意見 |
| □ offspring [ɔ́(ː)fsprìŋ] | 名 子，子孫，成果<br>類 descendant |

| | | |
|---|---|---|
| □ pass on A to B | | AをBに伝える |
| □ predator [prédətər] | 名 | 捕食動物，略奪者 |
| □ prepared for A | | Aの準備ができている |
| □ priority [praiɔ́:rəti] | 名 | より重要であること，優先（権） |
| □ protect [prətékt] | 動 類 | …を守る，…を保護する<br>defend |
| □ provide A with B | 類 | AにBを与える<br>supply A with B |
| □ puzzle [pʌ́zl] | 名 類 | 謎，解決できない問題　動　…を困らせる<br>mystery |
| □ related [riléitid] | 形 | 血縁関係の，縁続きの，関係のある |
| □ relative [rélətiv] | 名 | 親族，同類　形　相対的な，関係のある |
| □ rephrase [ri:fréiz] | 動 類 | …を言い換える<br>paraphrase |
| □ reproduce [rì:prəd(j)ú:s] | 動 類 | 生殖する，子を産む，繁殖する，…を再生する<br>breed / duplicate |
| □ resource [rí:sɔːrs\|rizɔ́:s] | 名 類 | （複数形で）資源，富，資質<br>supply / reserve |
| □ review [rivjú:] | 動 名 | …を再検討する，…を見直す，…を復習する<br>再調査，批評，復習 |
| □ secure [sikjúər] | 形 類 動 | 安全な，不安のない<br>safe<br>…を確保する |
| □ selfish [sélfiʃ] | 形 類 | 利己的，自分本位の<br>egoistic / self-centered |
| □ selfishly [sélfiʃli] | 副 | 利己的に，自分本位に |
| □ sentinel [séntənl\|-ti-] | 名 類 | 見張り<br>guard / watchman |
| □ separate [sépərət] | 形 類 | 個々の，別々の，離れた<br>individual |
| □ share [ʃeər] | 動 語法 名 | …を共有する，…を分ける，分担する<br>share A with B「AをBと共有する」<br>分け前，割当，役割 |
| □ sociable [sóuʃəbl] | 形 類 | 交際好きな，なごやかな<br>outgoing / friendly |
| □ succeeding [səksí:diŋ] | 形 類 | 次の，続いて起こる<br>subsequent / following |
| □ survival [sərváivl] | 名 | 生き残ること |

| | | | |
|---|---|---|---|
| □ thatched [θætʃt] | 形 | 草葺きの | |
| □ ultimately [ʌ́ltəmətli] | 副 | 最終的に，最後に | |
| | 類 | eventually / in the end | |
| □ undertake [ʌ̀ndərtéɪk] | 動 | …を引き受ける，…を始める | |
| | 類 | take on | |
| □ unique [ju(ː)níːk] | 形 | 独特の，たぐいまれな，特有の | |
| | 類 | distinct | |

## 参考文献

The Official Guide to the New *TOEFL iBT®*, p.283. McGraw Hill

Clutton-Brock, T.H., O'Riain, M.J., Brotherton, P.N.M., Gaynor, D., Kansky, R., Griffin, A.S. & Manser, M. (1999b) Selfish sentinels in cooperative mammals. Science 284:1640-1644.

# Unit 8 Keystone Species

## Integrated Task

Using specific examples, explain the concept of keystone species and its implications.

## Key Words

**keystone**
▶建築学で「かなめ石」と呼ばれる石で，アーチ状の構造の頂点に置かれます。構造上最も大きな力がかかるため，それが取り去られるとアーチ全体が壊れてしまうことになります。このことから転じて，「組織や論理の中で最も中心的な働きをするもの」という比喩的な意味で用いられます。今回は「群生生態学」(community ecology) に関する話題ですが，この分野で「キーストーン種」(keystone species) と呼ばれる種とはどのようなものでしょうか。

**ecologist / ecosystem**
▶ecologistは，ecology「生態学」の研究者を表す名詞です。ecologyとは生き物相互の関わり合い，および生き物とその生息環境の関わり合いを扱う学問のことです。また，生き物と環境とが関わり合って持続的に機能するまとまりをecosystem「生態系」と呼びます。今回は，ある岩場に生息するヒトデ (starfish) と他の甲殻類 (shellfish) とが，どのように関わり合っているかが理解のポイントです。

# Lecture 1  Original

**Listening**  講義を聴いてみよう。

① As the removal of a keystone
② The theory of keystone species was
③ The area originally contained
④ Paine found
⑤ When he removed
⑥ The number of invertebrate species
⑦ Paine concluded

American ecologist
Robert Paine
prey on
rocky tidal zone
mussels
starfish
Shellfish
invertebrates 15
rock surface
crowd out
invertebrates 8
ecosystem

**Speaking**  イラストを見ながら講義を再現してみよう。

## Script

①**As the removal of a keystone** in a building leads to the destruction of the whole structure, the removal of a keystone species results in a dramatic change in the ecosystem. ②**The theory of keystone species was** first postulated by an American ecologist, Robert Paine, who did an experiment in a rocky tidal zone. ③**The area originally contained** 15 species of invertebrates, including starfish, mussels, and other shellfish. ④**Paine found** that starfish preyed heavily on mussels, preventing the mussel population from multiplying. ⑤**When he removed** the starfish from the tidal zone, mussels rapidly increased in number, crowding out other organisms from the rock surfaces. ⑥**The number of invertebrate species** in the ecosystem soon dropped to eight species. ⑦**Paine concluded** that the loss of just one species can significantly damage the delicate balance of an ecosystem.

## Translation

①建築物のかなめ石を取り除くことが構造物全体の破壊につながるように，中枢となる種を取り除くと，生態系が劇的に変化することになる。②中枢種理論は，アメリカの生態学者であるロバート・ペインによって最初に唱えられ，彼は岩の多い潮間帯で実験を行った。③その一帯には，もともとヒトデやイガイやその他の甲殻類動物を含む15種の無脊椎動物が生息していた。④ヒトデはイガイを大量に捕食し，イガイの個体群が増殖することを妨げていることにペインは気づいた。⑤ペインが潮間帯からヒトデを取り除くと，イガイの個体群の規模が急速に増大し，他の生物を岩の表面から追い出してしまった。⑥この生態系における無脊椎動物種の数は8種にまですぐに減少した。⑦たった1つの種の喪失が，生態系の微妙なバランスを著しく損なう可能性があるとペインは結論づけた。

☞ スクリプトの文法ポイントについては，p.174～の**Grammar Notes**を参照しよう。

# Lecture 1　Paraphrase

**Listening**　別の表現を用いた講義を聴いてみよう。

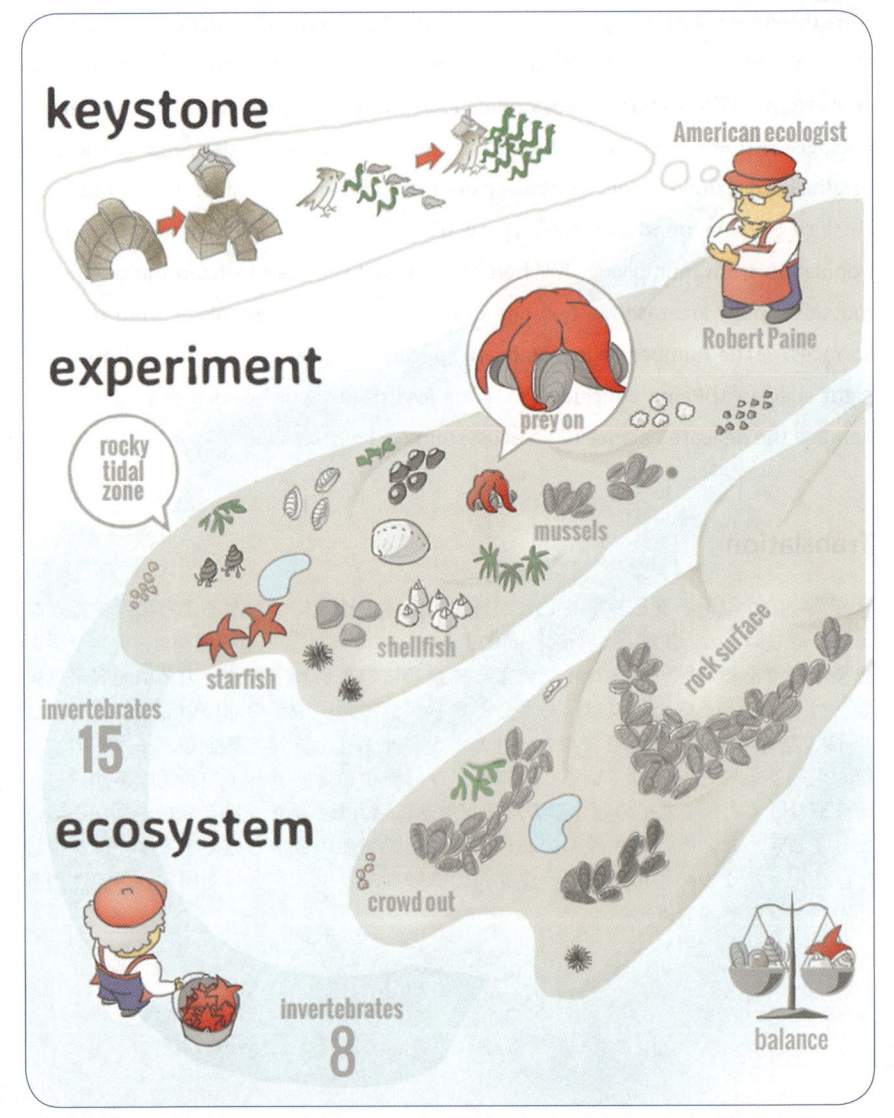

CD 52

keystone

American ecologist
Robert Paine

experiment

rocky tidal zone

prey on

mussels
shellfish
starfish

invertebrates
15

ecosystem

rock surface

crowd out

invertebrates
8

balance

**Speaking**　イラストを見ながら講義の内容を英語で説明しよう。

166

## Script

①Similar to how the loss of a key element in a building can lead to the collapse of the entire building, removing a **keystone** species can greatly affect an ecosystem. ②This idea of keystone species was first suggested by Robert Paine, an ecologist in the US who did an **experiment** in a rocky tidal area. ③When first approached, the area had 15 invertebrate species such as starfish, mussels, and other shellfish. ④Paine noticed that the starfish was eating large amounts of mussels, which kept the mussel population in check. ⑤Paine then took away all the starfish, and the mussel population soon pushed out many other creatures from the area, so much so that the number of species dropped to eight. ⑥This convinced Paine that the loss of a single species can dramatically affect an **ecosystem**'s fine balance.

## Translation

①建築物の重要な要素の喪失が建物全体の崩壊につながっていく可能性があるのと同様に，中枢種を取り除くことは，生態系に大きな影響を与える可能性がある。②中枢種というこの考えは，ロバート・ペインによって初めて提案されたが，彼は岩の多い潮間帯で実験を行ったアメリカの生態学者である。③その一帯の調査が始められたとき，そこにはヒトデやイガイやその他の甲殻類動物を含む15種の無脊椎動物が生息していた。④ペインはヒトデが大量のイガイを捕食し，そのことがイガイの個体群の増加を抑えていることに気づいた。⑤次に，ペインがヒトデをすべて取り除くと，イガイの個体群がその一帯から他の多くの生物をすぐに追い出してしまい，その結果，種の数は8種にまで減少した。⑥このことは，たった1つの種の喪失が，生態系の微妙なバランスに劇的に影響を与えることがあるということをペインに確信させた。

☞ パラフレーズのポイントについては，p.176〜の**Paraphrase Notes**を参照しよう。

# Conversation

**Listening** 講義に関連する会話を聴いてみよう。

Student A: Hi, David. Would you mind filling me in on the biology class from last week? If you could just give me the gist, that would suffice for now.

Student B: Sure, no problem. So last week we talked about keystone species. The professor used the African Elephant from the Serengeti Plains as an example in class.

Student A: Elephants? How so? It seems like all they do is eat and roam around.

Student B: Doesn't it though? But actually I thought it was cool.

①**He said the elephants eat …**

②**And even when the trees become out of reach, the elephants can still eat them by …**

Student A: I can see that.

Student B: ③**So this eating habit actually serves as tree population control, you know, to keep the trees from …**

And because of that, grasses can grow, and guess what?

④**Grazing animals such as zebras and antelopes feed on grass, and predators such as hyenas …**

Student A: But if, for some reason, the elephant is removed from the ecosystem …

Student B: ⑤**Then that would destroy the balance and some species …**

**Speaking** 上の会話文を見ながら音声を聴き、学生Bのパートを再現してみよう。

## Script

①**He said the elephants eat** small trees, such as the acacia.
②**And even when the trees become out of reach, the elephants can still eat them by** knocking them down with their strong feet.
③**So this eating habit actually serves as tree population control, you know, to keep the trees from** growing out of control.
④**Grazing animals such as zebras and antelopes feed on grass, and predators such as hyenas** prey on these herbivores in the plains.
⑤**Then that would destroy the balance and some species** would most likely disappear from the plains.


## Translation

学生A：ねえ，デイビッド。先週の生物の授業について私に教えてくれない？　もしあなたが私にちょっと要点を教えてくれれば，今のところそれで十分だと思うの。
学生B：もちろん，おやすいご用さ。先週，僕たちは中枢種について議論したんだ。教授は授業の中で一例としてセレンゲティ大平原のアフリカゾウを用いたんだ。
学生A：ゾウ？　どうして？　ゾウがすることと言えば食べたり，あちこち歩き回ったりすることくらいのように思えるけど。
学生B：本当にそうだよね。でも実は，僕はそれは素晴らしい例だと思ったんだ。①先生の話では，ゾウはアカシアのような低木を食べるんだって。②そして，ゾウが届かない所まで木が高くなっても，ゾウは強い足で木を蹴り倒して木を食べることができるんだ。
学生A：そうでしょうね。
学生B：③だから，このゾウの食習慣が実際に木の総数を管理するのに役立っているんだ。つまりさ，木が手に負えないほど成長するのを妨げているんだ。さらに，そのおかげで，草が成長できて，そしてどうなると思う？　④シマウマやレイヨウのような草食動物が草を常食として生きて，ハイエナのような肉食動物はそれらの平原の草食動物を捕食するってわけさ。
学生A：でも，もし何らかの理由で，ゾウが生態系から取り除かれると…。
学生B：⑤そうすると，それが生態系の均衡を崩して，一部の種はおそらく平原から姿を消すだろうね。

# Lecture 2　Original

**Listening**　新たな講義を聴いてみよう。

Let's continue our discussion on keystone species. Now, my question is, what do you do when the balance in one ecosystem is lost? You know, if one species grows out of control?

Well, let me tell you about this one case in Kenya, where people suffered from a parasitic disease called schistosomiasis. It is an infection caused by the parasitic worm called a schistosome, which lives inside a host species, the freshwater snail.

①**For one reason or another, the ecosystem of Kenyan rivers was disrupted and the numbers of the snail** …

②**The worms frequently infect** …

One study showed that about 2 million Kenyans, majority of whom were children, were infected.

③**Once infected, schistosomiasis can result in** …

Pretty scary, huh?

Well, to combat this disease, researchers introduced a biological control agent, namely Louisiana crayfish. Crayfish, you know, they look like miniature lobsters with red shells, big claws … anyway, they love to eat snails.

④**After the researchers released the crayfish into Kenyan rivers and ponds, the overall** …,

and so did the number of people infected with schistosomiasis.

⑤**This was the first time a biological control agent** …

**Speaking**　吹き出しを見ながら足りない語を補い，講義を再現してみよう。

Unit 8　Keystone Species

## Script

①**For one reason or another, the ecosystem of Kenyan rivers was disrupted and the numbers of the snail** dramatically increased, and so did the schistosome.
②**The worms frequently infect** the residents who are exposed to water.
③**Once infected, schistosomiasis can result in** internal bleeding, fever, fatigue, and sometimes death.
④**After the researchers released the crayfish into Kenyan rivers and ponds, the overall** number of the snail dropped,
⑤**This was the first time a biological control agent** has been successfully used to restore balance in an ecosystem.

## Translation

　中枢種についての議論を続けましょう。さて，皆さんへの質問は，ある生態系において，そのバランスが失われたら人はどうすればよいのか，ということです。ほら，もし１つの種が手に負えないほど数が増えてしまったらどうするか，ということですよ。
　では，こんな事例を１つお話ししましょう。人々が住血吸虫症と呼ばれる寄生虫症に苦しんでいたケニヤでの事例です。この病気は，宿主動物種である淡水巻貝の内部に住み着く住血吸虫と呼ばれる寄生虫によって引き起こされる伝染病です。①何らかの理由で，ケニヤを流れる川の生態系が崩壊し，巻貝の数が劇的に増え，その結果住血吸虫も増えたというわけです。②その虫は水に触れる住民によく感染するんです。ある研究によれば，約200万人のケニヤ人が感染したらしく，その大多数が子どもでした。③感染してまうと，住血吸虫症は内出血，発熱，疲労を引き起こし，そして時には死に至ることもあります。とても怖いですよね。
　この病気を撲滅するため，研究者たちは生物的駆除因子，具体的に言うとルイジアナザリガニを持ち込みました。ザリガニというのは，ほら，赤い殻を身にまとい，大きなはさみ持った小型のロブスターのような恰好をしたやつですが…とにかく，ザリガニは巻貝を食べるのが大好きなのです。④研究者たちがザリガニをケニヤの川と池に放したあと，巻貝の全体的な数は減り，そして寄生虫症に感染した人の数も減りました。⑤生物的駆除因子が生態系のバランスを回復するためにうまく使われたのは，この時がはじめてでした。

# Lecture 2　Summary

**Listening**　チャートを見ながら講義をもう一度聴き，Lecture Notesを完成させよう。（答えは右ページ）　CD 55

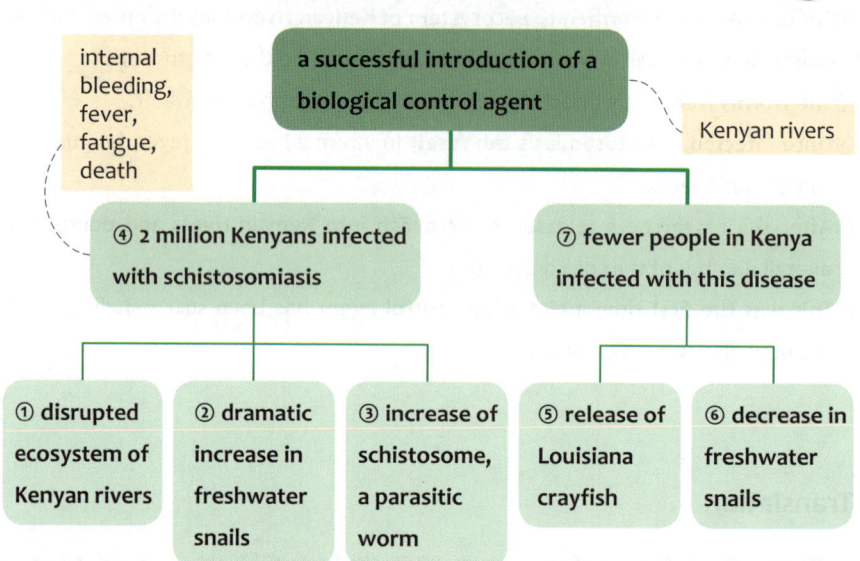

- internal bleeding, fever, fatigue, death
- **a successful introduction of a biological control agent**
- Kenyan rivers

④ 2 million Kenyans infected with schistosomiasis

⑦ fewer people in Kenya infected with this disease

① disrupted ecosystem of Kenyan rivers
② dramatic increase in freshwater snails
③ increase of schistosome, a parasitic worm
⑤ release of Louisiana crayfish
⑥ decrease in freshwater snails

## Lecture Notes

**TOPIC**
生物的駆除因子

**PURPOSE**
生物的駆除因子の導入による生態系制御の成功例を提示すること

**MAIN ARGUMENT**
主張：ケニアで行われた生物的駆除因子の導入により（　A　）のバランスを回復させることに成功した。
問題：ケニアの河川の生態系の（　B　）によって多くのケニア国民が住血吸虫症に苦しんでいた。
解決：住血吸虫症が（　C　）する淡水産巻貝の数を減らすために，生物的駆除因子として放たれたルイジアナザリガニによって事態が収束した。

**Speaking**　チャートを見ながら講義を要約し，声に出して言ってみよう。

Unit 8　Keystone Species

☞ 要約文（サンプル）を聴いてみよう。

## Summary

**The successful introduction of a biological control agent to Kenyan rivers** restored a balance in ecosystems and, as a result, saved the lives of many. Before the introduction, **two million Kenyans were infected with schistosomiasis**, a parasitic disease, which causes **internal bleeding, fever, fatigue, or even death**. The widespread tragedy started from the **disrupted ecosystem of Kenyan rivers**. A **dramatic increase in freshwater snails** naturally led to an **increase of schistosome, which is a parasitic worm** that dwells inside the freshwater snail. However, when they **released Louisiana crayfish**, the number of **freshwater snails decreased** significantly. Consequently, today **fewer people in Kenya are infected with this disease**.

## Translation

ケニアの河川への生物的駆除因子の導入は成功し，生態系のバランスを回復させ，その結果多くの人々の命を救った。導入前は200万人のケニア国民が住血吸虫症という寄生虫症にかかり，内出血，発熱，疲労そして死という症状を起こしていた。この拡大した悲劇はケニアの河川の生態系の破壊により引き起こされた。淡水産巻貝は激増し，当然の結果として，淡水産巻貝に住みつく寄生虫である住血吸虫も増加した。しかし，ルイジアナザリガニを放つと淡水産巻貝は激減した。その結果，現在ではこの病気に感染している人は少なくなった。

---

### Integrated Task

Using specific examples, explain the concept of keystone species and its implications.

---

☞ Lecture Notesの答え　A 生態系　B 破壊　C 寄生

# Grammar Notes

①**As** the removal of a keystone in a building **leads to** the destruction of the whole structure, the removal of a keystone species **results in** a dramatic change in the ecosystem.

▶物事を何かになぞらえて説明する方法の1つに，As S V ...., (so) S V 〜「…のように，〜」という表現があります。この文では「かなめ石を取り除くことが構造物全体の崩壊につながる」ことになぞらえて，「かなめ石に当たる種がいなくなると生態系に大きな変化が生じる」ことを説明しています。

▶ A lead to B と A result in B という「A（原因）から B（結果）が生じる」という意味の同義表現が効果的に使われています。このように，たとえば As S V ...., (so) S V 〜のような類似点を示す構文では，同じ趣旨の動詞表現を2度用いる必要がありますが，単調さを避けるために全く同じ表現を用いるのを避け，同義語や類義語を用いる傾向があります。

②The theory of keystone species was first postulated by **an American ecologist, Robert Paine**, who did an experiment in a rocky tidal zone.

▶ある人物名を，その肩書などと併せて示す場合，"［肩書］，［人物名］"という順序と"［人物名］，［肩書］"という順序があります。今回は"［肩書］，［人物名］"の順で，「アメリカ人生態学者，ロバート・ペイン氏（によって提唱された）」という感じです。このようなカンマ（,）の働きは音読を通じて，1つの「リズム」として身につけましょう。

③The area **originally** contained 15 species of invertebrates, **including** starfish, mussels, **and other** shellfish.

▶ originally は「もともとは」という意味の副詞です。ここでは「その後の変化」を示唆する働きがあることに注意しましょう。

▶ A, including B「B を含む A」は，A の具体例が B であることを表します。ここでは，15 species of invertebrates にどのような生き物が含まれるかを，具体的に示しています。

▶ A, B(,) and other X は「A や B などの X」という意味です。たとえば，math, science and other important subjects ならば「数学や理科などの重要な教科」という意味になります。

④Paine found that starfish preyed heavily on mussels, **preventing** the mussel population **from** multiplying.

▶ A prevent B from *doing* は「A は B が〜するのを妨げる」という意味ですが，「A が原因となって B が〜できなくなる」という因果関係をとらえることが大切です。ここで A に当たるのは "starfish preyed heavily on mussels" の内容です。「ヒトデがイガイを大量に捕食する」（原因）→「イガイが増殖できなくなる」（結果）というつながりを分詞構文で表しています。

▶ preventing 以下は分詞構文で，ここでは「結果」を表しています。... **and this prevented** the mussel population from multiplying と書き換えてもほぼ同じ意味です。

Unit 8　Keystone Species

⑤When he removed the starfish from the tidal zone, mussels rapidly **increased in number**, **crowding out** other organisms from the rock surfaces.

- ▶increase in numberは「数が増加する」という意味です。increase / decreaseという動詞を用いるときには，主語が「数や量の概念を含む名詞」であるのが原則です。例えば，The population increased.「人口が増えた」とは言えますが, The residents increased.「住民が増えた」とは言えません。The number of residents increased. とするか，The residents increased in number. とする必要があります。
- ▶crowding out ...は「その結果…を追い出すこととなった」という意味の分詞構文です。④のpreventing ...同様に「結果」を表している点に注意しましょう。

⑥The number of invertebrate species in the ecosystem **soon** dropped to eight species.

- ▶soonは「ほどなくして」という意味の副詞です。基準となるときから「それほどたたないうちに」ということです。その時間が短くなり「即座に」となればimmediately / instantlyを用います。

⑦Paine **concluded that** the loss of just one species can significantly damage the delicate balance of an ecosystem.

- ▶conclude that ...は「…と結論付ける」という意味です。観察，実験，議論などの最終段階として結論を述べるときに用います。

175

## Paraphrase Notes

①**Similar to** how the loss of a key element in a building can lead to the **collapse** of **the entire building**, removing a keystone species can **greatly affect** an ecosystem.

▶オリジナル①で用いられていた As S V ...., (so) S V ～「…のように，～」という表現が，Similar to ～「～と同様に」という表現を用いてパラフレーズされています。

▶単語レベルでは，destruction→collapse, the whole structure→the entire building, result in a dramatic change→greatly affect などの言い換えが見られます。

②This idea of keystone species was first **suggested** by **Robert Paine, an ecologist in the US** who did an experiment in a rocky tidal area.

▶オリジナル②で用いられていた postulate「提唱する」よりも平易な suggest が用いられています。

▶人物を紹介する表現では，オリジナル②とは逆に"[人物名]，[肩書]"の順になっています。"Robert Pain, who is an ecologist in the US ..." と，〈関係代名詞＋be 動詞〉を補うことができます。

③**When first approached**, the area had 15 invertebrate species such as starfish, mussels, and other shellfish.

▶オリジナル③では originally という副詞を用いて表されていた「もともとは…（だが後に～）」という意味合いが，When (it was) first approached「最初に調査された際には」という，より具体的な表現に変わっています。

④Pain noticed that the starfish was **eating large amounts of mussels**, which **kept** the mussel population **in check**.

▶オリジナル④と比べると，prey heavily on→eat large amounts of, prevent ... from multiplying→keep ... in check といった表現のバリエーションが見られます。

⑤Paine then took away all the starfish and the mussel population soon pushed out many other creatures from the area, **so much so that** the number of species dropped to eight.

▶so much so that ...は，「あまりにもそうなので，（その結果）…」という意味の表現で，接続詞のように用います。the mussel population soon pushed out <u>so</u> many other creatures from the area <u>that</u> the number of species dropped to eight と書き換えてもほぼ同じ意味です。オリジナル⑤と⑥の「イガイの増殖が他の種を駆逐する」（原因）→「無脊椎動物が8種にまで減少する」（結果）というつながりが，1文にまとめられています。

Unit 8　Keystone Species

⑥**This convinced Paine that** the loss of a single species can dramatically affect an ecosystem's <u>fine</u> balance.

▶ This convinced Pain that ... は「このことがペイン氏に…を確信させた」という意味です。オリジナル⑦の Pain concluded that ... よりも，「観察結果を受けて…を確信するに至った」という意味がはっきりと感じられる表現です。

## Expressions and Phrases

ヒントを手がかりにして，日本語に対応する英語表現を言ってみよう。

| 日本語 | ヒント | 英語 |
|---|---|---|
| □ 生物 | li___ or___ | living organism |
| □ 脊椎動物種 | ve___ sp___ | vertebrate species |
| □ 無脊椎動物種 | in___ sp___ | invertebrate species |
| □ 宿主動物種 | ho___ sp___ | host species |
| □ 肉食動物 | ca___ an___ | carnivorous animal |
| □ 草食動物 | he___ an___ | herbivorous animal |
| □ 雑食動物 | om___ an___ | omnivorous animal |
| □ 海の生き物 | se___ cr___ | sea creature |
| □ 海洋生態学 | ma___ ec___ | marine ecology |
| □ 生態系全体 | en___ ec___ | entire ecosystem |
| □ 恐ろしい捕食者 | sc___ pr___ | scary predator |
| □ 簡単に捕まる餌食 | ea___ pr___ | easy prey |
| □ 草原 | gr___ pl___ | grassy plain |
| □ 潮間帯 | ti___ zo___ | tidal zone |
| □ 小型のロブスター | mi___ lo___ | miniature lobster |
| □ 鋭いつめ | sh___ cl___ | sharp claw |
| □ 微妙な均衡 | de___ ba___ | delicate balance |
| □ 避けられない崩壊 | in___ co___ | inevitable collapse |
| □ 劇的な破壊 | dr___ de___ | dramatic destruction |
| □ 重要な要素 | si___ el___ | significant element |
| □ 表面構造 | su___ st___ | surface structure |
| □ 熱帯性の熱病 | tr___ fe___ | tropical fever |
| □ 寄生虫 | pa___ wo___ | parasitic worm |
| □ 細菌感染 | ba___ in___ | bacterial infection |
| □ 内出血 | in___ bl___ | internal bleeding |
| □ 肉体的疲労 | ph___ fa___ | physical fatigue |
| □ 地元の住人 | lo___ re___ | local resident |
| □ 大多数 | va___ ma___ | vast majority |
| □ 強制退去 | fo___ re___ | forced removal |
| □ 全体的な評価 | ov___ as___ | overall assessment |

## Unit 8　Keystone Species

□ 彼に前回の授業の要点を伝える

| br___ him about the la__ le____ | brief him about the last lecture |
| gi__ him the gi__ of the pr____ le__ | give him the gist of the previous lesson |

□ その重要性について彼を説得する

| co____ him of its si_____ | convince him of its significance |
| pe____ him of its im_____ | persuade him of its importance |

□ 生態系に影響を与える

| af___ the ec_____ sy___ | affect the ecological system |
| ha_ an ef___ on the ec_____ | have an effect on the ecosystem |

□ 生態系の破壊を引き起こす

| re__ in the de_____ of an ec___ | result in the destruction of an ecosystem |
| le__ to ec_____ di_____ | lead to ecological disorder |

□ 急速に増殖する

| mu_____ at a ra__ pa__ | multiply at a rapid pace |
| ra__ in_____ in nu____ | rapidly increase in number |

□ ザリガニを小川から取り除く

| re__ cr_____ from the br____ | remove crayfish from the brook |
| ta__ away cr_____ from the st__ | take away crawfish from the stream |

□ 草食動物を捕食する

| fe__ on gr_____ animals | feed on grazing animals |
| pr__ on he_____ | prey on herbivores |

□ 個体数を制御する

| ha__ co____ over the size of the po_____ | have control over the size of the population |
| ke__ the po_____ size in ch__ | keep the population size in check |

□ 珍しい病気に感染する

| get in____ with a ra__ di_____ | get infected with a rare disease |
| ca__ an un_____ in_____ di_____ | catch an uncommon infectious disease |

□ 健康な成長を阻む

| pr__ so__ gr____ | prevent sound growth |
| di___ he____ de_____ | disrupt healthy development |

179

# Word List

| | | | |
|---|---|---|---|
| □acacia [əkéɪʃə] | 名 | アカシア | |
| □affect [əfékt] | 動 | …に影響を与える | |
| | 類 | influence / have an effect on | |
| □agent [éɪdʒənt] | 名 | 因子, 代理人 | |
| □antelope [ǽntəlòʊp] | 名 | レイヨウ | |
| □biological [bàɪəlá:dʒɪkl \| -lɔ́dʒ-] | 形 | 生物学的な | |
| □bleeding [blíːdɪŋ] | 名 | 出血 | |
| □claw [klɔː] | 名 | 爪 | |
| □collapse [kəlǽps] | 名 | 崩壊, 衰弱　動 | 崩壊する, 失敗する |
| | 類 | breakdown | |
| □combat [kəmbǽt] | 動 | …と闘う | |
| | 類 | fight | |
| □consequently [kɑ́:nsəkwèntli] | 副 | 結果として | |
| □contain [kəntéɪn] | 動 | …を含む, …を収容する, …を抑え込む | |
| | 類 | include / comprise | |
| □continue [kəntínjuː] | 動 | …を続ける, 続く | |
| □crayfish [kréɪfìʃ] | 名 | ザリガニ | |
| □crowd out A | | Aを追い出す, Aを閉め出す | |
| | 類 | push out A | |
| □delicate [délɪkət] | 形 | 微妙な, 繊細な, こわれやすい, 優美な, 精巧な | |
| | 類 | fine | |
| □destruction [dɪstrʌ́kʃən] | 名 | 破壊, 破棄すること | |
| □disappear [dìsəpíər] | 動 | 姿を消す, いなくなる, 消失する | |
| | 類 | vanish | |
| □disease [dɪzíːz] | 名 | 病気, 疾病, 不健全な状態 | |
| □disrupt [dɪsrʌ́pt] | 動 | …を分裂させる, …を邪魔する | |
| □dramatic [drəmǽtɪk] | 形 | 劇的な, 劇の | |
| | 類 | striking | |
| □dwell [dwel] | 動 | 住む, 暮らす, (～ on Aで) Aについて考えを巡らせる, Aに固執する | |
| □ecologist [ɪká:lədʒɪst \| -kɔ́l-] | 名 | 生態学者 | |
| □ecosystem [íːkoʊsìstəm, é-] | 名 | 生態系 | |
| □element [éləmənt] | 名 | 要素, 元素, 少量 | |
| | 類 | component / constituent | |

## Unit 8  Keystone Species

| | |
|---|---|
| □ expose [ɪkspóuz, eks-] | 動 …をさらす，…を露出する，…を暴露する<br>語法 be exposed to A「Aにさらされる」 |
| □ fatigue [fətíːg] | 名 疲労，骨折り仕事<br>類 tiredness |
| □ feed on A | Aを食べて生きる |
| □ fever [fíːvər] | 名 熱，興奮状態 |
| □ fill A in | (人)に詳細を伝える，(用紙など)に記入する |
| □ fine [faɪn] | 形 微妙な，細かな，立派な，晴れた，元気な<br>類 delicate<br>副 見事に 名 罰金 動 罰金を科す |
| □ for now | 今のところ，さしあたり |
| □ freshwater [fréʃwɔ̀ːtər] | 名 淡水 |
| □ gist [dʒɪst] | 名 要点<br>類 point / essence |
| □ grazing [gréɪzɪŋ] | 形 草食の，放牧用の |
| □ herbivore [hə́ːrbəvɔ̀ːr] | 名 草食動物 |
| □ host [houst] | 形 宿主の，主催側の |
| □ hyena [haɪíːnə] | 名 ハイエナ |
| □ including A | Aを含めて |
| □ infection [ɪnfékʃən] | 名 感染，伝染病，影響<br>類 contagion |
| □ internal [ɪntə́ːrnl] | 形 内部の，体内の |
| □ introduction [ìntrədʌ́kʃən] | 名 導入，紹介，序論 |
| □ invertebrate [ɪnvə́ːrtəbrət] | 名 無脊椎動物 |
| □ keep A from *doing* | Aが…するのを妨げる<br>類 prevent [stop / hinder] O from *doing* |
| □ keystone [kíːstòun] | 名 かなめ石，かなめになる物 |
| □ knock A down | Aを倒す |
| □ lead to A | Aにつながる，Aを引き起こす<br>類 cause A / bring about A / result in A |
| □ lobster [lɑ́ːbstər\|lɔ́b-] | 名 ロブスター |
| □ majority [mədʒɔ́ːrəti] | 名 大多数 |
| □ miniature [mɪ́niətʃər\|mɪ́nə-] | 形 小型の<br>類 tiny |
| □ most likely | おそらく，たぶん |

# Word List

| | | | |
|---|---|---|---|
| ☐ multiply [mʌ́ltəplàɪ] | 動 | 増殖する，繁殖する，増える，かけ算をする，…を増やす | |
| | 類 | increase / grow / proliferate | |
| ☐ namely [néɪmli] | 副 | すなわち | |
| | 類 | that is (to say) / in other words | |
| ☐ organism [ɔ́:rgənìzm] | 名 | 生物，有機体，人間 | |
| | 類 | living thing / life form | |
| ☐ originally [ərídʒənəli] | 副 | もともと，元来は | |
| | 類 | at first / initially | |
| ☐ out of control | | 制御不能な | |
| ☐ out of reach | | 届かない | |
| ☐ overall [òuvərɔ́:l] | 形 | 全体の 副 [òuvərɔ́:l] 総計で，全体として | |
| | 類 | general / whole | |
| ☐ parasitic [pèrəsítɪk] | 形 | 寄生虫によって起こる，寄生する | |
| ☐ population [pɑ̀:pjəléɪʃən|pɔ̀p-] | 名 | 個体群，人口，住民 | |
| | 類 | inhabitant | |
| ☐ prey on A | | Aを捕食する | |
| ☐ removal [rɪmú:vl] | 名 | 除去，移動，引っ越し | |
| ☐ remove [rɪmú:v] | 動 | …を取り除く，…を取り去る，…を脱ぐ | |
| | 類 | take away / take off | |
| ☐ resident [rézədənt] | 名 | 住人，居住者 | |
| ☐ roam around | | 歩き回る | |
| | 類 | wander around | |
| ☐ scary [skéəri] | 形 | 怖い | |
| | 類 | creepy, frightening | |
| ☐ serve [sər:v] | 動 | …の役に立つ，…のために働く，（飲食物）を供する，（役割など）を果たす | |
| ☐ shell [ʃel] | 名 | 貝 | |
| ☐ snail [sneɪl] | 名 | カタツムリ，巻貝 | |
| ☐ suffice [səfáɪs] | 動 | 十分である | |
| ☐ take away A | | Aを取り除く | |
| | 類 | remove | |
| ☐ tidal [táɪdl] | 形 | 潮の，干満の | |
| ☐ tragedy [trǽdʒədi] | 名 | 悲劇，惨事 | |
| | 類 | disaster / misfortune | |
| ☐ widespread [wáɪdspréd] | 形 | 広範囲に及ぶ，普及した | |

| | | | |
|---|---|---|---|
| □ worm [wəːrm] | | 名 | （細長く脚のない）虫，寄生虫 |
| | | 動 | 徐々に進む |
| □ zebra [zíːbrə, zé-] | | 名 | シマウマ |

## 参考文献

Lodge, David M, Sadie K Rosenthal, Kenneth M Mavuti, Wairimu Muohi, Philip Ochieng, Samantha S Stevens, Benjamin N Mungai, and Gerald M Mkoji. "Louisiana crayfish (Procambarus clarkii) (Crustacea: Cambaridae) in Kenyan ponds: non-target effects of a potential biological control agent for schistosomiasis." *African Journal of Aquatic Science* 30, no. 2 (August 2005): 119-24. Accessed September 7, 2015. http://dx.doi.org/10.2989/16085910509503845.

# Unit 9 Decision Fatigue

## Integrated Task

Do you agree or disagree with the following statement?

*It is better to have more choices than having fewer or no choice.*

Use specific reasons and examples to support your answer.

## Key Words

**fatigue**

▶「疲労」という意味の名詞です。形容詞tiredの名詞形であるtirednessよりも堅い表現で、また「極端な疲れ」「疲弊した状態」を表します。fatigueには肉体的な（physical）なものと、精神的な（mental）なものとがありますが、講義の主題であるdecision fatigueとはどのような疲労なのでしょうか。その原因（cause）と結果（effect）を理解することが今回のポイントです。

**rational**

▶「理にかなっている」「理屈が通っている」という意味を表す形容詞です。reasonと同語源で、2つ以上の物事の間に、因果関係などの論理的なつながりを見出そうとする人間の知性の働き、つまり「理性」と深く関わりのある語です。否定形はirrationalですが、emotional（感情的な）なども対義語として挙げられます。「人がrationalでなくなるのはどのようなときか、またその結果どのようなことが生じうるか」と考えることが、講義を理解するためのポイントです。

# Lecture 1　Original

**Listening**　講義を聴いてみよう。

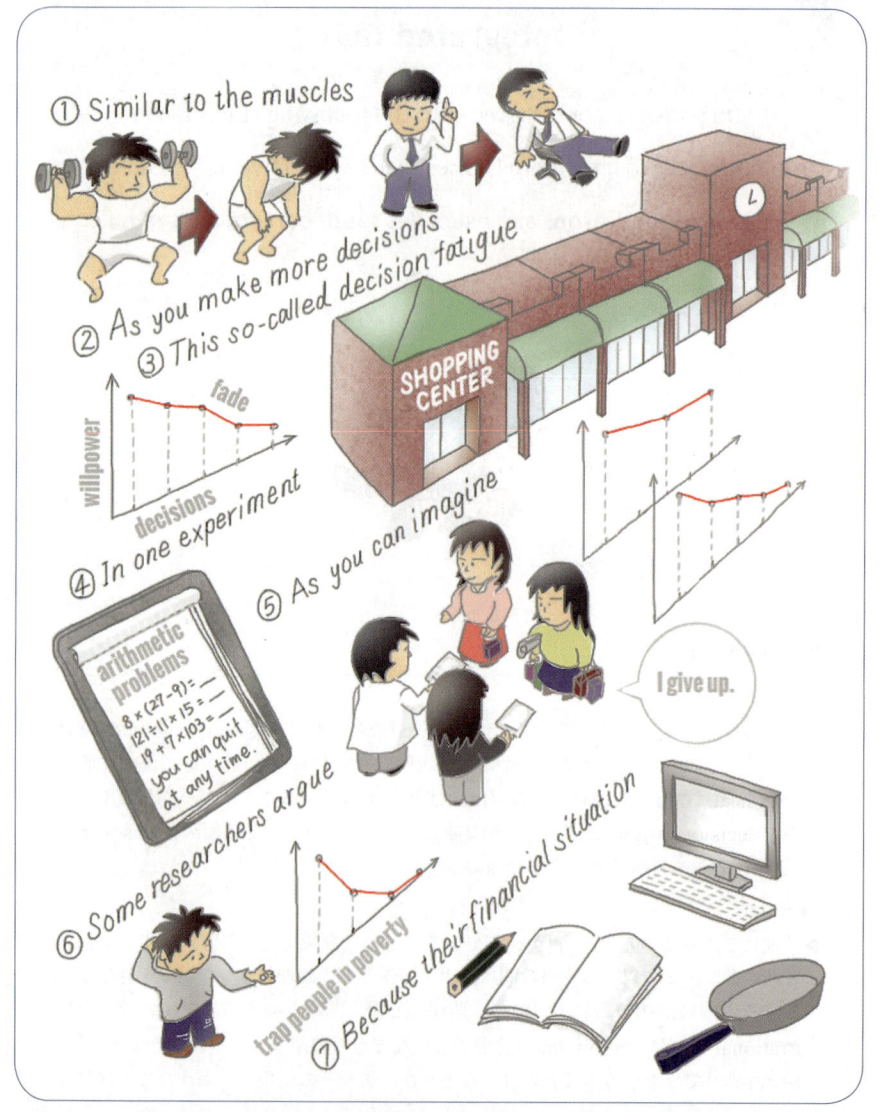

① Similar to the muscles
② As you make more decisions
③ This so-called decision fatigue
④ In one experiment
⑤ As you can imagine
⑥ Some researchers argue
⑦ Because their financial situation

**Speaking**　イラストを見ながら講義を再現してみよう。

## Script

①**Similar to the muscles** in your body, willpower can get fatigued when you use it repeatedly. ②**As you make more decisions,** the willpower fades, making it difficult to make rational choices. ③**This so-called decision fatigue** is easily observed in the shopping center, where many decisions are made in a short period of time. ④**In one experiment,** researchers asked shoppers to solve as many arithmetic problems as possible but said they could quit at any time. ⑤**As you can imagine,** the shoppers who had already made the most decisions in the stores gave up the quickest on the math problems. ⑥**Some researchers argue** that this decision fatigue could be a major factor in trapping people in poverty. ⑦**Because their financial situation** forces them to make so many difficult decisions, they have less willpower left to devote to school, work, and other activities that might help them escape poverty.

## Translation

①身体の筋肉と同様に，意志力も繰り返し用いると疲労することがある。②より多くの決定を下すにつれて，意志の力は弱まり，それが理性的な選択をすることを困難にするのだ。③この，いわゆる決定疲労は，ショッピングセンターで容易に観察される。ショッピングセンターでは短時間で多くの決定が下されるからだ。④ある実験で，研究者らは買い物客に「できる限り多くの計算問題を解くように。ただし，いつやめてもかまわない」と言った。⑤ご想像の通り，すでに店で最も多くの決定を下していた買い物客が，計算問題を解くのを最も早くやめてしまった。⑥一部の研究者は，この決定疲労は，人々が貧困から抜け出せなくなる大きな要因になりうると主張している。⑦財政状況が，あまりに多くの困難な決定を下すことを彼らに強いるため，貧困から逃れる助けとなるかもしれない学業や仕事などの活動に注ぐ意志力が，低下してしまっているのだ。

☞ スクリプトの文法ポイントについては，p.196〜の**Grammar Notes**を参照しよう。

# Lecture 1　Paraphrase

**Listening**　別の表現を用いた講義を聴いてみよう。　CD 59

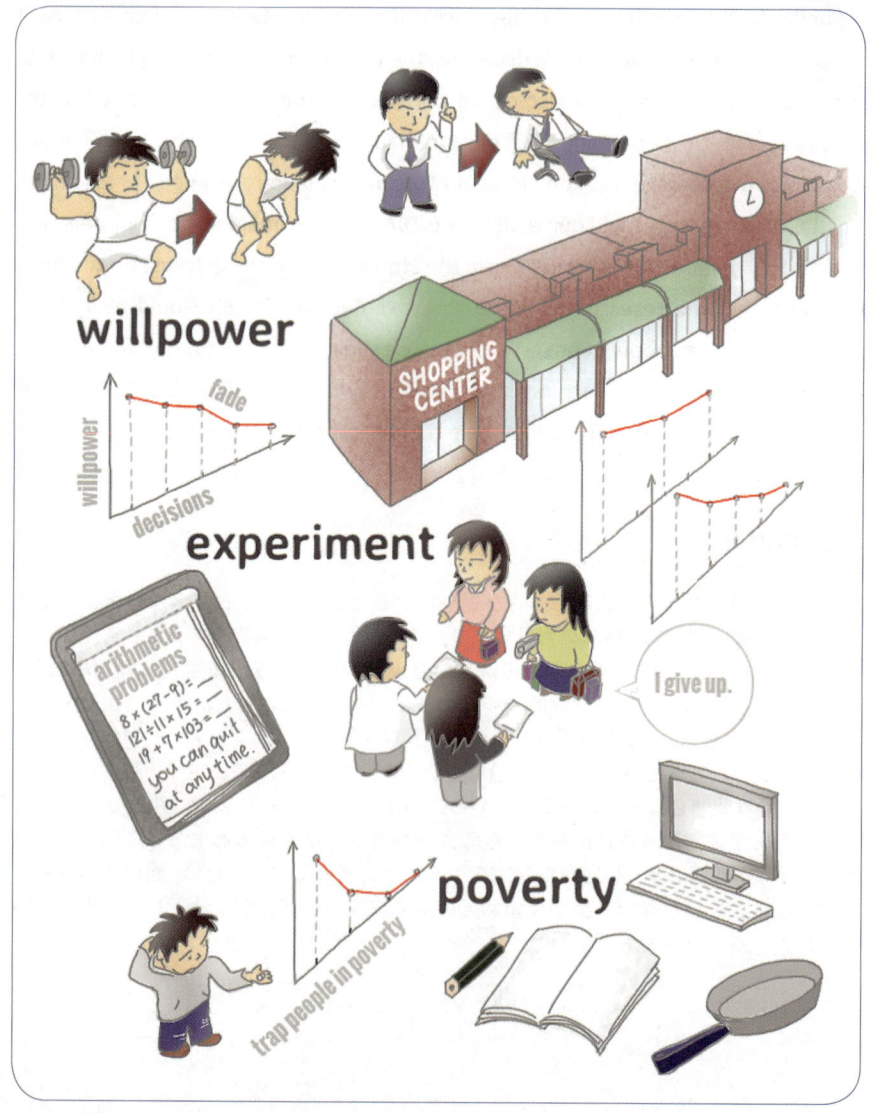

**Speaking**　イラストを見ながら講義の内容を英語で説明しよう。

Unit 9　Decision Fatigue

## Script

①Just like with your body's muscles, it is possible to tire out your **willpower** from repeated use. ②As decision-making increases, one's willpower is diminished, reducing the chance for an intelligent choice. ③This is called "decision fatigue", and you can readily spot it in a shopping center, a place where one must make numerous choices within a brief period. ④Researchers conducted an **experiment** there. ⑤They gave shoppers math problems and told them to do as many as they could, with the understanding that they could quit whenever they wanted to. ⑥Predictably, those who were already worn out from decision-making in the shops were the first to abandon the problem-solving. ⑦It is the opinion of some social scientists that "decision fatigue" plays a large role in keeping people poor. ⑧They are so worn down from the hard choices demanded by their **poverty** that they have little energy to give to schooling, career and other areas of life that could ameliorate the poverty.

## Translation

①身体の筋肉を用いるのとちょうど同様に，繰り返し用いると意志力を疲労させる可能性がある。②決定を下すことが増えるにつれて，意志力は弱まり，そのことが賢い選択をする見込みを減らすことになる。③これは「決定疲労」と呼ばれ，ショッピングセンター，つまり人が短時間で多くの決定を下さなければならない場所で容易に観察できる。④研究者らは，そこである実験を行った。⑤買い物客に計算問題を渡し，好きなときにやめてもかまわないという了解のもとで，できるだけ多くの計算問題を解くように言った。⑥予想通りに，すでに店で決定を下して疲れ果てていた客たちが，最初に計算問題を解くのをやめてしまった。⑦「決定疲労」は，人々を貧困から逃れられなくする上で大きな役割を果たしているというのが，一部の社会科学者の見解である。⑧そういった人々は，貧困によって要求される難しい選択に疲労困憊しているので，貧困状態を改善するかもしれない，学業や仕事や生活の他のさまざまな領域に注ぐ活力がほとんど残っていないのである。

☞ パラフレーズのポイントについては，p.198〜の**Paraphrase Notes**を参照しよう。

## Conversation

**Listening** 講義に関連する会話を聴いてみよう。  CD 60

Student A: This article on decision fatigue reminds me of doing Christmas shopping at the mall. Boy, do I get tired every year trying to buy things for my family!

Student B: Ha ha. But you know, I don't quite get it. You get tired because you spend hours walking around in a large, crowded mall, carrying many shopping bags. You are tired physically.

Student A: Well, according to the article, people who had already gone shopping did not want to continue solving math problems ①**because they were mentally tired from** …
If they were only physically tired, as you said, then they should be able to keep on solving problems, right?
②**I mean, math doesn't** …

Student B: You have a point there. But still, what's this about people trapped in poverty? Isn't that because there are no jobs available for them?

Student A: Well, that may be, but that's not the only reason.
③**I've read that facing difficult financial situations actually** …

Student B: Oh yeah? How so?

Student A: Imagine that your car broke down. Okay? Then you take it to a repair shop and the repairman tells you how much it will cost for the repair.
④**Then you'd have to decide whether to pay in cash, by credit card, take out a loan, or** …
⑤**When your mind is preoccupied with financial concerns like in this case, you lose your capacity to** …

Student B: So when you are worried about money, you cannot make the best choices …

Student A: … then you will have more monetary concerns, and the cycle continues!

**Speaking** 上の会話文を見ながら音声を聴き，学生Ａのパートを再現してみよう。  CD 61

## Script

①**because they were mentally tired from** making many purchasing decisions.
②**I mean, math doesn't** require physical strength.
③**I've read that facing difficult financial situations actually** lowers your cognitive functions.
④**Then you'd have to decide whether to pay in cash, by credit card, take out a loan, or** decide not to have it fixed.
⑤**When your mind is preoccupied with financial concerns like in this case, you lose your capacity to** give full consideration to other problems.

## Translation

学生Ａ：決定疲労に関するこの記事を読んで思い出したのよ，ショッピングセンターでのクリスマスの買い物のこと。本当に，毎年へとへとになるのよ，家族にプレゼントを買うのに。

学生Ｂ：ハハ。でも，よくわからないなあ。混雑した大きなショッピングセンターを歩き回るのに何時間も時間を費やすから疲れるんじゃないの。買物袋をたくさん提げて歩き回るんだろう。肉体的に疲れているんだよ。

学生Ａ：でも，この記事によれば，すでに買い物を済ませた人が計算問題を解き続けたがらなかったのは，①物を買う決定をたくさん下したことで，頭が疲れてしまったからなのよ。あなたが言うように，もし体だけが疲れているとすれば，計算問題を解き続けられるんじゃないの。②だって，計算問題は体力を必要としないのよ。

学生Ｂ：その点では君の言うことに一理あるけど，じゃあ，貧困から抜け出せなくなる人たちについては，どうなんだろう？　それは仕事の口がないからなんじゃないの？

学生Ａ：なるほど，それはそうかもしれないけど，それが唯一の理由じゃないわ。③どこかで読んだことがあるんだけど，金銭面で困難な状況に直面すると実際に認知機能が低下するんだって。

学生Ｂ：本当？　どうしてそうなの？

学生Ａ：じゃ，車が故障したと想像してみて。いい？　それで，車を修理に持って行くと，修理工が修理にいくらかかるかを告げるの。④そのとき，あなたは現金で支払うか，クレジットカードで支払うか，ローンを組むか，それとも修理をしてもらわないことにするか決めてしまわなければならないわ。⑤この場合のようにお金の心配で頭がいっぱいだと，他の問題を十分に検討する力を失うのよ。

学生Ｂ：つまり，お金の心配をしていると，最善の選択ができなくなって…

学生Ａ：…その結果，お金の心配が募って，悪循環がずっと続くのよ。

## Lecture 2  Original

**Listening**  新たな講義を聴いてみよう。

The world is full of choices. When you go to a cafe, for instance, you need to decide the size, flavor, and nearly all the ingredients of your coffee. Or when you go to a sandwich shop, you need to choose what type of bread, cheese, meat, dressing, and toppings you want. So naturally people get tired and think, "Aargh! Life would be so much easier if there weren't so many choices."

But that is not necessarily true.
①**Studies indicate that having fewer or no choices** …
②**According to such studies, when people know that they are being deprived of choice in life, they tend to** …,
such as feeling helpless and showing aggressive resistance, leading to exhaustion.

Let me give you one example. A study was conducted on two groups of university students who were thinking about applying to graduate school.
③**One group felt that they had to continue to graduate school because of** …
The other group had no outside pressure so the choice was completely theirs. Both groups were each given the same set of academic test questions and their test scores were measured. Can you guess which group scored higher on average? The group who had the choice.
④**In other words, having a choice** …
⑤**but having no choice — well, it causes people to** …

**Speaking**  吹き出しを見ながら足りない語を補い，講義を再現してみよう。

## Script

①**Studies indicate that having fewer or no choices** makes people feel more tired than having lots of choices.
②**According to such studies, when people know that they are being deprived of choice in life, they tend to** exhibit strong negative reactions,
③**One group felt that they had to continue to graduate school because of** pressure from parents, partners, or professors.
④**In other words, having a choice** mitigates the difficulty of performing unpleasant or onerous tasks,
⑤**but having no choice — well, it causes people to** feel fatigued and perform poorly.

## Translation

　この世の中，選ぶことで満ちあふれています。例えば，コーヒーを飲みにカフェに行くと，サイズ，フレーバー，そしてコーヒーに入れるものを，ほとんど全部決めなければなりません。あるいは，サンドイッチ屋に行けば，パン，チーズ，肉類，ドレッシング，トッピングに至るまで，どんな種類のものが欲しいのかを決める必要があります。そんなわけですから，疲れてしまってこう思うのも当然なのです。「うわーっ！　選ぶことがこんなに多くなかったら，人生はずっと楽だろうになあ！」
　しかし，それは必ずしも当たらないのです。①さまざまな研究によって，選択肢の数が減ったり，あるいは選択肢が全くなくなってしまったりすると，選択肢の数が多い場合よりも疲労を感じることが示されているのです。②そのような研究によると，生活において選択の余地が奪われているとわかると，無力感や攻撃的抵抗のような強い否定的な反応を示しがちになり，その結果，くたびれ果ててしまうというのです。
　一例を挙げてみましょう。大学院に出願しようと考えている大学生の2グループを対象に，ある研究が行われました。③1つのグループは，両親，パートナー，あるいは教授からプレッシャーをかけられて，大学院まで続けなければならないと感じていました。もう1つのグループは，外からのプレッシャーが全くなかったので，進学するという選択は全く本人のものでした。両方のグループが，それぞれ同じ学力テストの問題を解き，その後テストの点数が比較されました。どちらのグループの方が，平均点が高かったと思いますか？　選択肢のある方のグループだったのです。④つまりこういうことです。選択の余地があることで，不快で面倒な課題をやる大変さが緩和されますが，⑤選択の余地がないとなると…そうなのです，それで疲労を感じて，できが悪くなってしまうのです。

# Lecture 2　Summary

**Listening**　チャートを見ながら講義をもう一度聴き，Lecture Notesを完成させよう。(答えは右ページ)　CD 62

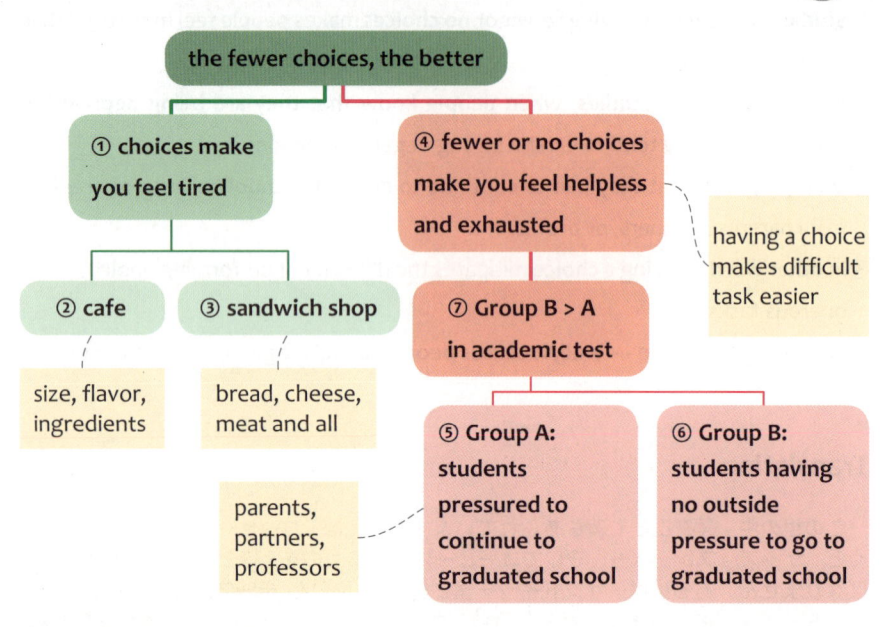

- the fewer choices, the better
  - ① choices make you feel tired
    - ② cafe — size, flavor, ingredients
    - ③ sandwich shop — bread, cheese, meat and all
  - ④ fewer or no choices make you feel helpless and exhausted
    - ⑦ Group B > A in academic test
      - ⑤ Group A: students pressured to continue to graduated school — parents, partners, professors
      - ⑥ Group B: students having no outside pressure to go to graduated school
    - having a choice makes difficult task easier

## Lecture Notes

TOPIC
(　A　)が人に与える影響

PURPOSE
(　A　)が人に与える影響には「決定疲労」のようなマイナスの面ばかりではないことを示すこと

MAIN ARGUMENT
主張A：選択肢の数が(　B　)ことは人を疲れさせる。
例　示：カフェやサンドイッチ屋での数多くの選択肢
主張B：選択肢の数が(　C　)または無いことは人を疲れさせる。
例　示：学生を対象に選択肢の有無が及ぼす影響を調べた研究

**Speaking**　チャートを見ながら講義を要約し，声に出して言ってみよう。

要約文（サンプル）を聴いてみよう。

## Summary

Some believe **the fewer choices, the better**, because **choices make you feel tired**. It is tiring to choose the right **size, flavor and ingredients** of your coffee at a **cafe,** and the right **bread, cheese, meat and all** at a **sandwich shop**. But others say **fewer or no choices make you feel helpless and exhausted**. In one study, they compared students who **felt pressured by their parents, partners or professors to continue to graduate school** and students who **had no outside pressure to do so**. When given an **academic test, the latter group did better**, because **having a choice made difficult tasks easier**.

## Translation

選択することで疲労するのだから，選択肢は少ない方が良いと思う人もいる。カフェではコーヒーのサイズ，フレーバー，そして他に何を足すか選び，サンドイッチ屋ではパン，チーズ，肉類の種類などを選ぶのは面倒である。しかし，人は選択肢が少ないか無い場合に無力感と疲労感を経験するのだと言う人もいる。ある研究は，大学院進学について両親，配偶者，あるいは教授からプレッシャーを感じている学生と外からのプレッシャーが無い学生を比較した。学力テストを課されると，後者のグループのほうが良い結果を出した。選択肢があることが難しい課題を簡単にしたからである。

### Integrated Task

Do you agree or disagree with the following statement?

*It is better to have more choices than having fewer or no choice.*

Use specific reasons and examples to support your answer.

Lecture Notesの答え　A 選択の余地　B 多い　C 少ない

## Grammar Notes

①Similar to the muscles in your body, willpower **can** get fatigued when you use it repeatedly.

▶ここでの can は「可能性」を表しています。「〜することがある」「〜しうる」といった日本語に相当します。

②**As** you make more decisions, the willpower fades, **making it** difficult **to make** rational choices.

▶As は，ここでは「…するにつれて」という意味を表しています。接続詞 as には，「…のように」（様態），「…なので」（理由），「…しながら」（時）など様々な意味がありますが，比較級など「変化を表す表現」を伴う場合，今回のように「比例」の意味になることが多くなります。

▶making ... は分詞構文で，直前の the willpower fades（意志の力が弱まる）という内容を受けて，「それが（結果として）…することを困難にする」と述べています。このように，文末に置かれた分詞構文は，「結果」を表すことがあります。

▶make it difficult to do ... は「〜することを困難にする」という意味です。make O C「O を C にする」を基本とした表現で，形式目的語と呼ばれる it が O の位置に置かれています。to do ... が，it の具体的な内容を表しています。

③This so-called decision fatigue is easily observed in the shopping center, **where** many decisions are made in a short period of time.

▶where は関係副詞で，where 以下は the shopping center がどのような場所であるかを説明しています。many decisions are made in a short period of time「短時間に多くの決定が下される」という説明が，同時に「決定疲労がショッピングセンターでよく見られる」という，前半の内容の「理由」となっている点に注目しましょう。... in the shopping center, because in the shopping center many decisions are made in a short period of time, と書き換えてもほぼ同じ意味です。

④In one experiment, researchers **asked** shoppers to solve as many arithmetic problems as possible **but said** they could quit at any time.

▶asked ... but said 〜は，研究者が買い物客に与えた一連の指示を表しています。研究者が出した指示を1つの文にまとめると，"Please solve as many arithmetic problems as possible, but you can quit at any time." などとなります。前半部は「依頼」を表す命令文なので ask O to do が，後半部は，「内容の伝達」を表すために，say (that) S V 〜が用いられています。

⑤**As** you can imagine, the shoppers **who had already made the most decisions in the stores** gave up the quickest on the math problems.

▶ ここでのAsは「…のように」という意味を表しています。続く主語がyou (=読者) なので「(この文章を読んでいる) 皆さんが想像するように」と述べていることになります。

▶ who は関係代名詞で，who had already made the most decisions in the stores は，the shoppersを修飾しています。「算数の問題を解くのをやめてしまった」時点で，すでに「最も多くの決定を下していた」のでhad (...) madeという過去完了形が用いられています。

⑥**Some** researchers argue that this decision fatigue <u>could</u> be a major factor in trapping people in poverty.

▶ Someは「一部の」という意味で，Some researchers argue thatは，「…だと主張する研究者もいれば，そうでない研究者もいる」という意味合いになります。

▶ couldは可能性を表しています。「…でありうる」「…かもしれない」といった意味合いです。慎重に断定を避けながらも可能性があることを伝える表現で，論文などの堅い文章によく見られます。

⑦Because their financial situation forces them to make so many difficult decisions, they have **less** willpower left to devote to **school, work, and other activities** that might **help them escape** poverty.

▶ lessは「より少ない〜」という意味です。ここでは「貧困状態にない人々に比べて…」(than those who are not in such a difficult situation) という比較対象が省略されています。このように比較を表す文では，文脈上理解に支障がない場合，比較対象を表すthan ...やas ...は，しばしば省略されます。

▶ school, work, and other activitiesは「学業，仕事などの活動」という意味です。〈a, b and other X〉は「a, bなどのX」という意味です。

▶ help O *do* は「Oが〜する一助となる」「O〜するのを促す」という意味です。目的語の後ろに動詞の原形 (=原形不定詞) を用いる点に注意しましょう。

## Paraphrase Notes

①**Just like with** your body's muscles, **it is possible** to tire out your willpower from repeated use.

▶ Just like with ... は「…（について）とちょうど同じように」という意味です。with は「…に関して」「…について」という意味で，it is possible ... 以下の「繰り返し使うことで疲れ果てることがある」という内容が，「体の筋肉についても言えるが，それと同様に…」という意味合いです。オリジナル①の similar to ... に相当する表現です。

▶ オリジナル①では，助動詞 can で表されていた「可能性」が，it is possible to do「…することがありうる」という表現でパラフレーズされています。

②As **decision-making increases**, one's willpower **is diminished**, **reducing the chance for an intelligent choice**.

▶ 基本的な文の構造はオリジナル②と同様ですが，you make more decisions が，decision-making increases とパラフレーズされています。more という比較表現が，increase という動詞表現に置き換えられている点に注目です。

▶ また，オリジナル②の make it difficult to make ... choices「選択するのを困難にする」という表現は，reduce the chance for an ... choice「選択の可能性を減らす」とパラフレーズされています。

▶ その他，fade → is diminished，rational → intelligent といった，語句レベルでの言い換えにも注目しましょう。

③**This is called** "decision fatigue", and you can readily spot it in **a shopping center, a place where** one must make numerous choices within a brief period.

▶ オリジナル③の，so-called ...「いわゆる…」という表現が，This is called ...「これは…と呼ばれる」という表現に置き換えられています。

▶ a shopping center, a place where ... では，カンマの後の a place where ... が a shopping center と同格の関係にあり，「ショッピングセンターとは，…な場所だ」と具体的に説明しています。わかりにくい場合は，a shopping center, which is a place where ... と，〈関係代名詞＋be動詞〉を補ってみましょう。また，より簡潔なオリジナル③とも比較してみましょう。

④Researchers conducted an experiment **there**.
⑤**They** gave shoppers math problems and told them to do as many as they could, **with the understanding that they could quit whenever they wanted to**.

▶ オリジナル④で，In one experiment researchers asked shoppers to ...「ある実験で，研究者たちは買い物客に…するように求めた」と，1文で表されていた内容が，ここでは，「研究者たちがそこ（＝ショッピングセンター）で実験を行った。彼ら（＝研究者たち）は買い物客に…」と2文で表現されています。there や They といった指示語で前後の文と結びついている点に注目しましょう。

▶ with the understanding that they could ...は「…してもよいという理解をもって」→「…してもよいという了解のもとに」という意味です。オリジナル④の but said they could quit at any time に相当する内容を表しています。

⑥**Predictably**, those **who were already worn out from decision-making** in the shops were **the first to** abandon the problem-solving.

▶ Predictably, ...は「予想通りに，…」という意味で，オリジナル⑤の As you can imagine, ...に相当します。

▶ オリジナル⑤の, who had already made the most decisions「それまでに最も多くの決定を下していた（買い物客）」という表現が，ここでは「原因」を表す from を用いて who were already worn out from decision-making「決定を下すことで，すでに疲れ果てていた（買い物客）」と「因果関係」の表現にパラフレーズされています。「下した決定の数」から「決定を下したことで疲れ果てている状態」へと，表現の焦点がシフトしている点に注目しましょう。

▶ A is the first to do は「A が最初に…する」という意味です。the quickest という最上級を使ったオリジナル⑤の表現と比較しましょう。

⑦**It is the opinion of some social scientists that** "decision" fatigue **plays a large role in keeping people poor**.

▶ It is the opinion of A that ...は「Aの意見は…というものだ」という意味で, It が形式主語, that ...が真主語となります。A argue that ...「Aは…だと主張する」というオリジナル⑥の表現からの言い換えが行われています。

▶ その他, be a major factor in ...「…の主要な要素だ」→ play a large role in ...「…において大きな役割を果たす」, trap ... in poverty「…を貧困から逃れられなくする」→ keep ... poor「…を貧しいままにする」といった言い換えが行われています。

⑧They are **so** worn down from the hard choices demanded by their poverty **that** they have little energy to give to schooling, career and other areas of life that could **ameliorate** the poverty.

▶ オリジナル⑦では，Because S V 〜, S V ...「〜という理由で，…だ」という文構造が用いられていましたが，ここでは S is so 〜 that S V ...「S はあまりに〜なので…」という構文で書かれています。so 〜 that ...の構文では，意味の上で「〜」が理由に相当することを確認しましょう。

▶ ameliorate the poverty は「貧困状態を改善する」という意味です。オリジナル⑦の help them escape poverty「彼らが貧困から逃れるのを助ける」に相当する表現です。

## Expressions and Phrases

ヒントを手がかりにして，日本語に対応する英語表現を言ってみよう。

| 日本語 | ヒント | 英語 |
|---|---|---|
| □ 体力 | ph___ st___ | physical strength |
| □ 筋肉疲労 | mu___ fa___ | muscle fatigue |
| □ 知的能力 | me___ ca___ | mental capacity |
| □ 神経衰弱 | ne___ ex___ | nervous exhaustion |
| □ 合理的な選択 | ra___ ch___ | rational choice |
| □ 数多くの選択肢 | nu___ op___ | numerous options |
| □ 弱められた意志 | di___ wi___ | diminished willpower |
| □ 意思決定の過程 | de___ -ma___ pr___ | decision-making process |
| □ 問題解決能力 | pr___ -so___ ab___ | problem-solving ability |
| □ 認知機能 | co___ fu___ | cognitive function |
| □ 知的な分析 | in___ an___ | intelligent analysis |
| □ 算術計算 | ar___ ca___ | arithmetic calculation |
| □ 再三の試み | re___ at___ | repeated attempts |
| □ 短い期間 | br___ pe___ | brief period |
| □ 予測される結果 | pr___ ou___ | predictable outcome |
| □ 外圧 | ex___ pr___ | external pressure |
| □ 骨の折れる仕事 | on___ ta___ | onerous task |
| □ 拒絶反応 | ad___ re___ | adverse reaction |
| □ 攻撃的な抵抗 | ag___ re___ | aggressive resistance |
| □ 進路選択 | ca___ ch___ | career choice |
| □ 入手可能な証拠 | av___ ev___ | available evidence |
| □ 学業成績 | ac___ pe___ | academic performance |
| □ 社会科学者 | so___ sc___ | social scientist |
| □ 購買決定 | pu___ de___ | purchasing decision |
| □ 主要成分 | ma___ in___ | main ingredients |
| □ 現金払い | ca___ pa___ | cash payment |
| □ 金銭上の懸念 | mo___ co___ | monetary concerns |
| □ 財政的要因 | fi___ fa___ | financial factor |
| □ 無力感 | he___ fe___ | helpless feeling |
| □ 悪循環 | vi___ cy___ | vicious cycle |

Unit 9　Decision Fatigue

□ 計画を実行する能力がある

| ha___ the ca_____ to ca_____ out the pl___ | have the capacity to carry out the plan |
| ha___ the ab_____ to co_____ the pr___ | have the ability to conduct the project |

□ その問題についてしっかり考える

| gi___ full co_____ to the pr_____ | give full consideration to the problem |
| gi___ that ma___ su_____ th_____ | give that matter sufficient thought |

□ 時間と労力を要する

| de_____ time and en_____ | demand time and energy |
| re_____ time and ef_____ | require time and effort |

□ 過度の労働で疲れ果てる

| be ex_____ from ov_____ | be exhausted from overworking |
| be fa_____ from ex_____ wo____ | be fatigued from excessive work |

□ 銀行からお金を借りる

| bo_____ mo_____ from the ba_____ | borrow money from the bank |
| ta_____ out a lo_____ from the ba_____ | take out a loan from the bank |

□ 反抗的な態度を見せる

| ex_____ a de_____ ge_____ | exhibit a defiant gesture |
| sh_____ a re_____ at_____ | show a rebellious attitude |

□ 危険をいとわない精神を奪われている

| be de_____ of a ri___-ta_____ sp_____ | be deprived of a risk-taking spirit |
| be di_____ from ta_____ ri_____ | be discouraged from taking risks |

□ 悲惨な状況に閉じ込められる

| be tr_____ in a di___ si_____ | be trapped in a dire situation |
| be st_____ in an ap_____ si_____ | be stuck in an appalling situation |

□ 悪影響を緩和する

| mi_____ the ne_____ im_____ | mitigate the negative impact |
| al_____ the ad_____ ef_____ | alleviate the adverse effect |

□ 同じ傾向を示す

| in_____ the sa_____ te_____ | indicate the same tendency |
| sh_____ an id_____ tr_____ | show an identical trend |

201

# Word List

- □ abandon [əbǽndən] 　動 …をあきらめる，…を見捨てる，…を捨てる
　類 give up / renounce / desert
- □ academic [æ̀kədémɪk] 　形 教養科目の，学問の
- □ aggressive [əgrésɪv] 　形 攻撃的な，積極的な
- □ ameliorate [əmíːliərèɪt] 　動 …を改善する，…を改良する
　類 improve / make better
- □ apply to A 　Aに出願する，Aに当てはまる
- □ arithmetic [èrɪθmétɪk] 　形 計算の，算数の　名 算術
　類 mathematical
- □ break down 　壊れる，故障する
- □ brief [briːf] 　形 短時間の，簡潔な
　類 short / concise
- □ capacity [kəpǽsəti] 　名 能力，定員，収容能力
- □ career [kəríər] 　名 仕事，職業，経歴
　類 profession / occupation
- □ chance [tʃæns|tʃɑːns] 　名 見込み，機会，可能性
　類 opportunity / possibility
　動 偶然…する
　語法 chance to do 「偶然…する」
- □ cognitive [káːgnətɪv, kɔ́g-] 　形 認知の，認識の
　類 perceptive
- □ concern [kənsə́ːrn] 　名 心配事，関心
　動 …に関係する，…を心配させる
- □ conduct [kəndʌ́kt] 　動 …を行う，…を管理する，…を導く，
　…を指揮する
　類 perform / carry out
- □ consideration [kənsìdəréɪʃən] 　名 考慮，検討，思いやり
- □ crowded [kráʊdɪd] 　形 混雑した，込み合った
- □ cycle [sáɪkl] 　名 循環，周期，サイクル
　動 自転車に乗る，循環する
- □ decision-making [dɪsíʒənmèɪkɪŋ] 　名 決定を下すこと，意思決定
- □ decision [dɪsíʒən] 　名 決定，決心，判決
　類 resolution / conclusion
- □ demand [dɪmǽnd|-mɑ́ːnd] 　動 …を要求する，…を尋ねる　名 要求
　類 call for / ask
- □ deprived of A 　Aを奪われている
- □ devote A to B 　AをBに捧げる

Unit 9　Decision Fatigue

| □diminish [dɪmínɪʃ] | 動 | …を減らす，…を小さくする，減少する |
| --- | --- | --- |
| | 類 | decrease / lessen |
| □dressing [drésɪŋ] | 名 | ドレッシング |
| □energy [énərdʒi] | 名 | 活力，精力，エネルギー |
| □exhausted [ɪgzɔ́:stɪd] | 形 | ひどく疲れた |
| | 類 | tired / fatigued |
| □exhaustion [ɪgzɔ́:stʃən] | 名 | 極度の疲労 |
| | 類 | fatigue |
| □face [feɪs] | 動 | …に直面する，…を直視する，(方向に) 向いている |
| | 名 | 顔，顔つき，表面 |
| □factor [fæktər] | 名 | 要因，因子 |
| | 類 | element |
| □fade [feɪd] | 動 | 弱まる，衰える，(色などが) あせる，(花などが) しぼむ |
| | 類 | weaken |
| | 名 | 色あせること |
| □fatigued [fətí:gd] | 形 | 疲労した，疲労困憊した |
| | 類 | tired / exhausted |
| □financial [fənǽnʃəl, faɪ-] | 形 | 財政上の，金銭的な |
| | 類 | economic |
| □flavor [fléɪvər] | 名 | 香り，味　動 …に味をつける |
| □graduate school | | 大学院 |
| □guess [ges] | 動 | …を推察する，…だと思う，言い当てる |
| | 名 | 推察 |
| □helpless [hélpləs] | 形 | 無力の，自分ではどうすることもできない |
| □intelligent [ɪntélɪdʒənt] | 形 | 賢い，知能の高い，頭のいい |
| | 類 | smart / clever / bright |
| □loan [loʊn] | 名 | ローン，融資　動 …を貸す |
| □lower [lóʊər] | 動 | …を低下させる，…を下げる，…を減らす |
| | 形 | 低い，下方の |
| □mall [mɔ:l] | 名 | ショッピングセンター |
| □math [mæθ] | 名 | 数学 (= mathematics) |
| □mentally [méntəli] | 副 | 精神的に |
| □mitigate [mítəgeɪt] | 動 | …を緩和する，…を和らげる |
| | 類 | moderate / ease |
| □monetary [má:nətèri｜mʌ́nɪtəri] | 形 | 金銭上の |
| | 類 | financial |

| | | |
|---|---|---|
| □ muscle [mʌ́sl] | 名 | 筋肉，腕力 |
| □ naturally [nǽtʃərəli] | 副 | 当然のことながら，自然に，天然に |
| □ negative [négətɪv] | 形 | 否定的な，消極的な，不賛成の |
| □ observe [əbzə́ːrv] | 動 | …を観察する，…である事に気づく，…を守る，…を述べる |
| | 類 | watch / examine / study |
| | 語法 | observe that S V …「…であることに気づく，…を述べる」 |
| □ on average | | 平均して |
| □ onerous [óunərəs] | 形 | 面倒な，わずらわしい |
| | 類 | tedious / tiring |
| □ opinion [əpínjən] | 名 | 意見，考え，評価 |
| | 類 | point of view / remark |
| □ outside [áutsàɪd] | 形 | 外側の  名 外側 |
| | 前 | …の外側に，…を除いて |
| □ perform [pərfɔ́ːrm] | 動 | …を行う，…を上演する，演奏する |
| | 類 | carry out |
| □ period [píəriəd] | 名 | 期間，時期，終わり |
| □ physically [fízɪkəli] | 副 | 肉体的に，身体的に，物理的に |
| □ physical [fízɪkl] | 形 | 肉体的な，身体の，物質の，物理的な |
| □ poverty [páːvərti \| pɔ́v-] | 名 | 貧困，貧乏，欠乏 |
| □ predictably [prɪdíktəbli] | 副 | 予想通りに，予想されるように |
| □ preoccupied with A | | Aのことで頭がいっぱいで |
| □ problem-solving [práːbləmsàːlvɪŋ] | 名 | 問題解決 |
| □ purchase [pə́ːrtʃəs] | 動 | …を購入する |
| □ quit [kwɪt] | 動 | やめる，…を中止する |
| | 類 | stop / cease |
| □ rational [rǽʃənl] | 形 | 理性的な，合理的な |
| | 類 | logical / reasonable |
| □ reaction [riǽkʃən] | 名 | 反応，反動 |
| □ remind A of B | | AにBを思い出させる |
| □ repair shop | | 修理店 |
| □ repairman [rɪpéərmæn] | 名 | 修理工 |
| □ repeatedly [rɪpíːtɪdli] | 副 | 繰り返し，しばしば |
| | 類 | frequently / again and again |
| □ role [roʊl] | 名 | 役割 |

|  |  |
|---|---|
| □ schooling [skúːlɪŋ] | 名 学業, 学校教育<br>類 education |
| □ situation [sìtʃuéɪʃən] | 名 状況, 情勢, 立場, 位置<br>類 state / condition / circumstances |
| □ so-called [soukɔ́ːld] | 形 いわゆる |
| □ solve [sɑːlv\|sɔlv] | 動 …を解く, …を解決する<br>類 resolve |
| □ spot [spɑːt\|spɔt] | 動 …を見つける, …を汚す 名 地点, 斑点 |
| □ task [tæsk\|tɑːsk] | 名 課題, 仕事<br>類 assignment / job |
| □ tire A out | Aを疲れさせる<br>類 exhaust |
| □ topping [tɔpɪŋ] | 名 トッピング |
| □ trap [træp] | 動 …を閉じ込める, …をわなで捕らえる<br>名 わな |
| □ unpleasant [ʌnplézənt] | 形 不快な, いやな<br>類 disagreeable |
| □ willpower [wílpauər] | 名 意志力, 自制心<br>類 self-control, self-discipline |
| □ worn down | 疲れきった, へとへとの |
| □ worn out | 疲れきった, へとへとの |
| □ worried about A | Aのことを心配している |

## 参考文献

Anandi Mani *et al.* Poverty Impedes Cognitive Function. *Science* 341, 976 (2013); DOI: 10.1126/science.1238041

Vohs, K. D., Baumeister, R. F., Twenge, J. M., Schmeichel, B. J., Tice, D. M., & Crocker, J. (2005). Decision fatigue exhausts self-regulatory resources—But so does accommodating to unchosen alternatives. *Manuscript submitted for publication.*

# Unit 10 Deceiving Eyes

## Integrated Task

Do you agree or disagree with the following statement?

*Seeing is believing.*

Use specific reasons and examples to support your answer.

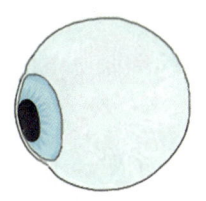

## Key Words

**vision**
▶今回のテーマである「視覚」を表す名詞で,「能動的・自覚的にモノを見る」という意味合いがあります。同義語のsightは「モノが視野に入る,見える」という意味合いです。講義では,「見る」という行為において,目が捉えた外部からの光の刺激に対して,脳がいかに「能動的に」働きかけるかが重要なポイントになっています。

**retina**
▶眼を構成する要素の1つである「網膜」を表す名詞です。外部から入ってきた光情報が,このretinaに届くことによって電気的な神経信号に変換されて,脳へと伝わります。目の仕組みをフィルム式のカメラに見立てたならば,水晶体(crystal lens)がレンズ(lens),網膜はフィルム(film)に当たります。

**physical**
▶physicalを辞書で引くと,「物理的な」「身体の」「空間的な」「自然の」などの訳語が並びますが,それらに共通する重要な意味は「実際に存在する」という意味合いです。講義では,physical(ly)という語がトランプのカードの「実際の大きさ」について述べる際に用いられています。これは,脳がinterpretした結果の「認識上の大きさ」との対比を明確にする働きをしています。

# Lecture 1　Original

**Listening**　講義を聴いてみよう。

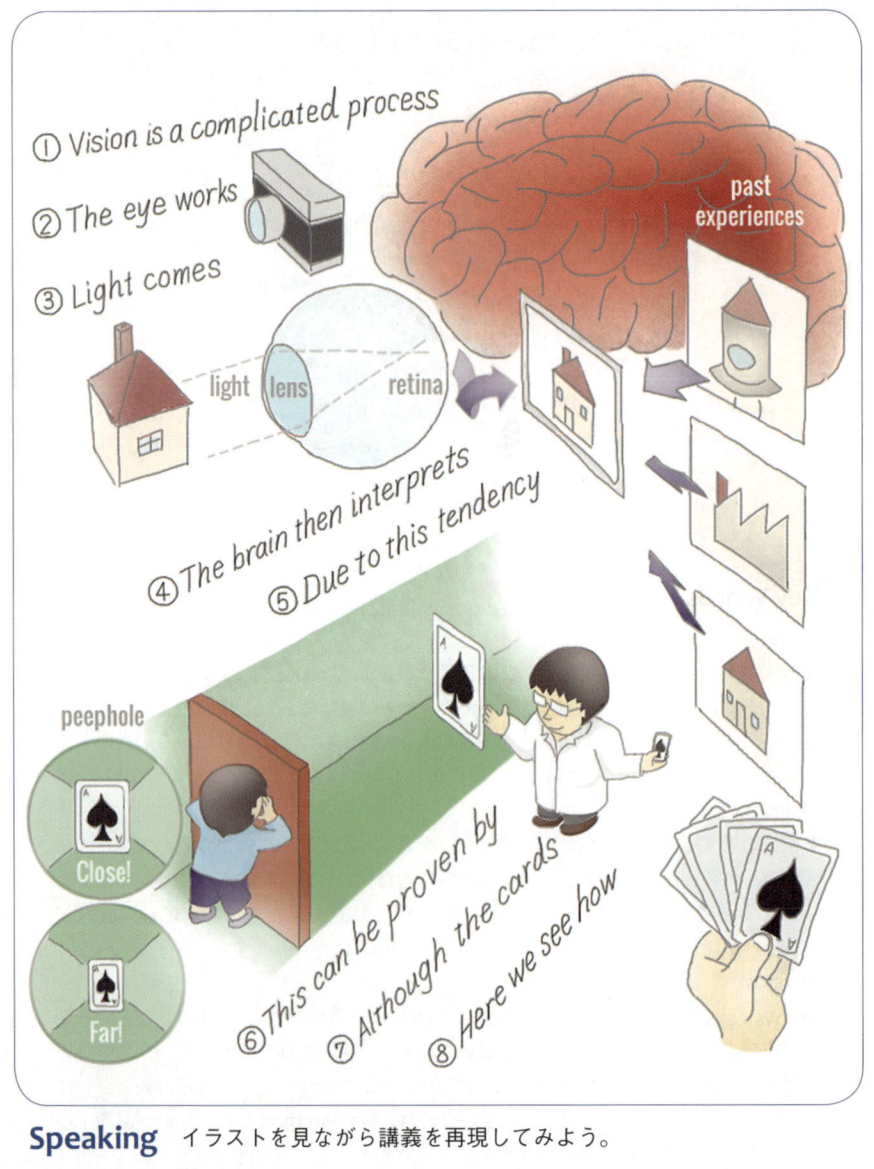

CD 65

① Vision is a complicated process
② The eye works
③ Light comes

light　lens　retina

past experiences

④ The brain then interprets
⑤ Due to this tendency

peephole

Close!

Far!

⑥ This can be proven by
⑦ Although the cards
⑧ Here we see how

**Speaking**　イラストを見ながら講義を再現してみよう。

208

## Script

①**Vision is a complicated process** in which the human eye and brain work together. ②**The eye works** like a camera, capturing detailed information of what we see. ③**Light comes** through the lens and leaves an image on the retina. ④**The brain then interprets** the image, selecting features that fit with the world pieced together from past experiences. ⑤**Due to this tendency** of the brain, we often see what we believe rather than believe what we see. ⑥**This can be proven by** having an observer look through a peephole at playing cards of different physical sizes. ⑦**Although the cards** are shown from the same distance, the observer reports that physically large cards are very close, while smaller cards are further away. ⑧**Here we see how** the brain has been deceived, convinced that the playing cards should be the same size.

## Translation

①視覚は人間の目と脳が協力して働く複雑なプロセスである。②目はカメラのように働き，私たちの目に入ってくるものについての詳細な情報を捉える。③光がレンズを通して入ってきて，網膜に像を残す。④その後，脳がその像を解釈し，過去の諸経験から組み上げられた世界に一致する特徴を選びだす。⑤脳のこの傾向のために，私たちは目にするものを信じるというよりは，むしろ信じているものを目にしていることがよくある。⑥このことは，観察者に覗き穴から物理的に大きさの異なるトランプ札を見せることによって証明することができる。⑦トランプ札を同じ距離から見せられても，観察者は物理的に大きなトランプ札は間近にあり，その一方で小さい方のトランプ札はそれよりも遠くにあると報告する。⑧このように脳は，トランプ札はどれも同じ大きさであるはずだと信じ切っているため，だまされてしまうのだ。

☞ スクリプトの文法ポイントについては，p.218〜のGrammar Notesを参照しよう。

## Lecture 1　Paraphrase

**Listening**　別の表現を用いた講義を聴いてみよう。

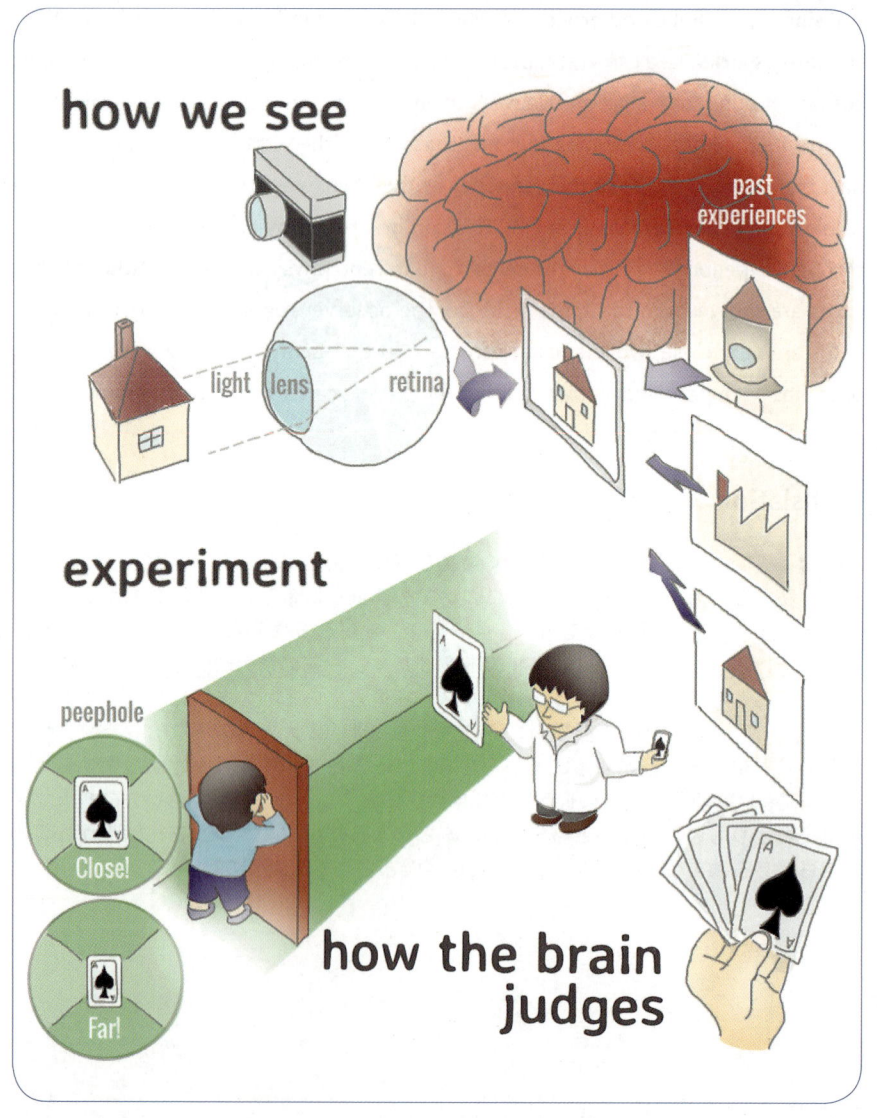

how we see

past experiences

light　lens　retina

experiment

peephole

Close!

Far!

how the brain judges

**Speaking**　イラストを見ながら講義の内容を英語で説明しよう。

## Script

①**How we see** is a complex activity involving eye-brain coordination. ②The eye is a camera, taking in whatever is in our line of sight. ③Light enters through the lens and deposits an image on the retina. ④The brain then translates this image, but it does so based on what it has learned from prior experience. ⑤As a result, seeing is not necessarily believing. ⑥This can be easily shown by an **experiment**. ⑦Look through a peephole into an empty tunnel with two playing cards of different sizes. ⑧One card is larger than a standard card, the other is smaller. ⑨Though they are at the same distance from your eye, you will think the larger one is closer. ⑩What this shows is that **the brain judges** distance by what it knows to be the normal size of things in sight.

## Translation

①私たちがどのようにして物を見るのかは，目と脳の協調した作業を伴う複雑な活動である。②目はカメラのようであり，私たちの視線の上にあるものはどんなものでも取り込む。③光はレンズを通して入り，網膜に像を残す。④その後で，脳がその像を解釈するが，それは以前の経験から学習したことに基づいている。⑤その結果，目にすることは必ずしも信じることにはならない。⑥このことは実験によって容易に証明することができる。⑦覗き穴から,大きさの異なる2枚のトランプ札が置かれた何もない通路をのぞき込んでみよう。⑧一方のトランプ札は標準サイズのトランプ札より大きく，もう一方は小さい。⑨トランプは目から同じ距離にあるが，大きなトランプ札の方が近くにあると思うだろう。⑩これが示しているのは，脳は見えているものについて脳が標準的な大きさであると認識しているものを基準にして，距離を判断しているということだ。

パラフレーズのポイントについては，p.220〜の**Paraphrase Notes**を参照しよう。

# Conversation

**Listening** 講義に関連する会話を聴いてみよう。

Student: Professor Jones, I've done the assigned reading for next week's class on vision, and, uh ... it says here that our brain perceives images based on past experiences.

Professor: That's right.

Student: But what does that mean? I couldn't quite get a grasp on the concept. Would you mind ...?

Professor: ①**Okay, so the key word here is ...**
②**That is, we see what our eyes expect to see based on ...**

Student: What do you mean?

Professor: ③**Information arriving at the retina — that is, the image the eye captures — is inherently ambiguous, um ... very vague, unclear, until our brain gives ...**
④**And that meaning comes from prior information, perhaps stored somewhere ...**
⑤**The brain then feeds it back to ...**

Student: So that example of placing two cards of different size at the same distance is... okay, the brain already knows that if something appears large it is close, and that if it appears small it is far away. But in this experiment the brain gets confused because it expects big things to be close and small things to be far?

Professor: You pretty much nailed it, Melissa!

**Speaking** 上の会話文を見ながら音声を聴き，教授のパートを再現してみよう。

Unit 10　Deceiving Eyes

## Script

①**Okay, so the key word here is** expectation.
②**That is, we see what our eyes expect to see based on** prior information our brain acknowledges.
③**Information arriving at the retina — that is, the image the eye captures — is inherently ambiguous, um … very vague, unclear, until our brain gives** meaning to the information.
④**And that meaning comes from prior information, perhaps stored somewhere** in the higher regions of our brains.
⑤**The brain then feeds it back to** the sensory cortex in the eye.

## Translation

学生：ジョーンズ教授，来週の視覚についての授業のために課題の図書を読み終えたんですけど，えっと，それには，私たちの脳は過去の経験に基づいて像を知覚する，と書いてあるんです。
教授：その通りだよ。
学生：でも，それはどういう意味ですか。その概念をまったく理解することができません。説明していただけないでしょうか？
教授：①構いませんよ。まず，ここでのキーワードは「予想」という言葉なんだ。②つまり，私たちは脳が認識している，以前の情報に基づいて，見えるだろうと予想しているものを見ているんだよ。
学生：どういう意味ですか。
教授：③網膜に届く情報，つまり目が捉える像は，脳がその情報に意味を与えるまでは，本来あいまいで，うーん，非常にぼんやりしていて，はっきりしないんだ。④で，その意味というのは，たぶん脳のどこか高い領域にでも蓄えられている，昔の情報がもとになっているんだ。⑤それから，脳がそれを目の中の感覚皮質にフィードバックするんだよ。
学生：だから，同じ距離に2枚の違う大きさのトランプを置いたあの例では…そうか，何かが大きく見えれば，それは近くにあり，小さく見えれば，それは遠く離れたところにあることを脳はすでに知っているということですね。しかし，この実験では，脳は大きいものが近くにあり，小さいものは遠くにあると予想するので，混乱してしまう，ということですね？
教授：だいぶわかってきたようだね。メリッサ。

213

# Lecture 2　Original

**Listening**　新たな講義を聴いてみよう。

In our last class we learned about how visual perception works. Now, I just wanted to take a moment to investigate optical illusions. You may have seen illusion shows, say, in Las Vegas, on TV, or on the Internet. Perhaps the simplest yet best-known optical illusion is the Muller-Lyer illusion. Here, a picture speaks a thousand words. Take a look.

Though the two vertical lines are of identical length, the line on the left with outgoing fins looks longer than the one on the right with ingoing fins. But how does it happen?

One explanation was offered by a British psychologist, Richard Gregory.
①**According to Gregory, the lengths of the images on the retina are still the same, but the brain …**
②**The brain tends to see those images as …**
If you would take another look, the line with the outgoing fins may start to look like, say, a corner of a house seen from the inside, and the line with the ingoing fins the corner seen from the outside.
③**The brain tells you that the actual length of the inside corner, which is part of a three dimensional object, should be longer than it looks just because it is …**
④**This influences …**
⑤**In this way, the brain's tendency to see things in perspective causes …**

**Speaking**　吹き出しを見ながら足りない語を補い，講義を再現してみよう。

# Script

①**According to Gregory, the lengths of the images on the retina are still the same, but the brain** interprets them in a unique way.
②**The brain tends to see those images as** perspective drawings of corners.
③**The brain tells you that the actual length of the inside corner, which is part of a three dimensional object, should be longer than it looks just because it is** farther away from you.
④**This influences** our perception.
⑤**In this way, the brain's tendency to see things in perspective causes** the distortion, and we call it an optical illusion.

# Translation

　前回の授業で視覚がどのように働くかについて学習しました。さて，今回は，少し時間をとって錯視について詳しく見ていきたいと思います。皆さんは，ラスベガスやテレビ，インターネットでイリュージョンショーを見たことがあるかもしれませんね。でも一番単純で，しかも有名な錯視はミュラー・リヤー錯視かもしれません。さあ，百聞は一見にしかず。実際に見てみましょう。
　２本の縦の線分は同じ長さですが，外向きの矢羽根のついた左側の線分のほうが内向きの矢羽根のついた右側の線分よりも長く見えます。でも，どうしてそうなるのでしょう。
　イギリスの心理学者，リチャード・グレゴリーによって１つの説明が提示されています。①グレゴリーによると，網膜に投影された像の長さは同じままですが，脳がそれを独特の方法で解釈するというのです。②脳は，これらの像を遠近法を用いて描かれた隅として見る傾向があるのです。もう一度見てみると，外側に向かった矢羽根のついている線分は，例えば家の隅を内側から見たものに，内側に向かった矢羽根のついた線分はそれを外側から見たもののように見えてくるかもしれません。③立体物の一部である建物の隅の長さは，遠くにあるのだから，線分の実際の長さは見た目よりも長いはずであると脳が伝えます。④これが視覚に影響を及ぼすのです。⑤このようにして，遠近法によってものを見ようとする我々の脳の傾向によって歪みが引き起こされ，それを我々は錯視と呼んでいるのです。

# Lecture 2　Summary

**Listening**　チャートを見ながら講義をもう一度聴き，Lecture Notesを完成させよう。（答えは右ページ）　CD 69

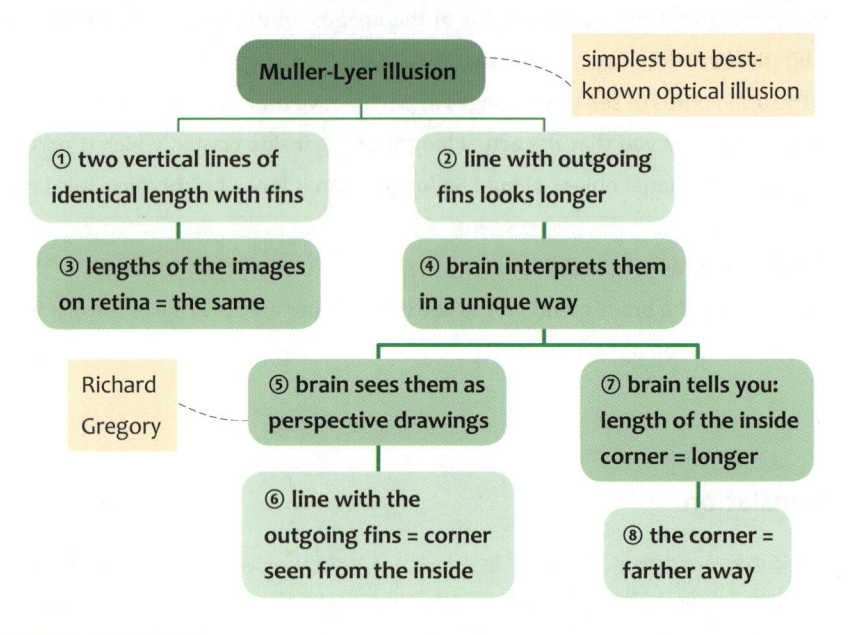

```
                    Muller-Lyer illusion ------ simplest but best-
                                                known optical illusion
        ┌───────────────────────┴───────────────────────┐
  ① two vertical lines of              ② line with outgoing
  identical length with fins           fins looks longer

  ③ lengths of the images              ④ brain interprets them
  on retina = the same                 in a unique way

        Richard      ⑤ brain sees them as        ⑦ brain tells you:
        Gregory      perspective drawings        length of the inside
                                                 corner = longer

                     ⑥ line with the             ⑧ the corner =
                     outgoing fins = corner      farther away
                     seen from the inside
```

## Lecture Notes

**TOPIC**
錯視（視覚的錯覚）

**PURPOSE**
ミュラー・リヤー錯視がどのように起こるかの説明を紹介すること

**MAIN ARGUMENT**
主　張：ミュラー・リヤー錯視は見たものを（　A　）と捉える脳の傾向によって引き起こされている。
理由①：脳は，矢羽根のついた線分を（　B　）で描かれた立体物と捉える。
理由②：視覚は，遠くにあるものの実際の大きさは見た目より大きいという認識の影響を受ける。

**Speaking**　チャートを見ながら講義を要約し，声に出して言ってみよう。

要約文（サンプル）を聴いてみよう。

## Summary

**The simplest but best-known optical illusion** would be **the Muller-Lyer illusion,** which compares **two vertical lines**. Although they are of the same length, **the one with outgoing fins looks longer** than the other. According to **Richard Gregory**, a psychologist, **the lengths on the retina are still the same**, but the **brain interprets them** differently because it **sees the lines as perspective drawings**. The **line with the outgoing fins is seen as a corner seen from the inside. The brain tells you the actual length should be longer than it looks because it is farther away.** This affects how we see, creating the optical illusion.

## Translation

ごく単純なのによく知られている錯視といえば2本の縦の線を比べるミュラー・リヤー錯視であろう。長さは同じなのに，外側に向かう矢羽根がついた線分のほうが，もう一方の線分よりも長く見える。心理学者のリチャード・グレゴリーによると，網膜上に写った線分の長さは同じままだが，脳は違う解釈をするという。それらの線を遠近法で描かれたものとして見ているからだ。外側に向かう矢羽根のついた線分は，建物の隅を内側から見たものに見える。遠くにあるのだから，線分の実際の長さは見た目よりも長いはずであると脳は考える。これが視覚に影響し，錯視を作り出している。

## Integrated Task

Do you agree or disagree with the following statement?

*Seeing is believing.*

Use specific reasons and examples to support your answer.

Lecture Notesの答え　A 立体（物）　B 遠近法

## Grammar Notes

①Vision is a complicated process **in which** the human eye and brain work together.
- ▶ in which 以下は a complicated process の内容を説明しています。Vision is a complicated process, and in this process the human eye and brain work together. と書き換えてもほぼ同じ意味です。

②The eye works like a camera, **capturing** detailed information of what we see.
- ▶ capturing …は，「目はカメラのように機能する」という直前の比喩表現に対して，「どのような点においてカメラのようなのか」をより具体的に記しています。このように，文末に置かれた分詞構文が，直前の内容を具体的に言い換えることがあります。

③Light **comes** through the lens and **leaves** an image on the retina.
- ▶ 1つの主語 Light に対して，comes … and leaves …と，2つの述語動詞が並べられた構造になっています。

④The brain **then** interprets the image, selecting features that fit with the world **pieced together from past experiences**.
- ▶ then は順序・前後関係を明示する副詞です。ここでは③で述べられた「光がレンズを通して入り，網膜に像を残す」という現象を受けて，「その後に脳がその像を解釈する」と順序を明示しています。
- ▶ pieced は過去分詞で，pieced together from past experiences 全体が直前の the world を修飾しています。

⑤**Due to** this tendency of the brain, we often see what we believe **rather than** believe what we see.
- ▶ due to A「Aのせいで」は理由を導く表現です。because of A, on account of A, owing to A などと書き換えることができます。
- ▶ A rather than B は「Bというよりも(むしろ)A」という意味です。ここでは，A に see what we believe，B に believe what we see が置かれ，「見るものを信じるというよりも，むしろ信じるものを見るのだ」と述べています。not so much B as A, more A than B, less B than A などと書き換えることができます

⑥This can be proven by **having an observer look** through a peephole at playing cards of different physical sizes.
- ▶ having an observer look …は，have O do「Oに〜させる」「Oに〜してもらう」を用いた表現全体が動名詞句になったものです。これが，by doing「〜することによって」という表現の一部となって，全体としては「このことは，観察者に…を見させることによって証明される」という意味になります。

⑦Although the cards are shown from the same distance, the observer reports that physically large cards are very close, **while** smaller cards are **further away**.

▶ while は対比的な内容を結びつける働きをしています。ここでは physically large cards are very close「物理的に大きなカードはとても近くにある」と，smaller cards are further away「小さいカードはそれよりも遠くにある」という２つの内容を「…に対して，一方〜」とつないでいます。

⑧**Here we see how** the brain has been deceived, **convinced** that the playing cards should be the same size.

▶ Here we see how ...は，直訳すると「ここに私たちは，いかに…かを見て取る」という意味ですが，実質的には As we can see here, ...「ここから見て取れるように…」や In this way, ...「このように…」といった表現に近いものです。ここでは，⑥⑦文の内容を受けて，「このように脳はだまされるのです」と述べています。

▶ convinced that ...は分詞構文で，脳が容易にだまされる理由を「トランプのカードは同じ大きさであるはずだと信じ込んでいるせいで…」と説明しています。

## Paraphrase Notes

①**How we see** is a complex activity **involving eye-brain coordination**.
- ▶オリジナル①のvision「視覚」という名詞が，How we see「私たちがどのように見るか」「モノを見る仕組み」という表現に変わっています。
- ▶involving eye-brain coordination「目と脳の共同作業をともなう」は，オリジナル①のin which the human eye and brain work togetherに当たります。work togetherという動詞表現を，coordination「協調した作業」という名詞に置き換えるのがポイントです。

②**The eye is a camera**, taking in whatever is in our line of sight.
- ▶オリジナル②では，like A「Aのように」という比喩を明示する表現（＝直喩）を用いてThe eye works like a cameraとなっていましたが，ここでは比喩を明示する語句をともなわない「隠喩（metaphor）」となっています。比喩であることが明らかであり，読み手の誤解を招く可能性がない場合は，隠喩が効果的に用いられます。

③Light **enters** through the lens and **deposits** an image on the retina.
- ▶オリジナル③のcomes，leavesが，それぞれ単語レベルで置き換えられています。

④The brain then translates this image, but **it does so** based on what it has learned from prior experience.
- ▶it does soはthe brain translates this imageの代用表現です。「その後に脳はこの像を解釈するのだが，それは（＝脳が像を解釈するのは）…に基づいてのことだ」というつながりです。
- ▶オリジナル④では，butなどの逆接表現はありませんでしたが，ここでは「その後に脳が像を解釈するのだが，(重要なのは) それが過去の経験に基づいているということだ」という意味合いでbutが用いられています。オリジナル④よりも明確に，「脳による像の解釈は，過去の経験に基づいている」という情報に焦点が当てられています。

⑤As a result, **seeing is not necessarily believing**.
- ▶"Seeing is believing."「見ることは信じることだ」「百聞は一見に如かず」という慣用句を用いて，オリジナル⑤の趣旨をはるかにコンパクトに表現しています。

Unit 10　Deceiving Eyes

⑥This can be easily shown by an experiment.

⑦**Look** through a peephole into an empty tunnel with two playing cards of different sizes.

⑧One card is larger than a standard card, the other is smaller.

▶オリジナル⑥では１文で表されていた内容を，実験の説明を切り離すことで３つの文に分けて表現しています。

▶実験内容を説明する際に，Look through a peephole ...「覗き穴から…を見てみよう」という命令文を用いることで，読み手に直接話しかけるような「臨場感」が生じています。

▶⑧は，カードの大きさについて，オリジナル⑥よりも丁寧に説明しています。「通常のカードの大きさ」を基準としたこの説明が，⑩の結論で生きてきます。

⑨Though they are at the same distance from **your** eye, **you** will think **the larger one is closer**.

▶⑦で命令文を用いた結果，youを主語とした文になっている点に注意しましょう。

▶オリジナル⑦と異なり，「大きい方が近くにあると思う」という説明にとどめています。「小さい方は遠くに見える」という点が自明だとみなされたからです。

⑩**What this shows is that** the brain judges distance **by what it knows to be the normal size of things in sight**.

▶What this shows is that ...は，「このことが示すのは…ということだ」という意味で，実験によって示される結論を導いています。オリジナル⑧のHere we see how ...に相当します。

▶by what it knows to be the normal size of things in sightは，「見えているものの通常の大きさだと脳が知っている大きさを基準として」という意味で，ここでのbyは判断基準を表しています。この説明は，オリジナル⑧のconvinced that the playing cards should be the same sizeに対応するものです。オリジナルでは, should「…のはずだ」という助動詞に「脳による解釈」が反映されていますが，こちらでは，そのことをより明確に説明しています。④の「過去の経験に基づいて解釈する」という内容を，より具体的に言い換えたものですね。

## Expressions and Phrases

ヒントを手がかりにして，日本語に対応する英語表現を言ってみよう。

| 日本語 | ヒント | 英語 |
|---|---|---|
| □ 認知心理学者 | co___ ps_____ | cognitive psychologist |
| □ 空論 | em___ th___ | empty theory |
| □ 複雑な概念 | co_____ co_____ | complicated concept |
| □ 一般的傾向 | ge___ te_____ | general tendency |
| □ 不明瞭な記述 | am_____ de_____ | ambiguous description |
| □ 詳細な観察 | de_____ ob___ | detailed observation |
| □ 予備知識 | pr___ kn_____ | prior knowledge |
| □ 内在する危険性 | in_____ ri__ | inherent risk |
| □ 緊密な連携 | cl___ co_____ | close coordination |
| □ 独自の特徴 | un____ fe_____ | unique feature |
| □ 曖昧な基準 | va___ st___ | vague standard |
| □ 脳の部位 | br___ re___ | brain region |
| □ 物理的刺激 | ph___ st___ | physical stimulation |
| □ 感覚皮質 | se___ co___ | sensory cortex |
| □ 水晶体 | cr___ le__ | crystal lens |
| □ 人間の網膜 | hu___ re__ | human retina |
| □ 視覚 | vi___ pe_____ | visual perception |
| □ 正常な視力 | no___ si___ | normal sight |
| □ 目の錯覚 | op____ il_____ | optical illusion |
| □ 視覚のひずみ | vi___ di_____ | visual distortion |
| □ 最も有名な例 | be__-kn___ ex___ | best-known example |
| □ 防犯用ののぞき穴 | se_____ pe_____ | security peephole |
| □ トランプ札 | pl____ ca__ | playing card |
| □ 透視図 | pe_____ dr___ | perspective drawing |
| □ ３次元の物体 | th__-di____ ob___ | three-dimensional object |
| □ 実際の距離 | ac___ di_____ | actual distance |
| □ 同一の長さ | id_____ le___ | identical length |
| □ 外向きの矢羽根 | ou__ fi_ | outgoing fin |
| □ 垂線 | ve___ li__ | vertical line |
| □ 水平運動 | ho_____ mo_____ | horizontal movement |

Unit 10　Deceiving Eyes

□ 鮮明な画像を捉える

| ca___ a sh___ im___ | capture a sharp image |
| pe___ a cl___ im___ | perceive a clear image |

□ どのように錯覚するか詳しく調べる

| in_____ how our ey___ are de_____ | investigate how our eyes are deceived |
| lo___ into how op____ de_____ wo___ | look into how optical deceptions work |

□ スケッチをもう一度見る

| ta___ another gl___ at the dr_____ | take another glance at the drawing |
| ha___ a se___ look at the sk_____ | have a second look at the sketch |

□ 好影響を認める

| ac_____ the po_____ im_____ | acknowledge the positive impact |
| re_____ the fa_____ ef____ | recognize the favorable effect |

□ 利点を確信している

| be co_____ of the me_____ | be convinced of the merit |
| fe___ co_____ about the ad_____ | feel confident about the advantage |

□ 誰かをだますつもりでいる

| in____ to de___ so___ | intend to deceive someone |
| ha___ an in_____ to fo___ so_____ | have an intention to fool someone |

□ その問題をしっかり理解する

| get a go___ gr___ of the pr_____ | get a good grasp of the problem |
| have a fi___ un_____ of the is___ | have a firm understanding of the issue |

□ 間違った前提に基づいている

| be ba___ on the wr___ pr_____ | be based on the wrong premise |
| be pr_____ on the fa___ as_____ | be premised on the false assumption |

□ 見過ごす傾向がある

| te___ to fa___ to se___ | tend to fail to see |
| ha___ a te_____ to ov___ | have a tendency to overlook |

□ 別の説明を提示する

| of___ an al_____ ex_____ | offer an alternative explanation |
| pr____ a di____ ac____ | provide a different account |

# Word List

| | | | |
|---|---|---|---|
| ☐ actual [ǽktʃuəl] | 形 | 実際の | |
| ☐ ambiguous [æmbígjuəs] | 形 | あいまいな，不確かな | |
| | 類 | vague / unclear | |
| ☐ assign [əsáin] | 動 | （課題など）を課す，…を指定する，…を割り当てる | |
| ☐ best-known [bèstnóun] | 形 | 最もよく知られている（well-knownの最上級） | |
| ☐ complex [kɑ̀ːmpléks \| kɔ́mpleks] | 形 | 複雑な，複合の | |
| | 類 | complicated | |
| ☐ confused [kənfjúːzd] | 形 | 混乱した，困惑した | |
| ☐ convinced that S V | | …だと信じ切っている，…だと確信する | |
| | 類 | assured that S V ... | |
| ☐ coordination [kouɔ̀ːrdənéiʃən] | 名 | 協調，調和 | |
| | 類 | matching / harmonization | |
| ☐ cortex [kɔ́ːrteks] | 名 | 皮質 | |
| ☐ deceive [disíːv] | 動 | …をだます | |
| | 類 | cheat / trick / mislead | |
| ☐ deposit [dipɑ́ːzət \| -pɔ́zit] | 動 | …を残す…を預ける，…を置く，…を預金する | |
| | 名 | 保証金，預金，堆積物 | |
| ☐ distortion [distɔ́ːrʃən] | 名 | 歪み，歪曲 | |
| | 類 | bend | |
| ☐ empty [émpti] | 形 | 何もない，空っぽの | |
| | 類 | bare, vacant, hollow | |
| ☐ expect to *do* | | …すると予期する | |
| ☐ expectation [èkspektéiʃən] | 名 | 予期，期待 | |
| ☐ experience [ikspíəriəns, eks-] | 名 | 経験，体験 | |
| ☐ feature [fíːtʃər] | 名 | 特徴，顔立ち 動 …を特集する | |
| | 類 | characteristic | |
| ☐ feed A back to B | | AをBにフィードバックする | |
| ☐ fin [fin] | 名 | ひれ，ひれ状のもの | |
| ☐ fit with A | | Aに合う | |
| ☐ illusion [ilúːʒən] | 名 | 錯覚，幻 | |
| ☐ image [ímidʒ] | 名 | 像，イメージ，画像，生き写し | |
| ☐ influence [ínfluəns] | 動 | …に影響を及ぼす 名 影響，勢力 | |
| | 類 | affect | |
| ☐ information [ìnfərméiʃən] | 名 | 情報 | |

Unit 10　Deceiving Eyes

| | | |
|---|---|---|
| □ ingoing [íngouɪŋ] | 形 | 内向きの，入ってくる |
| □ inherently [ɪnhíərəntli] | 副 | 本来的に，そもそも，生まれ持って |
| | 類 | innately / by nature |
| □ Internet [íntərnèt] | 名 | インターネット |
| □ judge [dʒʌdʒ] | 動 | …を判断する，…を推定する，…の審査をする |
| | 名 | 裁判官，審判 |
| □ length [leŋkθ] | 名 | 長さ |
| □ line of sight | | 視線 |
| □ nail [neɪl] | 動 | …をくぎで打ち付ける，…を見事にやる |
| | 名 | くぎ，爪 |
| □ normal [nɔ́ːrml] | 形 | 普通の，標準の　名　基準 |
| □ observer [əbzə́ːrvər] | 名 | 観察者，目撃者　評論家 |
| □ optical illusion | | 錯視，目の錯覚 |
| □ outgoing [áutgouɪŋ] | 形 | 外向きの |
| □ past [pæst\|pɑːst] | 形 | 過去の，前任の　名　過去 |
| □ peephole [píːphoul] | 名 | 覗き穴 |
| □ perceive [pərsíːv] | 動 | …を知覚する |
| | 語法 | perceive that S V …「…だと気づく」 |
| □ perspective [pərspéktɪv] | 名 | 遠近法，視点，全体的な見方 |
| □ piece A together | | （断片を）組み合わせる，まとめる |
| □ playing card | | トランプ札 |
| □ prior [práɪər] | 形 | 前の，優先的な |
| | 類 | previous / earlier |
| | 語法 | prior to A 「Aより前に」 |
| □ psychologist [saɪkɑ́ːlədʒɪst\|-kɔ́l-] | 名 | 心理学者，精神分析学者 |
| □ retina [rétənə] | 名 | 網膜 |
| □ say [seɪ] | 副 | 例えば |
| □ sensory [sénsəri] | 形 | 感覚の |
| □ somewhere [sʌ́mwèər, -hwèər] | 副 | どこかに，だいたい |
| □ standard [stǽndərd] | 形 | ふつうの，標準の，定番の　名　標準，基準 |
| | 類 | normal / typical |
| □ tendency [téndənsi] | 名 | 傾向，性質 |
| | 類 | inclination |
| □ that is … | | つまり… |
| | 類 | namely / in other words / that is to say |

| | |
|---|---|
| ☐ three dimensional | 立体の，三次元の |
| ☐ translate [trǽnsleɪt, trǽnz-] | 動 …を解釈する，…を翻訳する，…をわかりやすく説明する<br>語法 translate A into B「AをBに翻訳する」<br>類 interpret |
| ☐ tunnel [tʌ́nl] | 名 通路，トンネル 動 トンネルを掘る |
| ☐ vague [veɪg] | 形 ぼんやりした，漠然とした<br>類 unclear |
| ☐ vision [víʒən] | 名 視覚，視力，未来像，先見性，幻<br>類 eyesight / sight |
| ☐ visual perception | 視覚 |

参考文献

Hogenboom, M. (n.d.). *How your eyes trick your mind.* Retrieved September 2, 2015, from BBC FUTURE website: http://www.bbc.com/future/bespoke/story/20150130-how-your-eyes-trick-your-mind/index.html

McCarthy, M. (n.d.). *Müller-Lyer.* Retrieved September 2, 2015, from Online Psychology Laboratory website: http://opl.apa.org/Experiments/About/AboutM%C3%BCller-Lyer.aspx

Gregory, R. L. (1997) Knowledge in perception and illusion. Phil. Trans. R. Soc. Lond. B, 352, 1121-1128. Website: http://www.richardgregory.org/papers/knowl_illusion/knowledge-in-perception.pdf#search='Knowledge+in+perception+and+illusion'